Wakefield Press

Northern Territory Reflections

Richard Ryan (artist Danelle Bergstrom)

Richard Ryan began to practice as a chartered accountant in Darwin in 1971. With colleagues he built a significant accounting network with eight offices around Australia, three in the Northern Territory.

Following the Darwin cyclone he ultimately became Chief Executive of the fledgling Henry and Walker, the first industrial company in the Northern Territory to be listed on the Australian Stock Exchange and the first company in Australia to have an Indigenous Director. He chaired on two occasions the Menzies School of Health Research, which became Australia's leading institution in Indigenous Health Research. Other entities include Diamond Leisure Pty Ltd that operated casinos in Darwin and Alice Springs, and the NT Tourism Commission.

A leader in the formation of NT education institutions, which later became Charles Darwin University, he was recognised as Emeritus Chancellor and awarded an Hon. Doctorate of Letters. He is also a Companion of the Menzies School of Health Research and a Fellow of the National Heart Foundation.

Richard has also chaired a number of boards including Northern Territory Tourist Commission, Adelaide Festival Centre and Adelaide Festival Corporation. He served on the board of Port Adelaide Football Club, and has chaired and held directorships in a number of public companies both listed and unlisted, together with several statutory authorities for the Federal Government, including the Australian Government Solicitors Advisory Board, Federal Attorney-General's Advisory Board, and Indigenous Business Australia, and Director of the Northern Territory Treasury Advisory Board.

As Chair of the National Heart Foundation, he was awarded the Sir John Lowenthal Award for Outstanding Contribution to the National Heart Foundation. Other awards include Officer of the Order of Australia (AO) for his work with Indigenous people in the Northern Territory, the Australia Institute of Company Directors' Inaugural Distinguished Director of the Northern Territory, the National Centenary Medal, and Australia Day Council Achievers Award.

NORTHERN TERRITORY REFLECTIONS

1970s and Beyond

Richard Ryan

Wakefield Press

Wakefield Press
16 Rose Street
Mile End
South Australia 5031
www.wakefieldpress.com.au

First published 2026

Supported by a grant from the Government of South Australia.

Edited by Julia Beaven, Wakefield Press
Text designed and typeset by Jesse Pollard, Wakefield Press

ISBN 978 1 92338 855 0

NATIONAL LIBRARY OF AUSTRALIA

A catalogue record for this book is available from the National Library of Australia

CORIOLE
McLAREN VALE

Wakefield Press thanks Coriole Vineyards for continued support

Contents

Introduction

The Northern Territory was, and still is, fundamentally, significantly different from all the Australian States – physically, politically and economically. This unexplored territory, the so-called 'backwater' of colonial development on the northern coast of Australia, was settled by 'white fellas' who arrived from Britain with high hopes, unaware of the Indigenous population who had lived there for millennia.

It has long been thought of as a great economic opportunity and in earlier days a place to be safeguarded against Asian invasion. It is at least arguable that the Makassan trepang fishermen were the first non-Aboriginal visitors to the Northern Territory. They are reported to have come via Roti Island in Timor at least as far as Ashmore reef as early as the 17th century.

These visitors prospered for the next 200 years or so, shipping about 900 tonnes of trepang per year for sale to Chinese merchants until finally shut out by the newly federated Australia after 1901, as part of the White Australia Policy.

There are suggestions that Chinese traders may have also landed each December and left again on the trade winds in April with their booty. The Aboriginal population greatly discouraged settlement but were happy to trade.

Evidence of their camps on the coast from the Gulf country across Arnhem Land, to the Tiwi islands and WA, remains in the form of artifacts, tamarind trees, some genetic infusion, words in local languages, and records of Indigenous travel to Makassar. They are reported to have introduced gambling, alcohol and metal axes, and traded women, pearls and sandalwood in addition to allowing access to trepang.

European settlers were not so successful. The British tried three times to establish settlements, in 1824, 1838 and 1864, to demonstrate their claim to the territory and to establish a trading port before success with the establishment of Darwin in 1869. It was treated as part of NSW until the first attempt at an independent colony in 1846 and then annexed to South Australia in 1863. South Australia inherited high hopes for the Northern Territory as a gateway to Asian markets, and as a source of land to sell to settlers to develop agriculture.

Between the 1820s and 1850s, control over the Northern Territory was in the hands of the NSW Government. It oversaw the establishment of British military settlements in the Top End, predominantly to protect the North from invaders. South Australia had been colonised in the late 1830s and by the 1860s the South Australian Government was ambitiously stretching north, keen to possess this potential agrarian environment. In 1863 it enthusiastically took over the administration of the Territory, and within a few years, Port Darwin was established. This was followed in the 1870s with the building of a telegraph line linking Port Darwin to Adelaide. Significantly, Port Darwin was set up as a strategic base for the Overland Telegraph Line to connect the Australian mainland with the rest of the world.

Meanwhile, in the 1850s, gold was discovered at Bendigo and Ballarat, and inevitably there were searches for it all over the country, including in the Northern Territory. It was discovered around Pine Creek, attracting Chinese labourers.

The South Australian Government's ambitious vision of successful pastoral expansion northwards across Goyder's Line was never to occur. Goyder's Line, developed in 1865 by Surveyor-General George Goyder, is the line of reliable rainfall in southern Australia that separates land suitable for crops from drier grazing land. It helped potential pastoralists from Britain to decide where to farm.

Interestingly, in 1876 the Government of South Australia devised a scheme to attract settlers from Japan to migrate to the Northern Territory to grow sugar. In 1898 the Japanese Consul in Adelaide visited Tokyo to negotiate with Japanese capitalists for the sale of land on the Victoria River in the Northern Territory. The scheme had no real success; the South Australian Government eventually withdrew its support and it lapsed.

It was inevitable that by 1901, when the other States joined together as a Federation, the new Commonwealth Government would be deputed to take over responsibility for the administration of the Northern Territory. By the time this occurred in 1911, settlement in the Northern Territory was still insignificant.

It is interesting to note that according to *The Great Central State: The Foundation of the Northern Territory*, by Jack Cross, Wakefield Press (2011), South Australia (and by extension, the Northern Territory) had the most enlightened policies for dealing with the Indigenous (and women's) rights of any of the colonies. From 1856, Aboriginal men had the right to vote. Women's suffrage was granted in 1894.

The rest of Australia gave South Australia a choice at Federation, either they rescind Aboriginal people's or women's right to vote, they could not keep both. They chose women.

Dr Brian Reid in his monogram, *The Menzies School of Health Research: Establishment, 1978–1997*, perceptively wrote: 'In terms of the global colonial enterprise, settlement in the Northern Territory was insignificant so it is hardly surprising that it did not become a site for medical research.' Ironically, this very school of health research was to go on to become one of the most significant in the country. However, the 'empty North' syndrome that Reid's comment refers to was to haunt successive Federal Governments from the debating of the Northern Territory Acceptance Bill in 1910 and beyond. Throughout this period there was a complete disregard for the rights of the First Nations people who occupied the large land spaces of the Territory and had for millennia.

Unlike the rest of the population, they were not to become subject to any Commonwealth census until the 1960s.

With a European population of only about 3000, it was inevitable that this 'empty North' was feared to be open to attack and occupation by the Asian countries to the north and so, at the start of the First World War, attention was quickly focused on it. By the 1920s, Darwin with its population of Aboriginal and multinational people of 'mixed descent' had grown. Asian immigrants, predominantly Chinese, and a few Japanese, had begun to filter into the North, attracted by the emerging pearling and prawning industries in Broome and Queensland, and later in the Northern Territory.

It was at this point that the Commonwealth Department of Health officially became the 'Protector of the Aborigines'. Its policy of limited assimilation of people of 'mixed descent', which particularly applied to people living in town camps and on pastoral properties, led to the establishment of land reserves, where large groups or 'tribal' Indigenous populations dwelt.

Thus, the population of the Northern Territory was restructured into three categories: urban townships where Europeans and people of 'mixed descent' lived, pastoral properties with their Indigenous workers, and land reserves where Indigenous tribal groups lived in their own communities.

It is interesting to note the history and numbers of Chinese in Darwin in the early days. (Refer to Appendix K.)

In the 1940s, the Second World War descended on Darwin and the Northern Territory in a manner that, in retrospect, should have been predictable. It was brutal and damaging, and invariably highly disruptive. With the heavy bombing in 1942, which inflicted enormous physical damage and human suffering, Darwin became the nation's northern route offshore, as well as being the first Australian location to be bombed and disrupted; it was also, temporarily, the location of military command.

The Northern Territory, now a strategic Allied military base, became the home of troops, aircraft, shipping and all other military support. With this came new radio and aerial communications, and the appropriate civil engineering and associated works. After the war, Darwin remained the strategic defence base, in order for the country to protect its northern coastline.

The consequent improved communications and the building of the Stuart Highway and other major roads were a bonus for the city. For the first time the Top End became relatively easy to access, and so its population increased.

In the 1950s, with Paul Hasluck's appointment as the Federal Minister for Territories, 'assimilation' became a consideration. There was substantial investment in rural government settlements and in missions in the Northern Territory, and by the end of the 1950s, the local Northern Territory Administration had taken on significantly more responsibilities.

As if the Second World War's damage to Darwin's structures and the safety and confidence of its people hadn't been enough, in late 1974 Cyclone Tracy arrived. In financial terms, the cyclone ended up being a blessing in disguise. The rebuilding of the city generated an enormous amount of new work and significantly stimulated the economy. The remaining local labour forces were far too small to do the work alone, and there was a desperate need for sensible and sound government in order to build a new Darwin and a new life and to encourage investment and increase the population.

There was a growing need for the various communities and groups in Darwin to learn to co-exist and build a larger and more cohesive social force. Pastoralists might have believed that they were able to supply what Indigenous workers wanted, but this so-called 'paternalism' demonstrated by missions and cattle-station owners towards Indigenous groups was rejected with distain by virtually all the Indigenous workers. At the same time, the Northern Territory Administration was attempting to amalgamate some of the communities into local councils.

In 1966 the Aboriginal people's struggle for land rights and fair wages emerged with the very public strike and walk-off of the Gurindji people at Wave Hill Station. From the late 19th century, the cattle station had been run by the Vestey Group, a British pastoral company. The strike was led by Indigenous rights activist Vincent Lingiari, who as a young man had been a stockman at the station where the Indigenous workers were paid in rations, tobacco and clothing, thus receiving significantly less pay than the non-Indigenous workers. As the *Sydney Morning Herald* noted in Lord Samuel Vestey's obituary in 2021: 'The treatment by Vestey managers was symptomatic, rather than atypical, of Australian managers at the time.'

When the owners of the station refused to improve the Indigenous workers' pay and working conditions and to hand back some of the Gurindji land on which the station stood, Lingiari was elected as leader of the Indigenous workers. In almost Biblical fashion, he led his people in a walk-off as a protest against the work and conditions.

In his obituary in the *Sydney Morning Herald*, Samuel Vestey, the third Lord Vestey, was described as 'the half-Australian heir to a vast meat fortune and head of one of the richest families in Britain, owners of vast holdings in the Northern Territory and Queensland'. It also stated:

> The Gurindji 'walk-off' followed years of complaints from Indigenous employees at Wave Hill, but it was aimed at a much bigger target. Before 1968 it had been illegal to pay an Indigenous worker more than a specified amount in goods and money and in many cases, the government benefits for which Indigenous employees were eligible were paid into pastoral companies' accounts rather than to the individuals. Over the next decade, the Gurindji people gained nationwide attention and support for their campaign for their rights. The Wave Hill Strike which lasted over eight years, would reshape the relationships between Indigenous Australians and the broader non-Indigenous community, and 'morphed' into a major Federal issue when the Gurindji people demanded the return of their traditional lands.

The Whitlam Government called for a Royal Commission to 'recommend the most appropriate ways of recognizing and establishing Land Rights'.

Justice Edward Woodward's first report, in July 1973, recommended that a Northern Land Council and a Central Land Council be established to present the views of the Indigenous people. His final report led to the Federal Government introducing the Aboriginal Land Rights (NT) Bill 1975 into Parliament. It 'ensured that Aborigines [in the NT] could retain a traditional relationship with the land' and provided the economic base by 'giving them the right to negotiate with mining companies and receive Royalties', representing a reversal in government policy. Lord Vestey's obituary noted:

> It was Prime Minister Gough Whitlam who, in 1975, was to hand the Gurindji a lease over a small portion of Wave Hill, dramatically pouring its sand into the hand of their leader, Vincent Lingiari. The incident featured everywhere in the media and remains the mark of a significant moment in the nation's history. In effect, it allowed title to be transferred to Indigenous people, and granted them the opportunity to claim other land not owned, leased, or being used by someone else. When Gough Whitlam's Labor government was dismissed by the Governor-General before the legislation could be passed, the Fraser government that followed resubmitted it to Parliament virtually unchanged in 1976, at which point it was finally enacted. The actual Land Rights Transfer to the Gurindji people was therefore signed by Whitlam's successor, Liberal Prime Minister Malcolm Fraser.

The Commonwealth *Racial Discrimination Act 1975* also had a major impact, both in the Northern Territory and Australia-wide. But for this Act, the rights of Indigenous people to Native Title could have been removed by State governments. Queensland attempted this, prior to the finding of 'Native Title' by the High Court in the Mabo Case in 1992.

The Northern Land Council (NLC) in the Top End of the Northern Territory is now one of four in the Northern Territory. The others are the Central Land Council (CLC) covering the southern half, the Tiwi Land Council covering the Tiwi Islands north of Darwin, and the Anindilyakwa Land Council covering

Groote Eylandt in the Gulf of Carpentaria. The most important task and responsibility of these councils is consulting with traditional landowners and Indigenous groups who have interests in Country and its land use and management, and access for tourism, mining and other businesses. This can involve facilitating group negotiation and consensus building among scores of traditional Indigenous landowner groups, and many other impacted Indigenous people. While most of the Indigenous people in the NLC's area live in the region's major towns, there are also about 200 communities scattered over the lands in its area, ranging from small family groups on outstations to settlements of up to 3000 people.

The NLC has become the representative body with statutory authority for this area under the Commonwealth's *Aboriginal Land Rights (Northern Territory) Act 1976*. It also has responsibilities under the Commonwealth *Native Title Act 1993* and the Northern Territory *Pastoral Land Act 1992*.

Its Top End Zone is divided into seven regions, with regional offices in Palmerston, Katherine, Jabiru, Nhulunbuy, Tennant Creek, Ngukurr, Borroloola and Timber Creek. In 2022 it was estimated that there were 61,000 Indigenous people (approximately 30%) who formed a major part of the Northern Territory's population, and that they 'owned' some 50% of the land in the Northern Territory.

The Northern Territory Land Council stated in 2022 that, in many areas, a system of 'managers' and 'owners' operated. Land managers generally have maternal links to the land, landowners generally paternal links. Aboriginal landowners and managers have specific and complementary rights and obligations to ensure the spiritual and physical health of defined areas of land. All Aboriginal land is private property owned under special freehold title. It cannot be bought, acquired or forfeited. This is the strongest form of title in Australia.

The Aboriginal Land Rights (NT) Act 1976 has enabled Aboriginal people to gain inalienable freehold title to around 50% of the Northern Territory and, through the High Court's 2008 Blue Mud Bay decision, about 85% of the NT coastline. For the most part, Aboriginal landowners have the exclusive power to control the direction and pace of development on their lands. The public, in the form of government at various levels, has only limited rights to impose external development or conservation direction or constraints. Aboriginal land is not owned by individuals. It is granted as a communal title. Land is formally held by land trusts – groups of Aboriginal people who hold the title for the benefit of all the traditional owners and people with a traditional interest in the land.

In 1974, politically conservative non-Indigenous forces started agitating for self-government in the Northern Territory. They aligned to create the Country Liberal Party (CLP), which was publicly recognised and able to hold power for more than 20 years. The election for self-government was held in 1978.

It is interesting to note that despite an easy win to the Country Liberal Party there was a 15% swing to the ALP compared to the previous election. This impacted on CLP leadership. When CLP leader Geoff Letts lost his seat Paul Everingham took over and was to lead the party into self-government, becoming Chief Minister.

In real terms the platform for both parties was not hugely dissimilar – both parties supported eventual statehood and the recognition of uranium mining. The latter was bizarre, as the Federal Government did not at any stage agree to the transfer of mineral rights and did not consult the NT Government regarding the future of uranium mining.

In the 1978 election, the CLP gained almost all seats in the new fully elected Legislative Assembly and formed the first Northern

Territory Government. Legislative power in the Territory rests with the Legislative Assembly, which consists of the Administrator of the Northern Territory and the Members of the Assembly. However, it does so by a delegation of powers from the Commonwealth, rather than by constitutional right. This means that the Commonwealth maintains the power to overrule Northern Territory Government legislation and impose its own. This has occurred most frequently in the more remote areas of the Territory and includes the highly significant granting of Indigenous land rights. Commonwealth land use also remains prominent, particularly in Darwin and Katherine with the large defence force presence, and all the associated military bases and training and staging areas.

Commonwealth interests and other external agents and forces have retained a strong hold on power over a number of matters in the Northern Territory, even after 1978. The Federal Government has not transferred significant rights such as some mineral resources, national parks, native title and certain lands to Territory control. The Federal Government also has the power to disallow laws passed by the Northern Territory Assembly. This retention of powers has never applied to another jurisdiction.

The non-transference of power over mineral resources inevitably led to consequences and fall out. An example was the mining of uranium by the company ERA at Jabiru. Under the Hawke-led Federal Labor Government, which followed Fraser's Coalition Government, a policy of uranium mining was granted under licence. Even though the proposed mine site was on Northern Territory land, the Northern Territory Government was not involved in the process.

Another drama that emerged with self-government was that when the new government came into existence it literally had no public service of substance in place, and so the large government departments such as Education and Health were now the responsibility of local administrators, who had to take responsibility from the Federal Government. Infrastructure had to be developed for a new and expanding public service sector in the Northern Territory. Coincidentally Papua and New Guinea obtained independence at the same time. This was a blessing because it meant that when many of the Australian public service personnel who had worked offshore returned to Australia, a number of them chose to move to the Northern Territory. At least four of the new government departments in the Everingham era were headed by expats who had been working in Papua New Guinea.

Private sector activity at the time across the Northern Territory was essentially limited to mining and tourism, and for the most part these activities were conducted by companies headquartered outside of the Territory. There were very few locally based, large-scale investors. 'The Territory's economy was therefore highly dependent on external sources of financial investment tied to the extraction of minimally processed natural resources; this position remains even today. In the Northern Territory mining revenue accounted for over 20% of Gross State Product (GSP) in 2006/2007, while a similar amount was received from Commonwealth Government Transfers.

The political economy of peripheral export-dependent resource economies (also called staple economies), brings about economic, political and social/demographic risks. The dependence on external agents, be they resource companies or central governments, also means that opportunities for internal economic development with locally based industries are not realised. For example, between 2001 and 2006, about half of all new jobs created in Darwin were in the construction sector, which is again dominated by external investors.

The combination of the Northern Territory's small population, along with its very remote areas with Indigenous communities and its obvious lack of any form of a manufacturing sector, has all meant that its economy essentially has been based on the pastoral industry, along with tourism and mining . . . although minimal on a national scale.

Developments such as the Sheraton Hotels in Darwin and Alice Springs and Ayers Rock Resort (Yulara) have taken place, with the bulk of the funds for these either borrowed or provided by way of grants from the Federal Government, thus resulting in a huge outflow of capital from the Northern Territory Government.

A major project that did have a significant private equity was the establishment of casinos in both Darwin and Alice Springs by the Northern Territory Government with Federal Hotels.

Funding the administration of the Northern Territory will remain a real challenge.

One measure that caused national consternation was the 2015 sale of the port of Darwin – the most significant deepwater port along the north coast of Australia – to Chinese interests. It remains to be seen if the governments of both China and Australia enable this investment to evolve into the major trading port envisaged 150 years before, or it remains hostage to defence fears.

Subsequent media articles in the *Australian Financial Review* and *Northern Territory News* on 28 November 2024 revealed the port is facing troubling financial conditions. Matt Cunningham in the *NT News* reported the Chinese company that operates the port was considering the prospect of terminating the lease. However, management of the company stated that they were confident that all financial issues would be properly resolved.

Chapter 1

A New Era

I was just a ten-year-old when my father, only in his thirties, died from a heart attack as a result of his war wounds. His brother, Uncle Ron, came from the Northern Territory to stay with us and be with my father while he was dying and it was Uncle Ron who told me all about the Territory. In the 1950s the Northern Territory was, to most Australians who lived in the other so-called 'civilised' states, 'the last frontier', a territory to which struggling individuals fled. The two main communities of Darwin and Alice Springs were a cultural mix of rugged pioneer survivors, immigrants from East and Southeast Asia, and Indigenous people. And then there were the distant Outback areas where the Indigenous communities predominantly dwelt.

By 1971 the Northern Territory still had a population of fewer than 140,000 people spread sparsely across an area that is around 17.5% of the landmass of Australia. Approximately 25% of these people, or in total about 1.08% of Australia's population, were Indigenous. Being a territory, it was administered from Canberra. There were no locally publicly listed industrial companies, and significantly limited education and health resources. Successive Commonwealth Governments, for the most part, simply didn't comprehend the adversities faced in the Northern Territory, nor the aspirations of the Territorians, and so their funding was not fruitful. Paul Hasluck, Minister for the Territories in the 1950s and 60s, was one who identified the inadequacies of the Canberra administration and the inevitable frustrations it induced.

The mid 1970s to 2000s were exciting times for those living in the Northern Territory. Why was this so? Well, there was the new self-government learning the ropes, a young population trying to make a mark and help engage with a significant change in the Australian nation in relation to Indigenous people, and their role in society, particularly in relation to their land rights.

The introduction of self-government and the ensuant establishment of a public service resulted in the creation of departments of Education, Treasury, Health, Tourism, and the like. In addition, to stimulate tourism, the new government initiated the development of Yulara, the building of two new international hotels, and opened casinos in Darwin and Alice Springs – all of this coupled with the opening of Northern Territory Tourism offices around Australia. The education system was also completely overhauled, with the ultimate aim of establishing a university. Nowhere else in Australia provided so many possibilities.

Henry Walker Pty Ltd was created during this period. This small local contracting business was to become the first industrial company, resident in the Northern Territory, to list on the Australian Stock Exchange. This same publicly listed company had, for the first time ever in the corporate history of Australia, an Indigenous person as a director and Aboriginal and Torres Strait Islander Corporation (CDC) as a shareholder.

Where else in Australia could this happen?

The company not only had an Indigenous director, but as a public company it also entered into joint ventures with Indigenous communities of the region, also a first in Australia. Inevitably this caused huge changes, not only in the sleepy environment of the Northern Territory but for Australia and its people as a whole.

The Territory from the seventies onwards then, was an exciting and highly volatile place to be. It was changing from a place where fly-in fly-out experts were engaged to a place where they were predominantly local. Within three years, the four major national accounting firms that had never previously had a resident manager in the Northern Territory, all had resident partners.

Following Cyclone Tracy, the Northern Territory economy, which had been moribund, boomed. The Territory was becoming a destination in its own right.

It is also true that Northern Territory governments of both persuasions put the future of the Territory and its education, economy, and wellbeing in front of their careers as individuals.

Only history will show how effective these initiatives were, but I suggest that history is likely to be kind. My personal reflections, nevertheless, are simply a commentary about that time and the changes that occurred.

Chapter 2

Arrival in the Northern Territory

I was one of those attracted to the Northern Territory. As a young man I took my wife and children there in order to set up an accountancy practice. The primary motivation for my decision was to be with family, and make money and to do it with the support of my two favourite uncles, one of whom had lived in Darwin, the other in Katherine.

One of these, my uncle Ron Ryan, had an enormous influence on my life. An early Native Welfare Officer in the Northern Territory, he had gone to Elliot soon after the end of the Second World War to work as one of the few Patrol Officers. This role was similar to that of Patrol Officers in New Guinea at that time. Elliot is halfway between Darwin and Alice Springs on the Stuart Highway and about 250 km north of Tennant Creek so, like New Guinea, it was truly remote!

You have to wonder what it was that caused him to do this, in what was plainly a very challenging environment. It was, he said, because of something that happened to him during the war. It's a fascinating story, but one rarely discussed during his lifetime.

Ron was a member of an Australian Infantry Battalion (2/10th) that fought in New Guinea. They'd been under attack and at the end of the battle he was out on a lone patrol searching for fallen comrades when he found a critically wounded Australian soldier. He picked up the soldier and was carrying him on his back when in the distance a large Japanese patrol force approached. He acted quickly, lying down beneath the wounded soldier. Holding his breath, he lay perfectly still as a Japanese soldier stabbed a bayonet into the wounded soldier on top, killing him. Miraculously Ron survived, covered in the blood of the dying soldier. He survived because the Japanese soldier had assumed Ron was already dead.

Ron went to the Territory because he believed he must pay back a debt to society. He believed his life had been saved at the expense of his Australian colleague. I was very fortunate to have him as an uncle after my father died, and he became my foster father. My father had fought in the Second World War in the same battalion as Ron but was medically discharged after being wounded in Milne Bay and returned home to study oenology. Soon after he died of a heart attack. My mother had always told us that he had topped his oenology class at Roseworthy College. When I visited the College to admire his name on the College Honour Board, it was plain to see how he managed this feat. He was the only student to have sat the exam. His choice of studies however does help explain my love of red wine!

It was no doubt inevitable then, that when I left boarding school at Rostrevor College, where I had a Legacy Scholarship, I would choose to go to the Royal Military College at Duntroon. Engineering was a compulsory First Year subject there and it is ironic that many years later, as Managing Director of Henry Walker Eltin, I was to become a Companion of the Institution of Engineers, Australia.

After a couple of years at Duntroon, with its somewhat more sophisticated lifestyle than I'd had at school, I nevertheless resigned. Returning home to Adelaide, I enrolled to study Medicine at the University of Adelaide. This time I lasted 18 months before deciding again that this wasn't the course for me. However, I did have a very pleasant last two semesters sharing my wisdom in the University Refectory!

Attempting to get my somewhat dysfunctional life in order and, even more importantly, to get my black Triumph TR2 sports car repaired, I applied to the Education Department in South Australia for a position as a teacher. My mother had been one. Within days I found myself as a class teacher of 2G at Unley High School – a boys' class of 32 – in the days of class streaming. My official title was Temporary Junior Assistant on Probation for six months. I loved teaching and after six months rose to the giddy heights of Temporary Junior Assistant. While teaching I undertook accounting part-time and, two years later, I went to work with a large international accounting firm. I could not see a long-term financial future for me in the education system, even though it is one of the most rewarding positions I have held.

Meantime, Uncle Ron had ultimately settled in Katherine and married Ena Harvey, acting matron of the Katherine Hospital. The park south of the Katherine River, near where you travel over the bridge, is named in his memory . . . as is one of the bars in the Katherine Club.

My other uncle, my mother's brother Reg Gross, was in charge of the Department of Civil Aviation in the Territory during the 1950s and 60s. Writing about him in his 2003 obituary in the *Melbourne Sun*, Don Charwood said:

> In 1939, nine days after the outbreak of war, Reg enlisted in the RAAF. Trained as a navigator, he was posted to the renowned 10 Squadron, stationed at Mount Batten, on Plymouth Sound. The Squadron's Sunderland flying boats were engaged in the anti-U boat patrols from the English Channel down to the Bay of Biscay; they in turn were hunted by packs of long-

> range German fighters. As a navigator he directed the pilot's evasive action.
>
> He was awarded a Distinguished Flying Cross for his actions.
>
> Reg had previously joined the air traffic control branch of the Department of Civil Aviation and when he was repatriated from Britain after the war, he was given the task of setting up a training school in accordance with provisional international standards . . .
>
> In 1952, he was appointed Civil Aviation's Regional Director of the Northern Territory, a region seen to be in need of strong leadership as it was showing a tendency to go its own way.
>
> Reg's unannounced visits to all NT stations were cyclonic in nature and were followed by a deluge of telegrams and teleprinter messages demanding that operational shortcomings be set right before his next visit. These became known as Grossograms. Despite reverberations throughout the Northern Territory, Reg never lost his popularity, and many improvements were made.

Many people have heard about the infamous Russian spy incident known as the Petrov Affair. Uncle Reg as Director of the Department of Civil Aviation in the Northern Territory, had to run the gauntlet for the Federal Government. The Russian-bound aircraft carried two armed KGB agents who had forced Mrs. Petrov on board in Sydney when her husband defected from the Russian Embassy. The aircraft had to land in Darwin to refuel, and it was there that the Northern Territory Police disarmed one of the guards and rescued Mrs. Petrov, thus enabling her to return to her husband.

I still chuckle about how, as part of the operation, the police handed this very proper public servant, my Uncle Reg, a KGB revolver, which family legend says he put in a parcel and sent to the Secretary of the Department of Civil Aviation in Canberra.

No 007 here! But his life of drama had not ended. Having later settled in Melbourne, it was Reg as controller who led the search for Prime Minister Harold Holt when, in 1967, he was lost swimming at Portsea in Victoria. In 1974, Reg was recalled to Darwin, following the news on Christmas Eve of the devastation of the city by Cyclone Tracy. It was his job to coordinate the air evacuation of the homeless families to the southern states. He ended his career as the Australian member of the Council of the International Civil Aviation Organisation based in Canada.

As for me, after two years of practising as a chartered accountant in rural South Australia, I knew it was time for me to head to the Territory. And although I've now had homes in Sydney and Adelaide, along with an apartment in Paris, I guess that I felt I have never really left; arriving in the Northern Territory in 1971 felt like coming home to family.

Over the next decade we established, with partners, a series of accounting practices nationally, with three in the Northern Territory which specialised in general practice and insolvency. At one stage we had eight across the country, all of which had insolvency sections.

John Gamble and I looked after the accounting practices that were based in Darwin, Katherine and Alice Springs. The practice specialised in general management, taxation, insolvency and primary industry and Indigenous matters. It developed extensively into a powerhouse of primary industry. John specialised in that section and I worked predominantly in Indigenous and insolvency matters.

At its peak the practice would have been the forefront in terms of the number of Northern Territory cattle station clientele. This work often entailed travel by air or road to very remote locations. One week out west to Limbunya in the Kimberley; the next east along the Plenty Highway to Argadargada in the Georgina Basin. Many interesting characters, lots of tall tales and unforgettable experiences.

There was Ted, for example who had left school at age 14 and whose first job was in the employ of a drover who 'used to whip me with the hobble chains at least daily, whether I needed it or not'. Ted escaped this sadist after a year or two, tried to join the army, but was too young, and worked at stations around Queensland and the Northern Territory until – with a business partner – he managed to buy the Argadargada lease. Over the years Ted paid his partner out, raised five children and then bought each of them their own cattle station. John and I witnessed (and abetted) many remarkable success stories such as Ted's, and were proud to have been part of it.

There was the occasional downside of course. John sent one of our senior staff out to a Top End station by plane one day, to serve notice by a secured lender of default under mortgage. The staff member was met at the station's airstrip by a hard man toting a rifle, whereupon the staff member simply got back on the plane and returned to Darwin (with the papers).

The Indigenous work side of the practice grew at an enormous rate and was very rewarding, both financially and personally. A simple example was our involvement in the Community of Bamyili, 80 kms south of Katherine, population approximately 400 (also known as Barunga, among other names). We helped the financial aspects of the Community's building program, the general store and other matters such as how to establish and run a board of management.

In 1972 the government decided to start a buffalo eradication program, in order to eliminate brucellosis and bovine tuberculosis in the cattle industry.

In addition there was a drive by the government to build houses at remote Indigenous communities and provide some means of self-reliance. I flew out to the Bulman (400 kms from Darwin) on the edge of Arnhem Land to meet Indigenous families, living on country that teems with wildlife, including water buffalo. Bulman was accessible by road only in the dry season, and a 'mobile' abattoir was set up anew each year. It was a major operation; at the onset of the dry season a grader reconstructs the Roper River Road through to Bulman, and a fleet of modified Nissan 4WD trailers, fuel trucks, power plants, refrigeration units, accommodation units, and butchering rooms depart from Katherine. The buffalo are shot in the bush, winched onto trailers, and must be transported to the abattoirs in a limited time period. The meat is boxed, chilled, and most of it is exported to SE Asia within days.

These clients introduced us to a whole new world. We were delighted to be involved, and made many friends.

Territorians would be aware of names and places such as Yirrakla Business Enterprises, Jawoyn Association, Nelly and Tex Camfoo from Bulman, Willie Martin, Robert Lee, Beswick, Hooker Creek, and so on.

As a practice we were probably involved in at least 30 communities, all of which created incredibly rewarding work.

I was lucky to have several high-profile and national appointments, one of which was a business owned by 1985 *Australian* newspaper's *Australian of The Year* John David 'Jay' Pendarvis of Mudginberri Abattoir. It attracted huge national interest and led me to becoming involved in a broad array of industries and institutions, and a large variety of government and non-government boards, including listed and non-listed public companies. I went on to participate in decision-making and developments in higher and tertiary education, Indigenous communities, pastoralism, mining and tourism.

It was in the early 70s when, as the new accountant in town, I was recommended to Frazer Henry and Neville Walker to sort out the financial aspects of their fledgling company Henry and Walker. Little was I to know that by 1987 I would become Chief Executive of that company, and this would grow into my major career. Eventually we had 4500 employees nationally and internationally and worked in collaboration with multinational corporations both on and offshore. Nor could I have predicted that we would become national leaders in training and working with Indigenous people, our way paved by my foster father, Uncle Ron. Self-government for the Northern Territory meant self- determination and increased autonomy in Indigenous issues. It also meant considerable debt. Henry and Walker's associated expansion also had ramifications, some of which would sadly lead to its demise.

Chapter 3

Cyclone Tracy Hits

In the early 1970s, as one of the few Court Insolvency practitioners in the Northern Territory, it was inevitable that I would receive a significant amount of work from the banks, mainly in tidying up businesses; sometimes also their brutal liquidation and closure.

One appointment resulted in me driving thousands of kilometres from Darwin to a very small town. I was the official receiver and manager of its most prominent business – the town pub. I knocked on the door of the hotel and was met by a chap holding a loaded shotgun. 'No, it's not like that,' I said. 'You've got to be kidding! Let's have a drink and we'll sort it out. And to make you happy, I'll pay!' With a slight chuckle, he dropped the gun and muttered, 'No, you're not paying, I'm just angry!'

We both got quietly inebriated and, needless to say, we sorted it out.

Why do I still recall this so vividly? Well, this is how it was in the Northern Territory in those early days of the 1970s and, for that matter, beyond.

There is one significant incident that we all recall in fine detail. On Christmas Eve of 1974 the almighty Cyclone Tracy arrived and wreaked such indescribable damage to the town that it resembled Hiroshima after the Second World War. Prime Minister Gough Whitlam was in Greece for Christmas and responded promptly to suggestions he should return to Australia.

On 25 December 1974, ABC News reporter Suzannah Lyons described the devastation:

> Cyclone Tracy has been described as the most significant tropical cyclone in Australia's history and it changed how we viewed the threat of tropical cyclones to Northern Australia.
>
> Tracy was reported as a Category Four Cyclone. It was small but intense, the radius of the gale-force winds was only 50 km. It made landfall just north of Fannie Bay at 3:30 am on Christmas Day 1974 and passed directly over Darwin.
>
> Wind gust of 217 kph was recorded before the anemometer at Darwin Airport failed. The maximum wind gusts have been estimated at up to 240 kph.
>
> Darwin received 250 mm of rain in just 12 hours and debris indicated a four-metre storm surge at Casuarina Beach.
>
> Sixty-five people died, 49 in Darwin and 16 who were lost at sea. At least 90% of homes in Darwin were demolished or badly damaged.

The total damage bill came to around $800 million, or many billions in today's money. More than 30,000 Darwin residents were evacuated after the cyclone, many never returned.

I had been at Christmas drinks at the office an hour or so before this extraordinary turbulence engulfed us. Our home was in the eye of the cyclone and so initially it was completely still – no wind, no damage – so we gave the children their Christmas presents. When the second half of the cyclone hit us there were chunks of houses flying through the air and it was suddenly a vastly different, deafening and terrifying place to be.

I lay on the bed with two children beside me and my wife did the same with the smallest child. Thank God we did so, because suddenly, from nowhere, a huge steel girder flew through one window across the bedroom and went out through the window on the other side of the room and we were splattered with glass. It was a natural reaction to push the two children underneath me and protect them.

Families' homes were flattened, but it was the human loss that destroyed the soul. One baby was struck by one of the flying girders and killed instantly. A truly dramatic time, although our three children with the eldest just six years old, initially thought it was fun . . . well for a while. He spent a week dressed in his Christmas present, a Batman outfit.

In the days immediately after the cyclone I helped carry out the census of Darwin's suburbs. It was uncanny; the greetings different at every house we visited. Maybe one in three houses had a person with a weapon of some description, invariably a rifle. Others would say, 'Let's have a beer, mate!'

The other major role was emptying refrigerators and similar electrical appliances that had no power for at least a week. The refrigerators were packed with chicken and turkey that had been bought in preparation for Christmas lunch and dinner. Trust me, the smell and the odour was absolutely vile, so much so that we had to work with face masks on. It was an interesting experience and a dreadful job.

Why was this person working on the census? For two days prior I had worked on the back of rubbish trucks picking up the debris. The chap who ran it pulled me aside and said, 'Richard, I think you'd be better at doing the census work.' He knew my heart was not in the job and, frankly, I didn't have the physical ability and certainly not the talent.

After the cyclone, Darwin's population of 47,000 diminished to around 12,500. It had been truly horrific but, in retrospect, it had also been strangely exciting. My family survived, and I was relieved when my wife and our three small children took off for Adelaide, all sharing just two seats on the aircraft.

We all know the stories of behaviour on sinking ships; the odd ones determined to break the rules. Two men dressed as women in an attempt to board a rescue plane and several pretended to be so ill that they had to leave Darwin urgently. Uncle Reg supervised the entire airlift, the Darwin Airways Exit Strategy, as 25,000 people were evacuated by air in the first five days, and 10,000 left by car.

Darwin was now a city without water and power, and most significantly without direction. I stayed on for six weeks, dealing with the losses of my 20 key staff members, who also needed support. I found myself busy writing cheques for money that I didn't have. In fact, there was a time when I was overdrawn and owed the Commercial Banking Company of Sydney about a half-a-million dollars, which is over $4 million in today's money. The financial climate was extremely difficult. Many clients had lost their business and, in two cases, had suffered a death in their families, so how could I ask them to pay an outstanding bill? When I finally landed in Adelaide the drama caught up with me and, as we touched down, I burst into tears.

Cyclone Tracy changed many lives; it changed ours. Our previous plans to sell our Darwin house and business, all got lost in the washup. It did the same for another small and unknown business. Henry and Walker had the plant and equipment so desperately needed and they donated use of this gear to help in the monumental task of cleaning up Darwin, a gesture that would change their lives too. In the wake of Cyclone Tracy, Henry and Walker began to utilise skills that would develop their civil engineering and work for mining companies in remote areas. This horrific cyclone, by chance, created significant initial work for them in terms of plant hire, engineering and ongoing maintenance of public utilities.

Both men were highly skilled practical plant operators with unique abilities in operating and maintaining heavy machinery. Having met in the Northern Territory and become friends, they were smart enough to see that there were great opportunities to create a profitable business. These two established the partnership that was to become Henry Walker, the first home-grown publicly listed company in the Northern Territory.

In 1978 Henry and Walker was still small, but it was growing, inadvertently helped by the unlimited opportunities that had emerged in the wake of the 1974 cyclone.

Chapter 4

After the Cyclone

This, then, is the environment into which I walked in the latter part of the twentieth century. The small contracting company Henry and Walker became one of my clients. Their growth following Cyclone Tracy led them to become the largest ASX listed company in the Northern Territory, and one of the largest and most significant contracting and mining companies in Australia and internationally, working both onshore and offshore, with an annual turnover of more than AU$1 billion per year and more than 4500 employees. As a major ASX listed company, Henry and Walker had the capacity to negotiate with Indigenous communities regarding their land and mineral resources.

The volatile economic environment also led the Northern Territory Government to create the Northern Territory Treasury Corporation, a centralised borrowing authority that enabled funds to be obtained at competitive rates, both wholesale and retail, in the marketplace. These funds were used, in part, to develop tourism and create employment.

The Darwin casino, Don Hotel Casino, was established. Its success led to a new casino, Lasseters Hotel Casino, opening in Alice Springs in 1981. I was an initial director of the Northern Territory Treasury Corporation Advisory Board and later a director of the entity that would operate the casinos when they were resumed by the Northern Territory Government.

I was fortunate to witness these significant developments in the Territory, and to participate in the establishment of the Northern Territory Treasury Corporation, Henry and Walker Ltd, and the torrid times of the Territory casinos.

All three of these in an uncanny way were interrelated, because the government could not have taken over the casinos without appropriate funding from the Treasury Corporation, and Henry and Walker would have never been involved but for the government's interest in the Japanese company Kumagai Gumi, who were a major shareholder in Henry Walker, and who at the time wanted to establish a large presence in the Territory. But more of this later.

Successive Commonwealth Governments, for the most part, were unable to comprehend the adversities and challenges faced in the Northern Territory, and the aspirations of the Territorians always provided inadequate funding. One example of the shortcomings of the Canberra administration, and the inevitable frustrations this produced, had been identified by Paul Hasluck, who as Minister for the Territories (1951–1963) wrote a letter to the then Federal Treasurer Arthur Fadden seeking funding.

> I would myself have thought the claims of the people in the territory, who are more remote from the main centre of population and more deficient in opportunities for recreation, would be rated far higher than the claims of the sheltered, pampered, and unproductive inhabitants of the national sanatorium that is called the national capital.

Miraculously, funding was approved. You could argue that this situation continues today.

The Darwin Hospital was another example of the inadequacies of the Canberra administration. Prior to Cyclone Tracy, approval had been given for construction of the Casuarina Hospital in the northern suburb of Tiwi. It was to be based on the design of the distant Woden Valley Hospital in Canberra with its extremes of climate. This was blatantly not suitable for the temperate tropical climate that existed in the north. The provision of snow panels in the design, among other architectural and engineering specifications, ensured that locals, not unreasonably, illustrated Canberra's lack of understanding of the Northern Territory.

In 1974 the Whitlam Government passed an Act devolving the governance of the Northern Territory and creating a fully elected Legislative Assembly with 19 members. On 1 January 1977, the Northern Territory Public Sector was created and administrative powers relating to a number of State functions (such as police, fire brigades, local government and correctional services) were transferred from the Commonwealth to the Northern Territory. Other functions, such as health and education were progressively transferred. In 1978, under the Fraser Federal Government, the Commonwealth passed the *Northern Territory (Self-Government) Act 1978*, thus officially establishing the Northern Territory.

Chapter 5

Northern Territory Self-Government

Self-government in the Northern Territory meant state-like autonomy with its own Legislative Assembly and it gave the Administrator the power to grant or deny assent to proposed law. Following this, the first Ministry of the new Northern Territory Government was appointed, and the Legislative Assembly was given authority and responsibility for the finances of the government of the Northern Territory.

The 1978 Cabinet submissions and decisions show the challenges and opportunities that the newly self-governed Territory's first Cabinet was obliged to meet in order to establish a governance framework. Deliberations ranged over such matters as the introduction of new legislation following the transfer of powers from the Commonwealth, the establishment of various Northern Territory Public Service functions, approval of the 1978/79 budget, the establishment of government supply and tender boards, policy on regionalisation of government operations, civil works programs, law and order, motor vehicle registration charges, stamp duty rates, and government advisory committees. Significant among these was a submission relating to the establishment of casinos in Darwin and Alice Springs.

The Territory boasted a very young population during the late part of the twentieth century, with over 80% of the population in Darwin being younger than 45.

In 1979 the Northern Territory Government accepted responsibility for Health (on 1 January), Education (1 July) and the Supreme Court (1 October). This finalised the transfer of functions and the establishment of self-government. The Territory's first owned and operated insurance company (Territory Insurance Office) was opened on 2 July in the same year. It was the first in the world to create and issue crocodile attack insurance policies, which still operate in the Northern Territory today.

On 21 September 1979, Darwin's first interim casino opened at the old Don Hotel on Cavenagh Street. Laws controlling the operation of casinos in the Territory were agreed by the Administrator, paving the way for a mini casino to be built. The casino became a drawcard for high rollers and marked the point when Darwin matured, becoming a vibrant city and a popular destination for visitors. A second casino was constructed at Mindil Beach in 1981.

On 21 October 1979, Alice Springs was linked to the rest of Australia and the world with the acquisition of STD telephone dial-up. Tennant Creek, Elliott, Renner Springs, Three Ways and Frewena also benefited from the 13 repeater stations that were installed over a 580-km route, providing them with direct access to the rest of the continent and easing the burden of remote living through access to better communication.

The Territory's development continued in 1979 with tenders called for the construction of a naval patrol centre and boat worth $17.8 million at Larrakeyah, the opening of a new bridge over Warlock Ponds south of Mataranka, and the opening of the Smith Street Mall. Growth in the mining and industry sectors was also strengthening with the commencement of mining at Nabarlek, 250 km east of Darwin in the Arnhem Land Aboriginal Reserve, and the Ranger Uranium Mine near Jabiru.

Finally, at a time when Aboriginal land claims were still in their infancy, the Larrakia people lodged the Tenby Land Claim for Native Title over Darwin and surrounding areas. This is Australia's longest running land claim. Significantly, on 13 December 1979, Darwin was finally raised to the status of capital city. Dr Ella Stack, a prominent local physician and mayor at the time, was appointed its first Lord Mayor. Stage 1 of Kakadu National Park was proclaimed, and the Northern Territory Government entered into a lease arrangement with the Kakadu Aboriginal Land Trust. The Park has since been added to the World Heritage List and remains one of the Territory's key tourist attractions for international visitors.

The Shell tanker *Etalina* berthed in Darwin on 4 December with 150 Vietnamese refugees on board, following their rescue from the sea. It was one of many refugee boats to head for Darwin's shores in this period following the end of the Vietnam War. Interestingly, on board one of these many vessels was Hieu Van Le, who later became Governor of South Australia. He and his partner Lan are good friends of mine.

Chapter 6

Henry and Walker

The accountancy practice thrived. In 1962, Neville Walker and Frazer Henry had also identified the money-making potential of the broad landscape of this last frontier. Western Australian Walker and Henry from Queensland were highly skilled practical plant operators with expertise in operating and maintaining heavy machinery. Having met and become friends in the Northern Territory, they were smart enough to see that there were great opportunities to create a profitable business there.

John Gamble, a partner in the accounting practice who had lived in the Northern Territory for a number of years, contemplated writing a book about those times. He kindly shared his notes regarding Frazer Henry's description of how the company emerged. It is somewhat colourful:

> We started out contracting in 1962, after realising that we'd be better off going broke on our own than continuing as wage slaves. We bought an AC grader on finance with Tutt Bryant, the only firm that would finance us – they soon learned that we couldn't make the HP payments, but by that time the grader was way out on the Plenty River Road. There was Neville and I with a ute and one offsider, out in the bush for 18 months scraping roads through spinifex. We ended up with plenty of

work, but no bastard would pay us on time, so we were always on the tick for fuel and supplies.

We next bought a D7 Dozer and started on the Buchanan Highway later in 1962. I recall we worked on it for the princely sum of $4 per hour, including our labour.

We then began working on the Peko mines tailing dams, by which time we'd bought a second dozer. Paid off the old AC Grader too. Then on to the Tindal RAAF Base airstrip, and a number of outback jobs until we got a yearning for civilization, and so we moved to Darwin in 1965. Until then we were only really itinerant subcontractors.

We thought the job at Stokes Hill Wharf had finished. We'd just cut a huge slope out of the limestone outcrop, leading down to the flat industrial area below. The T&W Supervisor wasn't content, he had a nice tidy mind and wanted us to smooth out a few big rocks protruding from the face of the slope. Neville and I looked up at these bloody great rocks 60–70 m up, and wondered how the hell we were going to 'smooth' the lumps out?

Well, we ended up being lowered on ropes from the top of the cliff, drilled holes everywhere and plugged them with as much gelignite as we could stuff in our pockets. Maybe a bit more gelignite than was, with the benefit of hindsight, strictly necessary. All's well, up we go to the top to detonate the charges.

The first charge went off beautifully and bloody great chunks of rock soared into the air and rained down on the roof of the brand-new Stokes Hill Power Station. The roof obviously wasn't up to this barrage and the Manager of the Power Station came out and screamed obscenities at us from far below. Couldn't make out what he was saying 'cos Neville was yelling in my ear something about getting out of here and not waiting around while the other 19 charges went off.

> We heard later that the T&W Supervisor and his deputies were looking for the powder monkey responsible, probably intending to revoke his licence. We didn't have an explosives licence, so we made ourselves scarce for a few days. We later heard that two old WWII warriors took off down the track to Katherine when they heard the explosions. Thought the place was being bombed again.

Once established in Darwin, Frazer Henry and Neville Walker went searching for prime contracts that would provide a healthy income. The timing was right. Both the Federal Government and local council were planning major infrastructure projects in response to the decimation of World War II and the need to reinstate Darwin as Australia's northern gateway. There were city roads, port facilities, storm-water management and an airfield to be built, 'everything a modern emerging city needed'.

At the same time, they decided to look at developing their skills in contract mining.

Contract mining occurs when the owners of a mine employ the services of specialist contractors to conduct the various mining operations. Henry and Walker became highly experienced in contract mining, which saw a rapid expansion in Australia in the twentieth century and has since become a common feature in the mining of minerals – particularly gold, iron ore, coal and base metals. It is interesting to note that as the 21st century progressed, the dependence of mining companies on contract miners decreased due to the commercial and management issues that can arise.

Nevertheless, the contract mining procedures pioneered by Henry and Walker and others remain the base of operations.

Henry and Walker had a good relationship with the Territory Government. Both the government and the young company of Henry and Walker were new kids on the block. Several of the company's key personnel had close relationships with some of the Territory's politicians from both parties, which made communication easier. The broader contracting market also had very few players; most were restricted by their inability to bid on work due to technicalities of mining and their lack of local knowledge. The outcome was the inevitable 'easy fit' between Henry and Walker and government.

In a bid to reduce both their capital commitments and their exposure to risks in projects, major mining resource companies used contract miners who typically took on primary responsibility for production shortfalls caused by equipment failures, industrial disputes, and bad weather. The capability and reputation of the major contract mining companies grew with their increasing skill specialisation, especially in regard to the mining of low-grade ore bodies and of ore bodies located in remote regions.

One example of this is BHP. Australia's largest mining company engaged Henry and Walker to develop the Yandi iron ore mine in the Pilbara region of Western Australia. The venture was highly successful, with upgrades to the ore-processing plant and equipment. The contract was renegotiated until 2001, making the company responsible for building the additional new plant. This brought Yandi's capacity to 25 million tons per annum.

However, while Henry and Walker Ltd had developed a skilled and expanding contracting business in the 1980s and 90s, they did not develop certain necessary supplementary services. These deficiencies, discussed later, included fundamental requirements such as human resources and detailed reporting. Coupled with this, was the changing situation in terms of tenure on Indigenous land and Aboriginal land rights. The board of Henry and Walker made a strong decision to partner with Aboriginal communities wherever possible. This placed the company at a huge advantage over competitors whenever there was an opportunity of working on such land. It was also acceptable to the Indigenous owners of the mineral resources, and the resulting relationship gained a reputation for the company throughout the industry.

In 1981 Henry and Walker Ltd listed on the Australian Stock Exchange via a back-door listing of a company called Hollandia Ltd. Its board initially consisted of Malcolm Fricker (non-executive), a well-known corporate solicitor and former chair of Hollandia, Frazer Henry and Neville Walker (joint managing directors), Ted Bailey, CEO of AgServ Industries, and me (non-executive).

The board had an impressive set of skills. Malcolm Fricker had extensive public company experience, including being chair of several significant companies. Neville Walker and Frazer Henry were highly skilled in the company's core business. Ted Bailey was likewise highly proficient in the fields of marketing, procuring and maintaining technical equipment. I had significant experience in corporate restructuring and refinancing.

The listed entity of Henry and Walker Ltd had two wholly owned subsidiaries, Henry and Walker Contracting Company and the agricultural business AgServ, which sold trucks, cars and agricultural equipment. Henry and Walker diversified by acquiring a number of disparate businesses that included Territory Asphalt Roadways, prawning vessels, and air charter operations (Airnorth). For the company to grow and succeed, its capital had to be increased and substantial shareholders enlisted. The initial investor was the Japanese firm Kumagai Gumi Ltd; it was later joined by the Aboriginal and Torres Strait Islander Commercial Development Corporation (CDC) and its chair, Mr. Gatjil Djerrkura, was appointed as a director of Henry and Walker.

The investment by Kumagai Gumi and its Australian associated company Concrete Constructions Pty Ltd (which had built Parliament House in Canberra) was made during the financial years 1986/1987. The Australian Managing Director of Kumagai Gumi, Tony Mitani, and Concrete Constructions Pty Ltd Director, Graeme Beissel, were invited to join the board. Their skills immediately broadened Henry and Walker's base, and their national and international connections were invaluable. The company traded profitably for several years before it gradually got into a position where its debt levels needed closer management. It was this, coupled with an investment in the two new casino properties in the Northern Territory, that led to discomfort from both the banks and the general market.

Aboriginal and Torres Strait Islander Commercial Development Corporation (CDC), the legal entity that represented Indigenous people in Australia, became a second shareholder in 1993, and with other shareholders, including several major local and international institutions, and retail investors, the number of overall shareholders reached in excess of 5000.

In addition to Kumagai Gumi, Henry and Walker's other major shareholders included Toyota Tsusho Corporation (TTSO) of Japan, a wholly owned subsidiary of Toyota and its commodity-purchasing arm. TTSO acquired energy for the holding company (via coal and gas entities etc.) by purchasing raw materials, and other products that helped the manufacture of Toyota products. TTSO acquired a coal development licence in NSW and used Henry and Walker to help facilitate its entry into the market. I became chair of the TTSO coal company (Camberwell Coal Pty Ltd), and Neville Walker a director. Likewise, Masaaki (Matt) Fukahara, its managing director, became a director of Henry and Walker.

Henry and Walker also acquired 24.5% of a distributorship for Toyota Vehicles in Cambodia, with Toyota Tsusho and a

Cambodian company, Kong Nuon Import and Export Ltd, sharing the balance. This venture also included the establishment of a base in Cambodia for Henry and Walker's contracting division from which it attempted to win civil engineering and infrastructure development contracts in Cambodia. With this in mind, I became deputy chair of Toyota Tsusho Cambodia.

At the time, Toyota Tsusho was introducing Toyota vehicles into Cambodia. This was very difficult because the country was still reeling from the Pol Pot regime and dealing with significant levels of corruption. Ultimately it was a rewarding exercise. As an interesting aside, in the initial stages when I was actually resident in Phnom Penh, over 30 vehicles on site were stolen. Subsequent enquiries showed that they had been stolen by the police, but fortunately the army retrieved them for us at a small fee!

When I was appointed deputy chair of Toyota Tsusho Cambodia, my ego caused me to ask why I had been offered the position? Was it due to my many business talents and skills? The reply was 'No', because they 'needed a white guy', and I had 'blue eyes'!

After two unsuccessful contracting bids in Cambodia, due to the requirement to pay secret commissions, Henry and Walker decided that it could utilise its resources more efficiently elsewhere and ceased operations. Nevertheless, I remained on the board of Toyota Tsusho Cambodia.

Following presentations from BHP and other international companies, Henry and Walker extended its international operations into Indonesia and Chile. This move was highly successful, as we were employed by subsidiaries of companies that we had worked with before, such as BHP.

Chapter 7

Henry and Walker Hits Adolescence

Henry and Walker was publicly listed in 1981. By the mid 1980s, with the company's profligate spending habits, it had acquired – or was about to acquire – prawn boats, two small airlines, a crocodile farm, a gold mine and car yards, most of which didn't match the core business of contract mining and civil engineering.

An additional complication was that in 1983 Henry and Walker Ltd became involved in the partial property acquisition of the two casino properties in the Northern Territory. These casinos had been resumed by the Northern Territory Government via an entity called the Northern Territory Property Trust.

By 1987 a vastly different Henry Walker Group needed significant restructuring and, as some said in relation to the 'cowboys', there was a need for corralling. Sure, there was now a turnover in the $80 millions, but questions were being asked about the fast-accumulating debts, including by the Westpac bankers! The directors decided that the company must concentrate on its core business – contracting. This resulted in the need to implement certain structural changes, and it was decided that Neville Walker and Frazer Henry should voluntarily resign as joint managing directors, with Walker becoming chairman and Henry the director of engineering. I was to become managing director.

There was also another board appointment, with financial expert Peter J. Styles being invited to join the board.

I reported to the board and media that appraisal of the business revealed that it was 'out of kilter, with assets but no cash after several unfortunate investments, and it was suffering from the problem of being a large company in a small population base along with a bottlenecked management structure'.

The plan to turn the company around was 'pretty heady stuff' for Frazer Henry and Neville Walker, but to give them their credit, they and director Ted Bailey put in more than $1.5 million of their own funds and strongly supported all changes.

There was an urgent need to take immediate control of the finances. With the board having agreed to strongly commit to civil engineering and contract mining, the company undertook, with Westpac's blessing, a major disposal of all assets not related to core business.

The businesses that were retained all related to the core basic contracting, including the distribution of heavy vehicles, such as Toyota's four-wheel-drive vehicles (AgServ Industries), and light aircraft charters (Airnorth and Rossair) to enable the mobility of equipment and staff in remote areas.

Over the next few years, anything not relating to mining or contracting areas was sold. The total sales brought in $9 million. The company also diversified out of the Northern Territory to encourage core business growth, and to gain a broad geographic spread to help lessen the economic and climatic vagaries of a single region.

A positive relationship with our banks was imperative and the corporate headquarters was moved to Adelaide to be closer to the bankers with whom we needed to liaise. Westpac had moments of reticence, but the ANZ was brilliant. The strategy sold to them was that we had to go further into debt to make the company work, and to return to the core business of contract mining, capital was needed. A $24-million capital outlay was required for the necessary plant. It took a lot of talking and walking the streets, but we got it.

The contract mining management base was relocated to Perth due to the huge amount of mining activity in Western Australia and the seasonal nature of operations in the Northern Territory. We set a five-year company budget forecast that was stuck to religiously and developed a set of corporate objectives with the appropriate goals for each division of the company, along with a flat management structure.

All monies, including wages, were handled through the Adelaide headquarters, with a daily company cash balance. The financial controls could have been too tight, but it was important to know exactly where the company was at all times. Managing a rapidly growing contract company requires a set of skills based on strong core competencies to supplement the estimators (engineers), together with quantity surveyors and others who cost and program a contract and actually prepare the tender documents.

A number of new appointments were made:

Secretary and Legal Officer – Louise Hicks, chartered accountant and qualified solicitor who came directly from a large firm of national solicitors

Chief Financial Officer – Simon Robertson, chartered accountant with vast experience in professional accounting

Internal Auditor – Byron Brown, qualified accountant, and a long-time Henry and Walker employee with extensive experience in the industry

Don Murchland – an experienced practitioner in the field of corporate relations

Our team members were highly skilled professional operators supported by excellent coordinator Anthea Martin. The senior management team therefore comprised Director in Charge of Mining Frazer Henry, Chief Financial Officer Simon Robertson,

Legal Officer Louise Hicks, General Manager of Henry Walker Contracting John Jones, me as CEO, and such others as were needed. The team's decisions were passed to the board of the company for discussion and where appropriate for approval. This meant that greater attention was paid to both the process of bidding for work and to internal controls. There was much stronger corporate governance at every level, which had previously not been a priority. The asset changes created by the new structure attracted huge interest nationally in both the business sectors and the media. Alex Kennedy's article of 2 October 1992 in the *Financial Review* described the transformation in detail:

> The Henry Walker Group, the Northern Territory's only listed company, shopped until it dropped. This conspicuous consumer had by late 1987 amassed prawn boats, a gold mine, two small airlines, a crocodile farm, hotel, casino, numerous property interests and car yards, which sat uneasily and mostly unprofitably with its core business of contract mining and civil engineering.
>
> Its board consisted of four engineers, two lawyers and a marketing consultant, and its vague business plan was simply to keep growing and acquiring within the confines of the NT, seemingly with a view that expected tourism and mining booms there would carry its diverse interests up with them.
>
> Neither boom eventuated and Henry Walker found itself floundering with a turnover of $88 million and fast-escalating debts. The company, which after its listing in 1981 had been written up as one of Australia's most promising smaller stocks, had failed to live up to the expectation.
>
> Bain Securities and Day Cutten now recommend Henry Walker as a buy. During the past three years its shares have

risen from less than 19 to about 55. Last month it announced a record after-tax profit of $4.2 million, a 117% increase on the previous year, and an 18% increase in turnover from $152 million to $178 million. Debt has been halved from $44 million three years ago, while shareholders' funds have grown during the past year from $30.9 million to $34.5 million.

It is a vastly different Henry Walker Group. The purse is under the rigid control of managing director Richard Ryan, who has restructured the company. Its cowboy tendencies have been strictly corralled by him, with his 'plan the work and work the plan' ethos, and the company is now entering the fourth year of Ryan's five-year 'plan for prosperity'.

Ryan, who also is vice-president of the National Heart Foundation and chairman of its national finance committee, joined the Henry Walker Group in late 1987. Then a Darwin-based chartered accountant and company director, he had been accountant for the private interests of Neville Walker and Fraser [sic] Henry. He is vague about what made him take on their company, which was being referred to widely as a 26-year-old disaster. He says it went along the lines of 'it seemed like a good idea at the time' and 'I knew Walker and I knew Henry and I just felt we could make something of it' . . . The right track meant taking immediate control of the finances and organising the orderly disposal of all assets that were not core business or complementary, starting with property interests associated with the Darwin Casino. It had created 'a bad general perception about the company in the Territory'. The sales brought in $9 million . . .

Henry Walker has 700 employees, only four of them in its Adelaide corporate headquarters (finance manager, company secretary, group accountant and office manager) and half in the Northern Territory. More than a third of its business is conducted outside the Northern Territory – in line with Ryan's five-year plan.

The company also continues to decentralise, and an office was opened recently in Jakarta. Ryan wants to increase Indonesian operations to at least 10% of the company's turnover. At present, it has a $US10-million interest in a contract mining operation in the Lerokis Gold project at Wetar Island, near Timor, and is bidding for contracts in Indonesia worth $US100 million.

In Western Australia, Henry Walker has secured a $100-million contract to mine and mill 25 million tonnes of crushed iron ore at BHP Minerals' Yandi project, and other contract mining operations include the gold mines of Dominion Mining's Woolonga, Zapopan's Tanami and Western Mining's Goodall. It also has civil engineering contracts worth $35 million, including work for the BHP subsidiary Gemco on Groote Eylandt and work on the Second Cavalry Army Base in Darwin. It has engineering and mining work worth $220 million.

The company has been rationalised into three structured divisions. Its expanding contract mining and civil engineering division increased turnover by 45% last year to $103 million, taking its pre-tax operating profit from $2.76 million to $5.99 million. The small Darwin automotive division achieved a pre-tax profit of $1.33 million after being rationalised from five used-car outlets into one. Its aviation division, Airnorth (freight and passengers) and Rossair (which services aircraft across Australia), just broke even after its fleet was reduced from 26 to eight aircraft during the past year.

'The cars are there purely because they are profitable and

the air division because we actually utilise it ourselves, which saves a lot of money, and because I have a view that it will be profitable as we come out of the recession,' Ryan says.

The next financial year is the time to consolidate, according to the five-year plan, and Ryan says the company will assess all its operations and its management style. It also may be the first year that the plan is not firmly adhered to. 'We're not out there actively seeking, but if we find opportunities to strengthen our core business then I think we may be more flexible with the plan,' he says.

Chapter 8

Henry and Walker Grows Up

The 1980s had been a decade of significant corporate improvements and the group now needed to continue to grow, but with much tighter corporate governance and structures.

In January 1992, we opened a permanent resident office in Jakarta, Indonesia, through the Indonesian-controlled entity PT Darma Henwa, with the objective of further developing contract mining business there. PT Darma Henwa undertook contract mining for PT Prima Lirang Mining at the Lerokis Gold Project on Wetar Island, and coal mining operations for the BHP and Mitsu Mining subsidiary, PT Utah Indonesia, at the Petangis Mine in East Kalimantan.

In August 1995, the company won the Kelian River Diversion Channel contract for CRA. Valued at US$22 million, it was the largest civil engineering project the company had ever undertaken in that country. Total work on hand in Indonesia on 30 September 1996 was approximately A$70 million.

Henry and Walker's interests in the distribution and servicing of automotive vehicles and machinery was built upon AgServ Industries, the Northern Territory-based multi-franchise distributorship acquired in 1981. These interests had been expanded in 1988 through the acquisition of Darwin-based Toyota dealer, Bridge Autos. A radical change of direction emerged, given the company's focus on working in closer cooperation with Indigenous people.

Working with Aboriginal people was Frazer Henry's idea, and when this was approved by the board it became a major part of my role as Managing Director. It was my task to negotiate the joint ventures that were to make it a prominent leader in the industry. Unlike any other company at that time, we quickly entered into three arrangements facilitating closer co-operation with Aboriginal people.

The first was the Aboriginal and Torres Strait Islander Commercial Development Corporation (CDC), which invested $3.5 million by way of bank-guaranteed convertible notes in Henry and Walker. In 1993, the board invited the chairperson of CDC, Mr Gatjil Djerrkura, to join the Henry and Walker board, which ensured the company its unique place in Australian corporate history; the first public company in Australia to have an Aboriginal director. Gatjil Djerrkura was succeeded by Joseph Elu.

The first joint venture that the company undertook was with the Jawoyn Association and CDC. Mirrkworlk Joint Venture (MJV) was to undertake contract mining services for the Mt Todd gold mine near Katherine in the Northern Territory. The owner was Zapopan NL. The contract, originally valued at $160 million, was 50% Henry and Walker Group Ltd and 50% Jawoyn Association, in conjunction with the Aboriginal and Torres Strait Islander Commercial Development Corporation. All parties had equal board representation, and an intensive dual cross-cultural program was introduced, which continued until the contract was finalised. A detailed budget and employment strategy was also developed. The initial workforce, made up of 27 individuals, was increased significantly as the highly successful project developed. The commercial success of the MJV in September 1996 was heartening, and in January 1997 an eight-year contract valued at between $160 and $190 million commenced.

When ATSICDC became Henry and Walker's second major shareholder it was to the delight of both the company and the share market.

Significantly, Henry and Walker Ltd was the first company to also employ large numbers of Indigenous people in the north and north-west of Australia, a landmark achievement. Gatjil Djerrkura, chair of ATSICDC, acknowledged this, saying at the time that it would 'provide an appropriate basis that can help facilitate the involvement of local Aboriginal communities in the commercial development of land in which they have an interest'.

In just over two years the Mirrkworlk Joint Venture had not only grown into a profitable business enterprise, but also illustrated how different cultures and philosophies can be successfully interwoven to achieve a common goal. It was awarded the Northern Territory's 'Business of the Year for 1995' at the National Indigenous Business of the Year Awards. It was a huge success.

In 1996 Henry and Walker Ltd launched a third initiative, the Henry Walker Group Aboriginal Employment Strategy. Under this strategy, which was jointly funded by the company and the Commonwealth Department for Education, Employment and Training, we recruited and trained Aboriginal people for employment within the company's operations.

This included identification of procedures and policies that would encourage greater access for Indigenous people to job opportunities.

The Strategy was implemented at the company's operations at the Mt Todd gold mine and Groote Eylandt. By 31 October 1996, Aboriginal and Torres Strait Islander people accounted for 18% and 72% respectively of the company's on-site workforce in these locations. The strategy was progressively extended to other operations. Day-to-day operations on all joint ventures were run on a normal commercial basis with significant input from all the partners. Henry and Walker initially committed substantial monies to fund its share of the strategy's costs over the five-year period in which it was to operate.

It is interesting to note the raw population statistics of the Northern Territory recorded in the Australian Bureau of Statistics, Census and Population & Housing of 30 June 1971 and 30 June 1981:

Year	Non-Indigenous	Indigenous	Totals
1971	86,390	23,253 of which 14,705 Rural & Remote	109,643
1981	94,240	29,086 of which circa 17,000 Rural & Remote	123,326

These figures show how important and socially economic the Joint Mining Ventures were in remote areas, making up 21% (1971) and 23% (1981) of the population, due to their ability to provide work and income for communities.

Chapter 9

Ngarda Civil & Mining and Henry and Walker Joint Venture

In 2001 Henry and Walker, Ngarda (the Yindjibamdi word for Aboriginal people), Ngarli Yarndu Foundation Inc., and Indigenous Business Australia (formally ATSICDC or CDC), together developed a business model that they believed would give Indigenous people the training and skills necessary to meet the industry's needs and therefore creating a sustainable, long-term and profitable venture. The avenue that this created was to substantially increase Indigenous employment and involved the local Indigenous people in the benefits that flowed from the resource projects of Western Australia.

Ngarda Ngarli Yarndu Foundation Inc. was an independent body that represented the four wards of the ATSIC Ngarda Ngarli Yarndu (NNY) in the Pilbara region of Western Australia. It was established to alleviate poverty among the Indigenous people in the NNY region and aimed to raise funds and make investments that would generate long-term returns.

Indigenous Business Australia (IBA) is a statutory authority that facilitates Indigenous involvement in the private sector. It provides financial support to its Indigenous partners and liaison skills for bringing together interested local and industry-related organisations. It replaced ATSICDC due to changes in Federal Government policy and provided financial guarantees for Ngarda, as well as advice and expertise on issues in the wider business and Indigenous communities.

Within two years of operations, Ngarda and its founding partners won the '2003 Prime Minister's Award for Large Business Excellence'. The award recognised the mutual interest and determination of Ngarda's joint venture partners, the dedication of its employees and the vision of its clients, explaining why Ngarda was regarded as a commercially successful cross-culture organisation.

Ngarda Civil & Mining was the acknowledged industry leader in Indigenous employment in the Australian mining industry. It had a workforce of 168, 85% of whom were Indigenous people, with six apprentices, 47 trainees, and two Academy-based trainees. There were also 27 Indigenous personnel completing Certificate III in Metalliferous Mining Operations. Ngarda's portfolio of activities included tailings dam, ore handling and hauling, civils, stevedoring and ship loading, contract mining, earthworks, road and rail construction, mine site support services, haul rail maintenance, crushing and screening operations, environmental rehabilitation and services. It retained a strong reputation for high quality outcomes.

Ngarda's success was due to its culture of Indigenous leadership and the experienced industry managers that headed the company. The Indigenous leaders who led Ngarda were not afraid to lead their communities into new areas and challenges.

Accordingly, the entity took a people-centered, no-nonsense, old-school, anti-bureaucratic approach to recruiting, educating and inducting employees into the industry. It was so good to see this process introduced from Day 1 of the joint venture.

Because of the major role that it had with various Indigenous groups and communities, in both partnerships and joint ventures, Henry and Walker Ltd was invited to make a submission to the House of Representatives Standing Committee on the Aboriginal and Torres Strait Islander Commercial Development Corporation and its efforts. The company's submission to government detailed the concepts introduced to overcome many of the negative issues relating to doing business in Australia, and particularly in the Northern Territory. (Extracts from the full submission can be viewed as Appendix B.) In my opinion, sadly many of these negative issues still apply today.

Contracting is a challenging business to manage due to its nature and size, and despite the fact that the company was trading satisfactorily, there is always an enormous risk on certain contracts because of the very nature of the business. Most of the major contractors in Australia have been close to insolvency at some stage. John Holland, Theiss, and Leightons have all had their difficulties, but have overcome them through good management and by increasing the size of the balance sheet.

From early 1991, Henry and Walker was under considerable pressure from the market, shareholders, and investors to increase its size. In 1992 there were major shareholding changes in the company when the Japanese shareholder Kumagai Gumi decided to limit its exposure in Australia; the company that had played such a significant role in Henry and Walker's success decided to sell its shares. The 9.6% of shares it had held, were on-sold to institutions and retail investors.

Sometime later, Kumagai Gumi's associated company, Concrete Constructions, which also held 9.6% of Henry Walker Ltd, sold its share to Toyota Tsusho (TTS), the investment arm of Toyota, who became Henry and Walker's largest institutional shareholder.

The relationship between Toyota Tsusho and Henry Walker suited both parties. An example of this being Camberwell Coal, where Henry and Walker provided the professional expertise to develop the mine and Toyota Tsusho handled the finance and marketing of the finished product. Another was the assistance Henry and Walker provided to TTS in establishing the Toyota franchise in Cambodia and supervising the building of the premises in Phnom Penh.

Several of the Henry Walker directors, including Frazer Henry and myself, had major involvements in Indigenous issues.

In the late 1990s, for example, I was invited by the South Australian Government to chair a new eight-member task force to 'stream-line' the system of land access, including environment and native title issues in South Australia's mineral sector. It was our role to present a five-year plan to SA Premier John Olsen by September 1999. A series of workshops for the South Australian Farmers Federation included presentations by the State Government, Native Title Tribunal and Aboriginal Legal Rights Movement.

Chapter 10

Merger

In 1979 the independent company Eltin Ltd was created by a consulting group of three mining engineers and a metallurgist, who were all former employees of Western Mining in Western Australia. However, their focus changed two years later when they decided that consulting was not really their bent, and they began contract mining and eventually became a listed public company.

By 1986, Eltin had become one of the biggest underground contractors in Australia when it merged with MRSA Ltd, a significant open-pit, earth-moving contractor. Its activities were not dissimilar to those of Henry and Walker, but, interestingly, it was particularly strong in underground mining, a strength Henry and Walker did not have. Therefore, it was rational that the two companies should consider merging. This took place in the financial year ending 1998.

The merger was initiated because the new company provided the opportunity to develop a much healthier balance sheet, improve earnings per share performance, and client and operating efficiency that were beyond what either company could have achieved independently. This also created a much larger 'order book' and brought the new company broader engineering and mining capability.

These changes did have a downside in terms of people and management. The process resulted in the redundancy of 110 employees, mainly support staff, along with the additional abnormal costs. However, with goodwill, the merger was substantially successful, and these costs were more than outweighed by the benefits gained from the efficiencies it introduced and the business restructuring it delivered. The merger also resulted in marked improvements in the company's share trading performance. At year-end it was 22% higher than when the merger had been announced. The share price performance remained better than either Henry and Walker or Eltin could have reasonably anticipated as independent operators.

The merger also enabled a restructuring and upgrade of the Contracting Division, and as CEO of Henry and Walker, I was made CEO of the new entity, Henry Walker Eltin (HWE) in 1999. The order book was now more diverse, with a better spread of clients, industry and commodity sectors and geographical areas of operation.

Finally, combining the two businesses enabled a quantum leap in size. The company now ranked as one of the largest mining contractors in the world and, with total assets exceeding $700 million and annual revenue of over $1,200 million on a full year basis, and in excess of 4500 employees and contractors.

Its core skills included best practice people management, better fixed mobile plant and equipment, top utilisation and service delivery, mining and civil engineering, risk management and management of safety and environmental performance. All quality systems were certified to AS/NZS ISO 9002 and the environmental management systems were designed to satisfy AS/NZS 14001.

To summarise the new position, this newly assembled Henry Walker Eltin (HWE) had become a company with international operations in contract mining, civil engineering, environmental management and transport services. It had a relatively strong balance sheet with relatively low debt gearing.

HWE had its Corporate and Head Office in Adelaide, its major Contracting Division in Perth, and offices in most states. It also had operations in New Zealand, Ghana, Tanzania, Indonesia, Thailand, Jamaica and Chile. Importantly, its customer base included the world's leading mining companies and federal, state and local government agencies.

The new entity was listed under the name of Henry Walker Eltin Ltd (HWE) on the Australian Stock Exchange, and on 30 June 1999 it had 174.1 million shares on issue, held by approximately 7500 shareholders, and a market capitalisation of $355 million. With more than 4500 employees, HWE had excelled in a way that nobody could have predicted. It had won gold at the Olympics but, come to think of it, it had never trained for the Olympics and so inevitably there were problems on the run post the win.

Chapter 11

The Fall

Until 2000, HWE's growth in Australia and offshore was outstanding.

It had focused on the core business, while developing a work base that concentrated on rural and remote areas both domestically and internationally.

To be successful in any contracting business, the operating entity must be of significant size and have adequate capital to enable it to handle the risks that invariably arise, such as force majeure, a bad contract, the principal not having the ability to pay for work done, and a plethora of other matters. It is a fact that all major contracting companies in Australia have been placed under acute financial strain due to such issues at various times.

There was a huge growth in contracts that HWE had on hand from $180 million in 1991 to $1.1 billion in 2000. The number of employees increased from 635 in 1991 to 4500 in 2000. Ironically, however, the company was growing too quickly and, notwithstanding the increase in profit and revenue, the return was disappointing, as the rate of return generated by its operations was well below both budget and target rates.

The decline in HWE's profitability between 2001 and 2002 was attributable to a reduction on the return on the contracting assets, a small number of underperforming contracts in Australia, and then losses incurred in South American and Indonesian operations. Unfortunately, changes to key staff also caused major internal disruptions, which impacted on the group's corporate governance. This was recognised when net profit before tax of $23 million in 2001 resulted in a loss of $13.6 million the following year. The bulk of these losses were offshore, along with one Australian contract.

In 2000, after 15 years with HWE and having given it a lot of thought, I recognised that it was time for me to go. I submitted my resignation feeling that I had run my race and that it was time to move on, both for me and the company. However, my replacement did not arrive until 2001. The new CEO was Bruce James, and with his appointment the Head Office was shifted to Sydney, with the objective of bringing it closer to the banks and market trends. The Company continued to expand.

Sadly, its fortunes began to fluctuate. Essentially this occurred because the company had committed to several contracts without ensuring that the finances for the necessary plant and equipment contract were in place – a rare situation, but one that turned out to be highly significant. The rapid expansion led to a cash flow shortfall and the company needing a financial bail-out, so a rights issue of $42 million was made and was fully subscribed.

The Paterson Ord Minnett Review gave an update on and forecast for the company as of April 2003, as provided by HWE management. Westpac, concerned about the Company's cash liquidity, had an external draft review conducted that showed that Henry Walker Eltin should be able to pay its debts over time, but it would need time to do so.

The shortage of cash had occurred as a direct result of an Indonesian contract that had establishment costs of circa US$130 million. No initial finance had been arranged for this and consequently a significant portion of the operating cash flow was needed to support the establishment costs, which caused huge problems with current creditors.

The Demise of Henry Walker Eltin Ltd

It was then, and remains now, in my opinion that HWE should *never* have gotten into this financial position caused by both the prevailing laws and the financial circumstances of the time. It was an extraordinary experience, unforseen by any of the directors, who following advice given to them decided to put the company into voluntary administration. The reasons for this are summarised in the liquidator's report (see Appendix C).

Simply, the comments state that there was insufficient control over the cash flow and financial controls, as well as poor management and corporate governance – fundamentals of business!

It is important to note that when the liquidation was complete:

(a) all staff were paid in full;
(b) all creditors were paid in full together with any statutory interests on their debt;
(c) all shareholders received 18 cents per share in terms of a return of capita.

Distributions of this type are rare in terms of administration and insolvencies.

For shareholders to receive such a distribution, shows that Henry Walker Eltin should have never gone into liquidation, as shareholders actually received their distribution of capital only *after* every other class of creditor had been paid.

The story of HWE is a truly heroic story that never should have ended the way it did. This extraordinary Northern Territory company that started out as a two-man band and then gone on to be listed on the Australian Stock Exchange, inevitably ran headlong into trouble. The tragedies that followed this outcome illustrate that the current reforms being considered by the Australian Government are necessary.

Tragically, Chairman Neville Walker committed suicide as a direct result of the company's liquidation.

The company had a series of goals to meet to satisfy the banks and market, but unfortunately it did not reach them as promised.

Bruce James resigned in 2004 and was replaced as interim CEO by Robert Cleary. He in turn resigned on 8 February 2005.

This groundbreaking national engineering giant entered voluntary administration on 31 January 2005, during the peak of the mining boom, and this, in itself, generated enormous publicity in both the general and the financial press. The effect of liquidation was a tragedy.

Anne Hyland's article 'The Ghost of Neville Walker' in the *Australian Financial Review* of 2 April 2005 covers the story.

> Walker died just a week after the collapse of his company. He was Chairman of Henry Walker Eltin, one of Australia's largest contract miners and civil engineers. It was founded by Walker and his mate Frazer Henry in 1962, and the growth of Henry Walker, as a company was known in the early days, paralleled the advancement of the Northern Territory. The isolation of the outback meant HWE has virtually a monopoly on contracts for the Top End's infrastructure needs from road to ports.
>
> The company was, until its collapse, involved in a $1 billion Darwin waterfront development. But, from a business point of view, 'To commit to a project the size of Bengalon without the finance in place was just foolish.'
>
> The two men had outgrown Australia's north and had built a national and international corporation. So, Walker's death reverberated right through the Australian business community.

In the first instance it was the shock that a well-known and liked corporate identity had died so tragically. Second, there was an element of mystery about his death.

On 8 February, the *Northern Territory News* reported that Walker had died of a heart attack after a car crash, although there was no official statement, Walker had apparently climbed out of the wreckage and stumbled some 100 meters into the bush before dying. The NT Criminal Investigation Bureau is preparing to complete its report to hand to the coroner, Greg Cavanagh, who will then investigate the cause of death. The coroner's findings will not be released publicly unless there is an inquest.

But that does not matter to the close-knit community of Darwin, which has come to its own conclusion. It still grieves for Walker, the proud self-effacing, self-made millionaire, it loved and respected. It believes he committed suicide. For the 68-year old Walker, HWE was not just a job, it had been his life. As the company's expiry date neared, so did his.

'What really got him was that this was something he'd created and it was evaporating before his eyes' says Shane Stone, Liberal Party Federal President, and former Chief Minister of the Northern Territory . . .

Stone said, 'Walker had taken the company's collapse personally, feeling he had let people down, especially those Territorians who had been shareholders . . .

Walker was a knockabout bloke whose endearing quality of being able to respond to people on their own level drew individuals to him like bees to honey. It would allow him to build a powerful network that included members of Asia's political elite, US movie tycoon Kirk Kerkorian, Leighton boss Wal King and former prime minister Bob Hawke. On their honeymoon to the Top End Hawke and Blanche D'

Alpuget spent time with Walker on his property, fishing and visiting Kakadu.

While Walker mixed with the rich and powerful, he was equally at ease with the average person, including the odd foreign backpacker visiting Darwin. Strangers would often be treated to an impromptu guided tour of the city he loved and had helped to build. He was passionately proud of the NT and would happily run late for work in favour of taking visitors around Darwin.

At Walker's state funeral on 15 February [2005], son David spoke of his father's devotion to honesty at any cost. 'He was very proud of his word and I'm sure all of you here today would know why.'

For the last half of 2004, Walker had been engaged in a painful, humiliating, and desperate struggle to save his company. HWE needed at least $100 million, and he had approached the huge Australian construction firm Leighton run by good friend Wal King, but it was unable to help.

In late November, Walker took a big risk. He flew to Switzerland to strike a last resort deal with Glencore International, the feared commodities trader. Glencore is well-known in Australia where it has a reputation for ruthlessness. Its hunger for strategic mining assets here has earned it many enemies.

For Walker however, Glencore offered the prospect of corporate salvation and indeed the company agreed to throw HWE a lifeline and signed a conditional deal to provide financing just days before Christmas. But that lifeline snapped and so did Walker when Glencore declined to proceed on January 30. The company was put into voluntary administration the next day owing close to $350 million.

The buildup to the collapse was a period of enormous stress for Walker. His company had been visited by the Australian Securities and Investment Commission in December and the board directors were reminded of their exposure if the company were to trade insolvent. Walker and the board had been maneuvering to minimize the fallout to major clients such as BHP Billiton, Newmont Mining and Portman.

What made the corporate failure more exquisitely painful was that HWE was going to the wall during one of the biggest and most protracted booms in the construction and mining industries in Australian history . . .

Family members and friends of Neville Walker professed to never really knowing the man intimately as he wallpapered over his private life with a larger-than-life façade. Ask people what they know about Walker, and they will tell you about his red Cadillac that once chauffeured Marilyn Monroe, his interest in crocodile farms that sells skins to luxury retailer Hermes and his showcase property at Marrakai. On Marrakai Walker hosted foreign and domestic dignitaries and chief executives in a style that made Crocodile Dundee look like a wimp, skimming the top of crocodile waterways in his airboat and breezing past sleepy buffaloes . . .

The 19-year-old Walker arrived in the NT in the 1950's when it was real frontier country. He met Frazer Henry, and the visionary and pragmatic tyre-kicker soon developed a friendship, contracting business and a blood relationship after they became in-laws by marrying the Spanner sisters.

With their get on and do it attitude, the two men took the then civil engineering company from milestone to milestone. It became the NT's first listed company in 1981. But by 1987, when Richard Ryan, an accountant, was brought on as the company's managing director, the company was in trouble. It had grown too quickly with too many non-core assets, was cash poor and struggling with escalating debts. Those problems would be addressed with a personal cash injection by Walker and Henry, by a refocus and the disposal of non-core assets.

Richard Ryan noted that in 1987 the firm suffered from 'the problem of being a large company in a small population base, and with a bottlenecked management structure'.

On 18 August 2004, HWE released its full-year results showing the company was back in the black with $15.5 million net profit. But the good news wasn't to last.

In late October the board was ready to review first quarter earnings performance of the new financial year to see how the company was tracking against its budget. It hit the panic button at a board meeting on 24 October.

HWE's board was alarmed that it had not been aware of two unprofitable contracts. One was with Patrick Corporation. In March 2003, HWE trumpeted as 'a significant win' a $35 million contract with this company's container port operations in Brisbane to build a paved concrete container storage area as part of the new terminal at Fisherman Island.

However, it was essential that it be strong and therefore had to be reinforced by steel, which would represent a substantial cost. Yet in a blunder that was not discovered for months, an external estimator did not tender for the steel.

The other disastrous contract was with Ashton Mining. Later Bruce James stepped down and the company made provisions that would strip $16 million from its profit forecast for 2005 earnings, reducing them to at best break-even or a small loss. That was on 28 October and the timing of the downgrade could not have been worse.

HWE was trying to finalise a $US100 million ($130 million) long-term financing facility with international banks, led by Fortis, for its $US1.2 billion Indonesian coal-mining contract, known as Bengalon. HWE's board and management announced it had won the 10-year Indonesian project in May 2004. Bengalon was the largest contract for HWE and had doubled the order-book to $3.8 billion in June 2004. But its eagerness for growth meant the contract was seven times HWE's market capitalisation which led it to make a fatal error as summed up by a mining industry executive: 'To commit to a project the size of Bengalon without the finance in place was just foolish. I'd wring the neck of the Chief Financial Officer that did that to me.

To add to the calamity of a profit warning and a lack of fund on a key project was the growing risk that HWE might not be able to ultilise its domestic banking facility of $30 million. The profit warning had spooked the international and domestic banking syndicates and Westpac, which decided to increase the interest rate on the multi-million $ facility and accelerate the repayment schedule. These stricter conditions are said to have made it difficult for HWE's board and management to sell off non-performing businesses or offer redundancies to improve the company's outlook.

Westpac 'categorically' denied its conditions on HWE were too restrictive, compared to the deal that Glencore would propose, they were probably right . . .

Walker knew he had to find a white knight and fast. But before he leapt into action it would become apparent to the board that poor financial planning was not HWE's only problem.

The unprofitable contracts that had prompted the market

downgrade had exposed bad management decisions and complacency in parts of HWE. The Patrick contract also exposed a practice among some HWE managers to tender on civil jobs never intended to make money. Instead, the tenders were called 'strategic contracts' and were all about getting a foot in the door with a new client, a dangerous game in an industry that operates on fine margins with little room for error.

In 2004 the margin on earnings before interest and tax was a skinny 1.4 per cent.

The high cost of retaining and maintaining skilled staff and expensive machinery for contract mining and civil engineering demands reliable revenue flow and solid financial backing, in other words good risk management. Bad weather, incorrect geological maps, or wrongly priced contracts, as in the case of the Patrick job, can cause unexpected delays and change revenue forecasts. It's a tough balancing act as Walter Construction demonstrated recently when it went belly-up.

In November and December Walker approached Leighton, private equity investors and then finally Glencore to try to save his company. During this period, Walker and the board would also receive a routine visit from ASIC, which after the company's profit downgrade, wanted to review its solvency. Satisfied that HWE was solvent, ASIC reminded directors of their responsibilities should the company deteriorate.

Wal King confirmed to the Weekend AFR that his management had a look at HWE last year but declined to comment further. Analysts say Leighton's would have taken a risk bailing out HWE with a minimum of $100 million because the domestic banks probably would have insisted Leighton's also sign as guarantor to other HWE projects.

As things were looking more precarious for HWE, the

concern of BHP Billiton, Newmont and Portman's grew. It is understood they demanded to have security over the leases on HWE's equipment so they could continue to make payments and operate if the company folded.

Walker then turned to Glencore and using his extensive network of contacts, he got through to Ivan Glasenberg, the commodity trading firm's chief executive who agreed to meet him in late November, but it would be Steven Isaac, a director of Glencore Finance, who would deal mostly with Walker and HWE.

Glencore and HWE had already crossed paths. Glencore was the global marketer, excluding Japan, for the Indonesian Bengalon mine. It also owned a Jamaican bauxite mine where HWE was the contractor.

On 23 December, HWE released a statement that Glencore had agreed to help recapitalise the company to the tune of $100 million, which was subject to due diligence. But there were also other insurmountable conditions, HWE had to secure the $US100 million international banking facility, renew the $30 million Australian bank facility and resolve the dispute on the bleeding $200 million Ashton coal-mining contract in the Hunter Valley . . .

Henry Walker has always been in an awkward position of being too big to be small and too small to be big, but it's drive for growth saw risk management take a back seat. It learnt the harsh lesson that the bigger you are the harder you fall.

A fire sale of HWE's assets has already begun, with the Indonesian and African assets snapped up and several civil engineering businesses auctioned.

There is talk that, with the boon in commodity prices and the resources sector, the contract mining business may

> be refloated Answers may be forthcoming at the creditors meeting on 23 May.
>
> Walker is dead but there is a glimmer of hope that his dream may live, albeit in some smaller form, to grow again.

The sequel to these tragic events was covered in an article by Camden Smith in the *NT News* in February 2023 where he talked about how the 'final thread' linking one of the Territory's oldest and best -known businesses to its base had been severed and the Darwin operation relocated to Brisbane. He added that several weeks later co-founder, Chairman Neville Walker, died in a car crash.

Chapter 12

The Northern Territory Casinos

In 1978, while still in the process of rebuilding the Top End and the surrounding territory that had been destroyed by Cyclone Tracy, the new self-governing government decided that it needed to create a broader platform for employment, and that one of the avenues for this would be tourism. The logic behind this was simple; the resulting increased employment would lead to the development of further infrastructure, which in turn would provide yet more employment and a broader income tax base.

The Northern Territory's relative distance from the population centres of Australia, along with its physical adversities, had contributed to the region's challenges in attracting and sustaining social and economic development. Its economic base was described as narrow and fragile, in that it relied on minerals, oil and gas, along with restricted rural industries (essentially pastoralism and fishing) as its major forms of private sector production. So it was in this environment that the tourism industry developed and would eventually overtake pastoralism to become the Territory's second largest income producer, contributing 5.6% of the GSP.

Growth in the tourism industry inevitably made gambling an attractive option to both private investors and the government, and this was compounded by the casinos' potential to bring in revenue and taxation opportunities. Given the Territory's immediate Asian neighbours, the focus turned to 'tourism junkets' and 'high rollers'.

With this in mind, the government included in its various submissions to the public and other parties a paper that related to the establishment of casinos in both Darwin and Alice Springs. This proposal was to become part of the CLP platform for 1978, which argued that casinos should be introduced in order to improve employment in both hospitality and tourism. This was tacitly agreed to by the Labor Party led by Bob Collins.

The first casino licence was granted to Darwin's Old Don Hotel in Cavenagh Street in 1979 and, on 21 September, the new casino opened as the Don Casino, with the new laws controlling the operations of casinos in the Territory being agreed to by the Administrator. As only the second functioning casino in Australia (beside the Federal Casino in Tasmania), the Don Casino had real in-house cash-payment gaming machines. This was enough to put it way ahead of other clubs and hotels across the country.

Federal Hotels Ltd, led by John Haddad, held the Tasmanian casino licence, and because of this hands-on experience, Federal Hotels was selected to operate the Don Casino. Given Darwin's geographic position on the doorstep of the hypothetical 'junket operators' and 'high rollers' from South-East Asia, the next step was to attract them to the new casino, and in this process stimulate growth in hotel accommodation and related jobs across the broader retail trade.

Fortunately, as the post-cyclone Darwin, now re-built, began to emerge as a popular destination for visitors, the new casino become a drawcard for the high rollers. The Northern Territory Government, buoyed by this success, expanded its policy to include both a new casino to be built on land at Mindil Beach – land that had a native title claim on it – and another casino in Alice Springs. Federal Hotels, with government backing, arranged its own finance to develop and operate both the Mindil Beach Casino in Darwin and Lasseters Golden Reef in Alice Springs.

Officially opened in April 1983, these two casinos attracted tourists, in particular those who gambled for high stakes from South-East Asia. It is interesting to read comments from the 2014 Attorney-General John Elferink (MLA) when on 1 January 2014 the '1983 Cabinet Records' were released:

> 'The opening of the $30 million Casino Resort Hotel was one of the biggest events on Darwin's social calendar in 1983 and, in December that year, Territorians went to the polls and re-elected the CLP Government in a landslide victory with the CLP claiming 19 seats to the ALP's 6 seats.
>
> 'Paul Everingham remained Chief Minister, Noel Padgham-Punch became the Territory's first female Cabinet Minister and many of this Cabinet's decisions helped shape the Northern Territory we know today.'
>
> The Northern Territory government's assessment of tourism's economic potential led to its elevation within the cabinet hierarchy when the portfolio became part of the Chief Minister's responsibilities. That re-evaluated status indicated a new, stronger government approach to development; 'developmentalism' was declared highest priority, with Chief Minister Everingham taking charge of Community Development, Industrial Development and Tourism Development.

Effectively the Northern Territory Government underwrote the casinos both in Darwin and Alice Springs, by awarding Federal Hotels, the operator, exclusive rights.

In a bid to promote tourism and jobs, the Northern Territory Government also financed and implemented the building of Sheraton Hotels in Darwin and Alice Springs and created the Yulara Resort. These projects were sold to the electorate as support for private enterprise and economic development, but given the huge costs involved, they could be criticised as an over-optimistic outlook about tourism's potential in the Northern Territory.

It comes as no real surprise that the government gradually came to believe that the Federal Government's national tourism advertising had not applied sufficient high-level marketing to attract the maximum number of big spenders.

Importantly, it was even more firmly of the opinion that Federal Hotels had not met its implied charter in attracting tourists to the Northern Territory.

Given this background, and unbeknown to the public, the NT Government had begun negotiations with both Aspinall Holdings of London (a London casino that specialised in *very* high rollers), and the American Greate Bay Casino Corporation (Pratts) of Atlantic City, to become involved with the casinos in order to achieve the numbers and the revenue that it wanted.

In 1984 the Everingham Government publicly announced there was a need for a change of casino operators and indicated it was attempting to procure operators from overseas who had high-level reputations and corresponding positive financial records. Its argument was that the promotion of the casinos in the tourism – and particularly international tourism – gambling markets had not been of the high standard that the government had expected from the current operators.

With this as the main focus, in March 1984 Paul Everingham flew to London to meet with the flamboyant British millionaire zoo owner, gambler, and casino operator John Aspinall. They met at Aspinall's private members club, with its reputation of being one of the world's most exclusive gambling establishments. Surely Everingham would not have been surprised to find that the other dinner guests were Australians Kerry Packer and transport tycoon Sir Peter Abeles, both inveterate gamblers and also good friends.

No coincidence, then, that back in mid-1983 they had also been seen together in Darwin at the Mindil Beach Casino.

In October 1984, after the somewhat audacious compulsory acquisition of the casinos from Federal Hotels by the Everingham Government, Aspinall's became one of the proposed operators of both Northern Territory casinos. Prominent and highly respected journalist, Alan Ramsey, writing in the *National Times* on 9–15 November 1984, described what had occurred. Alan Ramsey said that Everingham claimed it was he who choreographed it all:

> When Everingham arrived at the Aspinall Club for dinner he said that he was 'surprised' to find the dinner guests included Packer and Bob Hawke's old mate, transport tycoon Sir Peter Abeles.
>
> Everingham says it was coincidence. He did not know nor expect Packer or Abeles would be there. He also insists neither was involved in his talks with Aspinall on the future of the Northern Territory's two casinos in Darwin and Alice Springs. 'As I recall, Kerry Packer spent most of the evening abusing me as a fool for going into Federal politics.'
>
> And that, says Everingham with exaggerated innocence, leaning forward to look you straight in the eye and putting his hand over his heart, is the only occasion he has ever seen Aspinall and Packer together, 'honest it is'.
>
> Well so what?
>
> Why shouldn't Packer and Abeles be in London at a private dinner party in a ritzy gambling club? After all both men like to gamble and Aspinall's is about the best place to do that if you can afford it.

Meantime, Alan Ramsey quizzed Everingham:

> But what about Kerry Packer and John Aspinall?

> Well, Everingham admits he was aware of their visit to Darwin last year. Yes, he'd even heard that Packer had run into some unpleasantness when he wanted to gamble at the new casino.

The 'unpleasantness' had been about Packer's lines of credit. He was angry about being kept waiting while telephone calls were made. Everingham later denied that he had had breakfast with Packer and Aspinall and, in particular, he denied that Packer had suggested that somebody like Aspinall would run a vastly better operation than the current incumbents.

Nevertheless, following this auspicious episode, Aspinall Holdings *was* selected by Everingham to jointly operate the casino licences in Darwin and Alice Springs, in conjunction with US hotel operator Pratt Hotels Corporation, which managed a chain of some 32 hotels, including the Sands Hotel/casino complex in Atlantic City, New Jersey.

Theoretically, Aspinall's role in the Darwin venture was to run the exclusive upstairs private gaming tables for the wealthy patrons, while Pratt's was to operate the ground-floor gaming tables that were seen as primarily catering for the locals. In the year before it came to the Northern Territory, Aspinall's had turned over almost $50 million with just six London tables for its elite clientele. In contrast, Sands was used to having 60,000 gamblers per day at its 80 tables in Atlantic City. In short, both of these groups were highly experienced at doing what they did best and so appointing them both to Darwin and Alice Springs made sense, given what Everingham was aspiring to achieve. The government therefore officially proposed that Sands and Aspinall's become the operators of the two casinos; this new entity became Diamond Leisure.

For the offshore licence holders to be able to operate in Australia under Australian law, they had to have approval from the Foreign

Investment Review Board (FIRB). However, the FIRB put a 90-day freeze on the proposed transfer of the two Northern Territory casino licences while it scrutinised the deal for the Federal Treasurer Paul Keating.

As a professional company director, I was asked to be interim chairman of Diamond Leisure until such approval was granted. Similarly, until the transfer was either approved or rejected, Aspinall's/Pratt would put in a professional of their choice, Christopher Raphael, to run the Darwin Casino for Diamond Leisure.

Raphael, the 42-year-old Calcutta-born Briton, had managed Aspinall's first exclusive London casino, the Clermont Club in Berkley Square. It was the haunt of dukes, MPs, tycoons and wealthy playboys. Aspinall sold it to the Playboy organisation in 1972, and Raphael went to the US in 1980 to become vice-president of Playboy's Atlantic City Casino operations. In 1981 he switched to the Sands Hotel as its Director of International Marketing.

If the FIRB approved the deal, Aspinall's and Pratt would get 100% ownership of the Darwin and Alice Springs licences and, most significantly, they would have a monopoly on casino gambling in the Northern Territory. As Alan Ramsey said:

> It's a cosy arrangement that proposes a mere 8% a year gaming tax in return for the NT Government getting a third of the partnership's gross profits after five years.
>
> Or so Everingham claims.
>
> As yet nobody has seen the agreements signed with the partnership, even though Everingham forced his compulsory acquisition bill through the NT Legislative Assembly in August and personally conducted the physical takeover of the Darwin hotel/casino in a bizarre 3 am ceremony on 30 September.

As interim chair, I was obliged to step into the blinding lights of the media at an Everingham-organised media conference for the official takeover. His chosen time was an extraordinary 3 am in the morning. It was a nightmare. Despite the irregular choice of the time, all the media packed in and surrounded Everingham and me. It was easy for Everingham, the politician, to thrust the papers into my hands, as chair of this new conglomerate.

There I was with media lights and cameras pointing at me as I attempted to explain to the assembled crowd that these big changes had all gone very well, and that there would be the best of outcomes for the casinos and indeed the Northern Territory.

Brian Johnstone's reported in the *Australian*, on 2 October 1984, about this 3 am news conference announcing the change of ownership:

> ***Casino Party Turns Sour***
> FEDERAL Pacific Hotels was officially expelled by the Northern Territory Government as the owner-operator of the two casino-hotels it has built in Darwin and Alice Springs yesterday – with no idea how much it will be paid for the property.
>
> The Country Liberal Government invoked compulsory acquisition legislation and handed over the licence to the new casino owners, the Territory Property Trust, which combines Australian, Japanese, American and British business interests.
>
> Mr Everingham said the Territory's only public company, Henry and Walker Ltd, would have a controlling 57 per cent interest in the trust.
>
> Japan's third largest construction company Kumagai Gumi would have 14 per cent and leading British casino operator Aspinall Holdings and the Pratt Hotel Group, operator of Sands Casino in Atlantic City, would each have 10 per cent.

> 'The remaining 9 per cent of the units have been set aside for further participation by Territory and Australian business interests,' Mr Everingham said.
>
> Mr Everingham handed Mr Richard Ryan, interim Chairman of Diamond Leisure, the new gaming and liquor licences before the press conference ended. The licences will be renewable each year.
>
> Mr Everingham said the Chairman of the Northern Territory Development Corporation, Mr Ray McHenry, signed an agreement on Friday with Pratts and Aspinall in London which appointed them joint operators of the two casinos.

The publicity relating to the major dispute between Federal Hotels and the government over both the valuations of the casinos and their final price (Federal Hotels valuation was $73 million versus the government's $47 million) did not help to settle matters.

In addition, the Opposition was saying that if it had been known that the government intended to take over the casinos during the time of the election, it would have resulted in the CLP losing power.

> Opposition Leader Mr Bob Collins has meanwhile described the Northern Territory Government's silence over the purchase and ownership of the casinos as an 'absolutely bloody disgrace'.
>
> Mr Collins said, 'It's clear if the Government came clean on the deal it would destroy any credibility Paul Everingham's got left.
>
> 'The Government is not acting as anything other than a banker for Henry and Walker so it can get 57% of the casinos,' he said.

> Mr Collins suggested there should be a shareholders meeting in the casino. He said, 'The 130,000 owners of the casinos – the Territory population – should have a meeting in Sweethearts Bar. Because we own it we can have free beer, throw the dress regulations out of the window, and get $1000 worth of gambling chips!'

Importantly, Sands and Aspinall's could still not take control of the casinos until the FIRB approval was obtained. This was compounded by the inability to settle the Territory Property Trust, which could not be done until FIRB approval was obtained. In addition, fierce opposition had arisen to a proposal to resume the residential land at Myilly Point adjacent to the Darwin Casino.

Interestingly, the Alice Springs *Centralian Advocate* newspaper strongly supported the takeover:

> Sale of the Alice Springs and Darwin Casinos in a development deal involving a golf-course estate in Alice Springs and the old Darwin hospital site marks the start of a very bold venture indeed for the Northern Territory. Let's hope it all works, for the sake of the developers and the Northern Territory Development Corporation, which is backing the loan of the Australian interest.
>
> New management of the two casinos and the involvement of the Northern Territory public company, Henry and Walker, is certainly of enormous significance to the Territory.
>
> More significant, perhaps, is the opportunities for promoting two of the Territories major tourist attractions through overseas interests.

The *Centralian Advocate* article provided some of the history that had led to the proposed 1984 deal.

> It was a bold move by Federal Hotels to apply for the casino licences and invest in the bricks and mortar to make them a reality. While the Darwin casino is doing reasonably well, the Alice Springs casino hasn't really taken off in terms of revenue. The hordes of 'wealthy Asian gamblers' that were expected just haven't materialised in Alice Springs and not too many in Darwin either.
>
> The failure to promote both establishments worldwide cannot be entirely blamed on Federal Hotels. The relatively few overseas tourists is both a reflection on Australia's isolation and the complicated logistics of promoting overseas without a network and backup to make it effective.

And the paper offered free advice on how the Federal Government could best boost the venture's chance of success, considering the challenges of geographic isolation.

> Pratt Hotels and Aspinnalls are experienced operators on an international scale, with links to make promotion work. The Federal Government and the airlines now must work on the same sort of scale to develop both Alice Springs and Darwin as international tourist destinations. We will need more international and domestic flights to cater for the needs of visitors – and surely, at last, not just upgrading but total redevelopment of the Alice Springs and Darwin air terminals.

The Darwin *NT News* also supported the takeover in the following opinion piece:

> The surprise at the takeover of the Territory Federal Hotels casinos was the announcement of the participation in the Territory Trust of the giant Japanese construction company, Kumagai Gumi.

The company's entrée into the Territory could have far-reaching consequences for development in the future. Kumagai Gumi is not exactly a household name in Australia, but it is already involved in massive projects in New South Wales, Victoria, South Australia and Queensland. In Adelaide it is the $150 million redevelopment of the Adelaide Station, a project that will also include a casino. The company will take 50% equity in the project.

After Henry and Walker, Kumagai Gumi has taken the biggest share of the equity in the Territory Property Trust which is to own the casinos.

It would be surprising if the company did not become heavily involved in the redevelopment of Myilly Point and Alice Springs condominium project near the golf course. The company has been operating in Australia for only three and a half years and has managed to chalk up business worth over $1000 million.

The developments Kumagai Gumi is involved in range from coal mines to casinos, shopping centres to a ski-tube railway. An advantage of the company which would no doubt have marked appeal for the Northern Territory Government, is that it is able to raise huge sums of money to get projects completed.

Mr Tony Mitani, the company's Managing Director in Australia, is in Darwin at present not only to mark the change of ownership of the casinos but to set up an office. In its Australian projects the company has striven to use Australian construction companies and no doubt will do the same if it becomes involved in Territory projects.

Of great importance to the future of tourism in the Territory, Kumagai Gumi could prove to be an invaluable ally

> in attracting the mass Japanese market to visit here as part of a package.
>
> Past fears in the Territory about foreign investment have hopefully been dissipated. Such fears have no place in an economy which needs above all to develop. Territorians should be seeking to welcome such development.

But back to Brian Johnstone's inciteful description of the 3 am debacle, published in the *Australian* on 2 October 1984:

> It was no great surprise when journalists learned last week that Mr Everingham would convene a news conference and celebration party at Mindil Beach Casino at 3 am yesterday, the normal closing time.
>
> But one can predict with confidence that it was his last scheduled pre-dawn get-together with reporters. Simply put, the much-touted event was a disaster. Mr Everingham convened the news conference to hand over new gaming and liquor licences to a consortium of British, Japanese, United States and home-grown business interests.
>
> The legislation was timed to take effect from 3 am. Senior executives from all parties, except the aggrieved Federal Hotels, had been assembled alongside Mr Everingham in the casino's convention centre.
>
> But the convention centre chandeliers provided the only sparkle. Mr Everingham was tired, his manner perfunctory.
>
> 'I decided to have this press conference at 3 am because I thought you would all be sleepy and confused,' the bleary-eyed Chief Minister confessed. If this was the cue to cut the questions and get stuck into the lavish food and grog, the media wasn't interested.

The compulsory acquisition of the casinos had been the stormiest takeover in the Northern Territory's brief but colourful corporate history. Details of the new financial arrangements have been the subject of so much disinformation, the media was intent on gaining details on the scant information contained in a government press release.

Mr Everingham sensed this, fielded a few questions with curt replies and then remarked: 'I think you guys are not very lively this morning – what say we go and have a drink.'

He stood up as the laughter subsided, but the questions kept coming.

Asked about the possible involvement of Elders IXL in the new deal, Mr Everingham said negotiations were continuing.

'We hope they will come in, but we have been talking and this is what I should emphasise . . . we have been talking to quite a number of parties because we were approached by a considerable number of parties many months ago. Elders IXL is one of those groups, they are a very substantial group, and we would be interested in doing business with them and we hope negotiations can be concluded.

'But let me say this . . . eh . . .'

He turned to Mr Richard Ryan, Chairman of the new operating company, Diamond Leisure, and asked in an audible whisper: 'How do you say they are not needed but we'd like . . . eh?'

Mr Ryan bailed him out. 'In simple terms, as far as Elders is concerned the opportunity is still there if they wish,' he said.

Mr Everingham immediately turned to Mr Ryan, thrust a piece of paper into his hand, and declared unceremoniously: 'There's the licence.'

> He started walking away, then stopped in the face of persistent questions. 'I think that these questions are . . . you know, you are not really on the balls of your feet this morning, chaps,' he chided.
>
> 'Do you want to come downstairs and have a drink, you guys?'

The article turned to the fortunes of the embittered Federal Hotels managing director Mr John Haddad, who left the casino 10 minutes after Mr Everingham began his news conference. It described him as:

> neither sleepy nor confused. He was bitter. 'What Mr Everingham did was just too much. We had a wake downstairs, and he was having a party upstairs. We did not even have a chance to get out. We hadn't even finalised the deal when he was up there boasting about it.'
>
> Mr Haddad said that he had not been invited to the handover. He was speaking at the Federal Hotels-owned Don Hotel, which was replaced by Mindil Beach as the company casino in Darwin. Mr Haddad said Federal Hotels had a business which would give the new owners and operators a cash flow of nearly $3 million a month.
>
> 'What equity have they got in it – $3 million?' he asked. 'We had $30 odd million in it.'
>
> Mr Haddad said reduced tax provisions for the new operators and the small amount of equity required enabled them to take it out of the cash flow.
>
> 'If I bought your business today, you would hand over the keys and I would hand you a cheque. No cheque, no business,' Mr Haddad said.
>
> 'As from today our cash-flow in the Territory is finished. We

> have no money from the Government. We should walk away from this with $50 million, but that's not the case.
>
> 'The Government has appointed a valuer. There is no time on when he [Mr Everingham] must come back with an evaluation and there is no time when the Government must release the information. When the Government decided to do that we will get 90% of the valuation. If we are not happy with the valuation, we can go to the independent tribunal.'
>
> Mr Haddad said every reason Mr Everingham had put up for pushing his company out had been refuted. 'Mr Everingham has consistently said Federal did not have the financial or managerial capacity to develop the casinos.'

It was inevitable that the compulsory acquisition would result in a barrage of major media releases. The Northern Territory Government now had several spot fires to fight, the largest concerning Federal Hotels persistent statements that it did not want to sell the casinos. Peter Wilson in the *NT News*, 16 October 1984, wrote:

> Federal Hotels revealed they were 'reluctant' sellers of their two Northern Territory Casinos.
>
> Managing Director Mr John Haddad said the Government told his company if it did not sell it would be putting back tourism in the Territory. He said Federal Hotels has intended to stay in the Territory for many years. 'We are long-term developers; we did not initiate this project,' he said.
>
> 'When they [Aspinalls and Pratt] come here they will have to perform under the conditions established by the Northern Territory Government. That is a plus for Australia. English casinos do not have anything like the controls in Australia and the casinos in Atlantic City are totally different to ours.

> 'They rely tremendously on poker machines, 60% of their business comes from the slots as they call them. Aspinalls do have a good reputation although they have very small casinos in London. They concentrate on four or five people that may be capable of turning over a million pounds on one table.'
>
> The Chief Minister Mr Paul Everingham said, 'Aspinalls had world-wide contacts with the wealthy gamblers of Asia and the Middle East. London, in money terms, is probably the serious gambling capital of the world.'
>
> He said the Northern Territory Government had letters of commitment from Aspinall and Pratts Hotels of the US on the joint venture agreement and hoped to be in a position within three or four months to table the Heads of Agreement in the Legislative Assembly.
>
> 'These people say they want to get into Asia because they believe there is a great market there,' he said. He said Hong Kong, Macao, Malayasia and Indonesia were closed to them for various reasons so they had decided on the Northern Territory.

Back at the office, both the government and I made repeated requests to the Federal Treasurer Paul Keating for his and FIRB's approval for the casinos, but our requests were continually rejected. The Federal Board had put a 90-day freeze on the transfer of the two Northern Territory casino licences while it scrutinised the deal for the Treasurer.

The *NT News* editorial described it thus:

> The Federal Treasurer, Mr Paul Keating, has been asked to urgently reconsider his decision to block the NT Government's takeover of the Darwin and Alice Springs casinos.
>
> Territory Property Trust chairman, Mr Richard Ryan, made the request in a telex to Mr Keating yesterday.

The Territory's new elected Chief Minister Mr Ian Tuxworth also sent a message to Mr Keating asking for the decision to be reconsidered.

Mr Keating announced yesterday he had an interim order under the Foreign Takeovers Act prohibiting for 90 days proposals by the foreign interests to lease and operate the two casinos. This followed a formal objection to the Foreign Investment Review Board by Federal Pacific Hotels.

Mr Ryan who is also Chairman of Diamond Leisure, pending FIRB approval, said he 'noted with dismay reports of Mr Keating's decision'.

Mr Ryan, who is also a director of Henry and Walker, said, 'The success of the substantial Australian investment in the trust, hinged on early reorientation of the casino enterprise. (Henry and Walker plan to take 57% controlling interest in the property trust).

'In the absence of any Australian operators with demonstrated ability to access international markets, (the) introduction of wide-ranging expertise is vital to our success' the telex said.

'I am therefore at a loss to understand your position and to fathom what can be gained by a final decision. A great deal of work has been put into structure an arrangement under which the interests of this trust, those operators and the public are all served.

'I am fearful that this whole balance may now be disturbed by the uneasiness which has now been caused.'

In a statement issued in Darwin Mr Tuxworth said there was no valid reason for any holdup.

'The Federal Treasurer, Mr Keating, has in front of him all the information he needs to go ahead with approval.' He said,

> 'The proposed new operators and the Territory Government had supplied all the information requested by the FIRB and his Government had detailed the reasons for not allowing Federal Hotels to continue as the casino operators.'
>
> He said he understood Mr Keating was supportive of foreign investment in casinos in Western Australia, South Australia (Kumagai) and Queensland.
>
> 'What possible objections could there be to a similar investment in the Territory?' he asked.
>
> Mr Tuxworth said while the deferral of FIRB approval would not affect existing operations it could delay the immediate plans for upgrading the casinos. Mr Tuxworth and Mr Ryan both attended a meeting in Darwin yesterday which was called when Mr Keating's decision became known.

The Treasurer's continual withholding of approval resulted in a plethora of angry exchanges between the parties, exacerbated by the fact that the former Territory Chief Minister Paul Everingham had now been elected to Federal Parliament.

> ***Deferment 'Cheap Political Stunt'***
>
> Former Chief Minister, Mr Paul Everingham, last night described attempts by the Federal Government to defer the take-over of the Territory's two casinos by the Territory Property Trust as a 'cheap political stunt'.
>
> Federal Treasurer, Mr Paul Keating, said late yesterday the Government wanted 'more information' about foreign participation in the trust before approval would be given by the Foreign Investment Review Board (FIRB).
>
> 'It's nothing more than a stunt motivated by the election,' Mr Everingham said. 'Creating jobs or anything else obviously

> doesn't matter. Whatever scant respect I had for the Hawke Government – I've got not one scintilla now.'
>
> He said, 'The FIRB had recently approved a $45 million project in South Australia. Yet here they are holding back. There was no indication (before the election was announced) of any problems.'
>
> The international marketing director of Pratts Hotels, Mr Chris Raphael, said his company had nothing to worry about over the delay in the FIRB deferment: 'We feel optimistic that at the end of the day their agreement to our participation, and that of our partners, Aspinall's, will be forthcoming,' he said.
>
> 'There is absolutely no reason why we should be turned down and we are not worried about the delay at all,' Mr Raphael said.
>
> Chief Minister, Mr Ian Tuxworth, was unavailable for comment last night, but has called an urgent meeting of all parties at 9 am today. Mr Everingham who pushed the compulsory acquisition legislation through the Northern Territory Parliament before his resignation this week to contest the Federal election, will also attend.

Although a formal Heads of Agreement had been signed to determine the value of the casinos, the acrimonious dispute regarding the purchase price had yet to be settled. This process had actually started prior to the formal acquisition of the casinos by the Northern Territory Government. Two valuers were to assess the properties and the average of their valuations (so long as it was no less than $47.1 million and no more than $55 million) was to be the agreed sale price. The government's valuers came up with a total of $44.2 million. Federal Hotel's valuation was $44.5 million, to which they added another $28.8 million for the cost of land

and improvements. The average of the figures was $59.4 million, which in Federal Hotel's eyes set the amount at $55 million as per the agreement. However, the government's final offer was $47.1 million. Despite the hyperbole, both parties were keen to settle. The difficulty was the gap between the two numbers. After some months settlement was finally agreed at $49.5 million.

As Michael Lawrence pointed out in the *Sydney Morning Herald* on 17 November 1984, a federal election was looming, and plainly it was not in the Federal Government's interest to delay FIRB approval any further now that the settlement finally had been reached.

> In a bid to avoid embarrassment ahead of the election, the Federal Government will allow the proposed acquisition by foreign interests of the Darwin and Alice Springs casino complexes.
>
> The Treasurer, Mr Paul Keating, said last night 'an interim order under the Foreign Takeovers Act had been revoked, allowing the Territory Property Trust transaction to proceed.' Mr Keating criticised the Northern Territory Government for passing emergency legislation to take the leases from Federal Hotels.
>
> 'Considerable public concern has been expressed about the impact on investor confidence of the Northern Territory Government's decision to compulsorily acquire the casinos from Federal Hotels,' said Mr Keating.
>
> 'At a time when Australia clearly needs a substantial increase in the level of private investment expenditure, it is difficult to reconcile such government action with the national interest. We can only hope that this (the compensation) agreement will allay investors' concerns about the manner in which the

> complexes were originally acquired from Federal and that this unfortunate episode had done no permanent damage to investor confidence, in particular in the Northern Territory, but also in the rest of Australia.'
>
> The transaction did not appear to breach foreign investment guidelines, as Henry and Walker, the Territory's only listed company, was to acquire a majority interest in the casinos. The foreign interests, through London based Aspinall's group, the Pratt group of the US and the Japanese company Kumagai Gumi, will hold collectively less than 40 per cent.

To help finalise matters I had to meet with the casino operators. I rushed home, packed, said goodbye to my wife and boarded the next plane destined for the US. On the flight I caught up with my sleep. Many hours later when we finally landed I disembarked into freezing winter conditions complete with snow. The flight attendant glanced at my attire and politely asked if I'd forgotten to get off earlier. Had I missed my stop? Given that my attire consisted entirely of thin fabric pants and a short-sleeved shirt, it was not an unreasonable query. Hence my urgent shopping for winter gear before I ventured to the Playboy-like Sands Hotel and Casino in Atlantic City.

The meetings occurred and then I was shown to my bedroom, which was larger than a normal house, its ceiling covered in mirrors. I was asked by the butler if I would like anything more. No, I said, as I headed off to sleep.

After meeting with the management of Sands, I boarded Concorde and flew to London to meet with Aspinalls. There followed enough incidents for a full-length movie. First there was the problem with their chauffeur who had been sent to meet me at Heathrow Airport and forgot where he had left his vehicle. We spent 90 minutes searching for it. Eventually we headed for Curzon

Street. At 11 am London time several notables were playing stud poker at £5000 a hand.

A luncheon engagement for three followed, for which I would have normally at least offered to pay. Given that the bill turned out to be £3000 (something like $20,000 in 2025) I became somewhat taciturn.

Then back to the reason I was in London . . .

While FIRB approval enabled Sands and Aspinall's to legally take control and operate the casinos, it put the Territory Property Trust as the owners of the properties, in an urgent need to settle and restructure its finances.

The Northern Territory Development Corporation was a Northern Territory-controlled entity used to promote development within the Territory. The chair/CEO was Ray McHenry, a senior Northern Territory public servant.

Funds were required for the Henry and Walker contribution of 57%, and possibly also for Kumagai Gumi at 14%. As interim chair of Diamond Leisure and the Territory Property Trust, and a director of Henry and Walker, it now became my major role to find the funds for the refinancing.

Ultimately, a loan of approximately $20 million was obtained from the State Bank of South Australia with the loan supported by guarantees from Kumagai Gumi and the Northern Territory Development Corporation.

The Trust at this stage had the following unit holders.

Henry and Walker	57%
Kumagai Gumi	14%
Sands (Pratt)	10%
Aspinall's of London	10%
Northern Territory Development Corporation	9%
	100%

The final issue that had to be settled was a major dispute over the resumption of land at Myilly Point. The government had considered the feasibility of building a new hotel and possibly a new airstrip on the point, along with upgrading the Darwin Airport. The potential development was strongly opposed by the residents, many of whom were either very senior public servants or wealthy 'captains of industry' who would be forced to relocate.

As Malcolm Ormiston reported in the *NT News* on 17 October 1984, the plan was ultimately abandoned as too difficult:

> The Northern Territory Government has told the owners of eight properties on Myilly Point that they will not have to leave the point.
>
> A spokesperson for the owners said they had been told the units would blend in with the development. The other three properties belong to the Paspaley family. The family has apparently been told it will not have to leave Myilly Point.
>
> Instead, they would be given three other blocks on the point and compensated for the disruption to their lives. It is understood negotiations between the family and the government are still proceeding. The family did not wish to comment and the Lands Minister, Mr Marshall Perron, was tied up with the Assembly sittings yesterday.
>
> Since the controversy over the four historic homes the government has said one of the houses, Audit House could remain, but the fate of the others is still in doubt.

In March 1984, Ivor Davies in *Business Review Weekly* published the following article that explained how funds were paid through borrowing structure:

> It has long been known that the Northern Territory Government, led by former Chief Minister Paul Everingham (now Federal MHR for the Northern Territory), took the casinos from Federal Hotels Ltd for a sum slightly more than $50 million in the early hours of October 1 last year.
>
> The political backlash of the Northern Territory Government's attack on Federal Hotels Ltd continued in Federal Parliament last week when Treasurer Paul Keating called the expropriation 'confiscation . . . vandalism'.
>
> But it has not been revealed just how little the shareholders of Henry and Walker Ltd have put at risk. Last week H&W company secretary Patrick Armitstead confirmed for BRW that his company had invested a total of $10,000 to buy 57% of the two casino properties, through the Territory Property Trust.
>
> Armitstead also confirmed that $10,000 was the maximum H&W shareholders had at risk in the casino venture. He said that the remainder of the company's so-called 'equity' contribution to the casino purchase, orchestrated by the Everingham Government, had been borrowed from the banks.
>
> Questioned by BRW, Armitstead said that these loans were off the balance sheet and not secured on H&W's other assets—which include civil engineering, property development, vehicle dealerships and prawn fishing in and around the Northern Territory.

While several points in the article are incorrect, it does set out the correct principles in that the total borrowings were paid into the Territory Property Trust. The entity holding the investment was called the Coonawarra Unit Trust (CUT) and the loan of circa $20 million was offset by the asset investment in the Territory Property

Trust entity, which was supported by the guarantees from the third partners. It was 100% debt financed!

In 1985 the casino was renamed the Diamond Beach Hotel and Casino and was managed for a brief period by the joint venture partners. In 1986 Aspinall's bought out Greate Bay's equity for $1 million and acquired all the units in the Territory Property Trust at par. The acquisition of these units meant that Henry and Walker, Kumagai Gumi and the Northern Territory Development Corporation were no longer involved in the casino operations/ property either directly or indirectly. As an aside, the CUT (Henry Walker) lost over $3 million dollars through this transaction.

After becoming Chief Executive Officer of Henry and Walker, I resigned from both Diamond Leisure and the Territory Property Trust. The transaction that was supposed to take three or four months had taken approximately three years of all of our lives. However, as the 'takeover' and changes did help in terms of increasing tourism numbers in both Darwin and Alice Springs, you could perhaps argue that it had all been a success!

However, it certainly wasn't a success for Henry Walker.

(Please refer to Appendix E for various media releases relating to the casino acquisition, disputes and sales.)

Chapter 13

The Saga of Aspinall/Pratts, Federal Hotels and Me

It is tempting to say that as chair of the new Casino group and therefore witnessing it all, I could have written interesting articles, but frankly it was incredibly labour intensive dealing with the acrimonious parties involved.

Federal Hotels had quite reasonably assumed that it had a 15-year monopoly agreement guaranteed by legislation. It had not been paid a cent in return for the seizure of its multi-million-dollar investment and was understandably bitter, given it had built both hotel/casino complexes from scratch and had been with them for five years, and the new Darwin casino had been open only for a single year before being transferred to an overseas group. The pain was exacerbated by the fact that the new operators were to be taxed only 8%, whereas Federal Hotels had had to pay 20% on its Darwin operations and 15% on the Alice Springs venture. Federal Hotels had been haggling with the government since March, first about the sale and then compensation for the takeover. The government refused to go past a total of $47.1 million, while Federal Hotels insisted on $55 million. And painfully it all dragged on.

Interestingly, John Aspinall and his US counterparts each paid $3 million for the licence under their new joint company Diamond Leisure. And it was my task to oversee it. I made a number of trips to London, Atlantic City and Singapore to deal with Aspinall, Sands and their colleagues, which generated sufficient material for a high rating movie.

John Aspinall had left his first casino to concentrate on his private life, which included his private zoo and wildlife park in Kent. His great loves were gambling and animals, and his various 'social activities'. His love of animals was displayed throughout his new Mayfair club in Curzon Street, where a variety of wildlife paintings adorned the walls of gaming rooms. When the lure of the gaming tables called him back, he set up the Curzon Street Club in association with financier James Goldsmith (a man who drove motorboats between social commitments). When they floated 20% of the shares in the club on the unlisted securities market, they valued its operations at more than $90 million.

It was Aspinall's gambling interests and his club that created media attention in Australia, but in London it was the unfortunate incidents surrounding his zoo in Kent that hit the press. The Aspinall Zoo had a record of housing difficult animals, and consequently this led to the accidental death of three staff; two were mauled by tigers and one was crushed by an elephant. Then there was the tiger that escaped and was finally shot in a suburban backyard. Despite these obvious dangers, Aspinall still ventured into his tigers' cage to play with them, and when the Northern Territory casino appointment was confirmed, he said that he had received 'a letter from the Northern Territory Government asking me if I was interested in taking some animals, but the quarantine laws are so strict here I won't be able to'.

The air of opulence that pervaded his Mayfair club, on the other hand, was something that he was both keen and able to bring to the Australian casinos. He was emphatic that there would be major changes and upgrades, and that this would all reflect his reputation for dealing in high stakes with high rollers.

'We are specialists in big gamblers, and we hope to attract the big players from the Far East,' he explained to Janine Perrett when she interviewed him in London for a *NT News* article of 2 December 1984, headlined 'A Flamboyant 'King' Moves into Darwin'.

Aspinall had said there would be a special private gaming room with more than 20 luxury suites for the sole use of the big gamblers from as far away as Tokyo and Seoul. He believed that he could also lure Muslim gamblers from South-East Asia, where Islamic fundamentalists had enforced the closure of casinos.

> Obviously proud of his reputation, he points out that already the Darwin casino is being inundated with Asians who have heard he has taken over and say: 'Ah, Mr Aspinall, you know how to treat us.'
>
> As yet, the facilities for these gamblers are not there, so all he can do is 'cover them with apologies' and tell them to come back in a year when it is finished.
>
> When John Aspinall talks about the 'big gambler', he is talking from the experience of his own club, which allows only that select group of 'established gamblers who are prepared to risk at least 3000 British pounds a night'.

As the Aspinall team moved into the Northern Territory casinos, they successfully applied to raise the minimum gambling limit from $50 to $200. Aspinalls was quick to assure Australians that the small punter would not be pushed out, and that it was for this very reason that the Northern Territory Government wanted the US partner that operated the Sands chain in their deal.

The Northern Territory Administration and Australian Gambling Authorities *Casino Licensing and Control Act 1984* recorded the following in a submission:

> They [Sands] specialise in the 'bedrock' or 'grind' action as it is known in the States. 'They are experts in the games for

> small players such as slot machines,' he said. Mr Aspinall believes Federal Hotels was not running the casinos 'with any imagination'.
>
> For a man whose club reported pre-tax profits of around $22 million last year and is expected to do even better when it reports in the next few weeks, he is incredulous that Federal 'could not even make a profit' from the Australian operations. For this reason, he totally supports the Northern Territory administration and Australian gambling authorities, which he describes as 'sensible'.

Nevertheless, the Casinos Affair caused a major political and financial scandal. It dominated the press, and bitter arguments arose, led by the Chief Minister Paul Everingham and the then Leader of the Opposition Bob Collins. The following extract from the Minutes of the Legislative Assembly, dated 21 August 1984, gives an indication of the vitriol between the parties:

> Mr B. Collins (Leader of the Opposition) moved—
>
> That this Assembly censures the Chief Minister for the ineptitude with which the negotiations with Federal Pacific Hotels have been conducted in respect of the acquisition of their hotel Casino operations in the Northern Territory with particular reference to—
>
> 1) The assertion by the government that the clause 16 (3) of the Casino agreement allows for the compulsory acquisition by the government of all the Casino hotels when it clearly fails to do so
> 2) The carriage by the government of high level and detailed negotiations through the Northern Territory Development Corporation of developments requiring

the use of assets owned by Federal Hotels without invoking clause 16 (3) of the agreement thereby placing those negotiations outside the ambit of the legislated agreement with Federal Hotels

3) The deliberate campaign of public denigration of the performance of the Federal Hotel Casinos by the government in the face of excellent record of operation and community support
4) The failure of the government to conduct all negotiations with Federal Hotels on the basis of the existing agreement signed in good faith by Federal Hotels and the government and attached as a schedule to the Casino License and Control Act.

The government confirmed that the casino licences had been stripped from Federal Hotels on the grounds that they had been conducting inadequate marketing. Compulsory acquisition was to be made by government legislation; the property ownership would remain in Australia, and the entity owning the properties would rent them to the overseas joint operators Greate Bay Casino Corporation (Pratts) of Atlantic City and Aspinall Holdings of London. The property owners' group, as detailed earlier, was to be called the Territory Property Trust, and it would have a consortium of investors. The Northern Territory Government, keen to get Australian investors, approached Henry and Walker as well as the Japanese company Kumagai Gumi to see if they would consider taking equity in this entity. Kumagai Gumi encouraged the idea of Henry and Walker becoming involved, as it was still a major shareholder in the company at the time. However, there were major questions from the Opposition and media about the Trust and, in particular, about the financing and structure in which

Henry and Walker and Kumagai Gumi were now invited to have a financial interest.

Despite vociferous opposition from both Federal Hotels Ltd and the Northern Territory Opposition, the legislation was duly passed. The future owner of the properties, the Territory Property Trust, was also established and as interim chair of Diamond Leisure and non-executive director of Henry and Walker, I was asked to also chair the Trust for an initial interim period of three to four months. However, again the FIRB issue arose. Approval was essential for the Trust to be properly settled and it took forever to come through! But it was eventually settled.

It is interesting to note the subsequent history of the Darwin casino. In 1995 Aspinall's sold the property to MGM Grand for US $75 million plus the assumed debt of $13 million in 1995. It was renamed the MGM Grand Darwin. In 2004, the SkyCity Entertainment Group purchased it from MGM Grand for $195 million to use as a hotel, and the hotel took ownership on 23 July 2004. SkyCity sold the hotel to an American company called Delaware North in April 2019 for $188 million. Delaware North changed the property's name to Mindil Beach Casino and Resort, to reflect both one of its original names and its modern facilities. The Alice Springs Casino has also been rebranded as Crown Plaza Alice Springs Lasseters, and is no longer part of the original group.

All of this made for a very long story because it had even more changes in ownership than the original Darwin Casino. First from Aspinall's to Ford Dynasty, and then when Ford Dynasty looked for a change, it went to the Intercontinental Hotel Group in a franchise agreement. This occurred in 2016 and enabled the operation to trade under the Crown Plaza Banner. There were extensive renovations, and in April 2021 the Hotel Casino was sold to the hospitality group Iris Capital for $105 million.

In retrospect, the compulsory acquisition on the part of the government was probably a success. Tourism numbers increased significantly over the next three decades and exceeded one million visitors. Employment in industry also grew strongly, as did certain types of infrastructure.

Would that have happened if Federal Hotels had kept ownership? Who knows – but with their limited finances they would probably not have had the same level of success.

So why did the two parties – the Northern Territory Government and Henry and Walker – get involved in casinos in the first place? Both parties were 'new' and keen to develop the North, and they also knew each other well. The government saw the attraction of promoting tourism in order to lure people to the Northern Territory, increased taxes and an association with Kumagai Gumi, and Henry and Walker came in to help and hoped to receive financial benefit.

In the long term the government probably achieved its objective of more jobs and increased tourism, but from Henry and Walker's perspective the transaction was unprofitable, with a total loss of around $5 million. In retrospect, they should not have been involved as closely as they were.

I can't resist repeating that this whole saga of the Northern Territory casinos is perfect material for a feature film. There are the two lead actors, the wealthy British socialite John Aspinall and the handsome Christopher Raphael from Atlantic City. There are the politicians Paul Everingham followed by Ian Tuxworth and Bob Collins, at logger-heads. Not to forget the walk-on parts for Kerry Packer and Peter Abeles as the wealthy players at the tables. And then there are all the crowd scenes, including those teeming with the media. And somewhere, lurking up the back, there I am dutifully impersonating Jacques Tati as Monsieur Hulot in *Mon Oncle*.

Chapter 14

Charles Darwin University

Background

Darwin had always been different from other towns and cities in Australia with its mix of inhabitants from all over, and so, not surprisingly, it was a town without tertiary or advanced education institutions. It is reasonable to say that in the postwar 1940s there was little in the way of any adult education in the Northern Territory, and nothing would have been further from the thoughts of its administrators at the time.

The South Australian Government had agreed to provide primary and secondary education in the Territory, with the Commonwealth bearing all costs. The first high schools in fact were only created in the early 1960s. These were located in Darwin and Alice Springs. Standards of education were so low that in 1950 the Administrator approved the introduction of evening continuation classes to enable students in Alice Springs to reach the South Australian Intermediate standard of secondary schooling. In 1951, supervised study classes were provided for apprentices in Darwin, along with courses in typing, shorthand, French and other subjects needed for the examinations for the Third Division of the Commonwealth Public Service.

Nancy Giese, who was a great leader of education in the Territory and who later became chair of both the Darwin Community College and the Darwin Institute of Technology (DIT) and, much later, Chancellor of the Northern Territory University, described the education scene in 1954, as recorded in CDU Archives:

> Darwin had a population of about 9000 and all educational needs were catered for in a single institution known as the Darwin Higher Primary School, which offered primary education and three years of limited secondary education and included the Adult Education Centre, for which the Headmaster of the School was also the part-time Registrar. Provision of services was a joint responsibility shared between the Commonwealth government, which accepted overall financial responsibility and provided buildings and physical resources, and the State of South Australia, which supplied staff and curriculum.

As the population grew, so too did the demand for adult education. Between June 1957 and June 1958 enrolments in Darwin grew from 270 students in 19 classes to 606 in 32. In Alice Springs they grew from 89 students in 12 classes to 110 students in 11 classes. These variants increased the Administrator's workload and meant that significant changes were needed.

With a total of 19 teachers and over 500 enrolments, it became obvious that the task of administering and developing adult education was too much for anyone to handle part-time. In June 1958, the South Australian Department of Education therefore recommended the appointment of a full-time principal to the Adult Education Centre in Darwin. The Territory Administrator had already decided on a three-part strategy: to develop internal training courses in the Public Service; to develop an Adult Education Centre in preference to a Public Service Institute; and to develop courses at university level insofar as this could be arranged within existing facilities. The South Australian proposal took the Territory a step closer to the development of the Administration's ultimate goal of providing tertiary education.

The first principal of the Adult Education Centre was Harold Garner, who held the position for 14 years. He was responsible for the entire Northern Territory Adult Education System, excluding Indigenous communities. By 1961, the Centre offered courses that covered many different groups, including matriculation subjects, and developed programs for apprentices, which had previously not existed. Between 1968 and 1972 it introduced classes for external students in professional subjects, under agreement with the University of Queensland.

Garner was a wonderful principal, and highly regarded by both staff and students. Hundreds turned up on enrolment week at the Adult Education Centre with the flexibility and informality needed to meet the obvious wide range of educational needs.

In 1973 the Centre was absorbed into the Darwin Community College, with its classes continuing until the College opened in 1974. The Community College was governed by a council of 15 members, with Bishop Ken Mason as the inaugural chair and Dr Joe Flint first principal. Nancy Giese became chair following Mason's retirement.

Over time, the College offered both Technical and Further Education (TAFE) courses, along with tertiary courses that included teaching. It developed a collaboration with the University of Queensland and the College ultimately developed a School of Aboriginal Studies, and merged and later formed the Northern Territory University with a relatively large extension service for external students, together with a community radio station.

Importantly, in order to continue the process of developing tertiary education in the Territory, a University College of the Northern Territory serviced by the University of Queensland was also created.

Due to the Northern Territory Government's wish to establish a university, however, there were a number of reviews of its role and place in the community. The name of the institution was changed to the Darwin Institute of Technology (DIT) and it would later merge and form the Northern Territory University.

By the mid-1970s there was an obvious need for more education and a desperate need for technical training in the skills required for the rebuilding of the city. In 1984 I became involved with Darwin Community College. I went to the first meeting, in December of that year, and it was at that meeting that its name was changed to the Darwin Institute of Technology (DIT). The government appointed Kevin Davis, a former schoolteacher and respected public servant, as Head of School and the new principal.

Formation of Northern Territory University

Baiba Berzins and Peter Loveday's excellent book *A University for the Territory: The Northern Territory University and Preceding Institutions (1949–1999*), on which I have drawn, details the development of education in the Northern Territory up to the creation of Charles Darwin University. After the ravages of Cyclone Tracy there was an increased need for skilled workers, and with the new self-government there was a similar need for government officers. These issues combined to focus on educational needs in the Territory.

In 1985, encouraged by the new government's desire to prove itself, there was a move to create an 'on the ground' dual sector (TAFE and higher education) institution. In practice this meant that the DIT would merge with the embryonic University College of the Northern Territory (UCNT), which had been established about 12 months earlier. In January 1989 DIT combined with UCNT to form the Northern Territory University.

At last, with its first legitimate university, the Territory was attempting to address the many demands for education and training.

Initial position of the university

The university was opened on 28 April 1989 by the then Minister for Education, Tom Harris. The inaugural vice-chancellor, Professor Mal Nairn, hailed from rural Queensland and was a graduate of both the TAFE and tertiary sectors, a perfect choice. The initial council of 25 members chose the Chief Justice Austen Asche AC, QC as the first chancellor, and Nancy 'Nan' Giese OBE as deputy chancellor. Other appointments included Professor Jim Thompson and Professor Ron McKay.

Austen Asche had completed his early education at Darwin Primary School in the 1930s and subsequently went on to study Law at the University of Melbourne. He had a long and distinguished career in law that included roles as Chancellor of Deakin University and First Judge of the Victorian Family Law Court. He ultimately became Chief Justice of the Supreme Court of the Northern Territory. He was made a Companion of the Order of Australia in 1994 and became Chancellor Emeritus of Charles Darwin University when he was appointed as the Administrator of the Northern Territory.

Nancy Giese was born in Brisbane and educated at Brisbane Girls Grammar School. She later trained at the University of Queensland, where she qualified as a teacher. She came to the Territory in the 1950s, and with her background in teaching worked hard to develop the educational, social and cultural life of Darwin in an array of positions including Northern Territory Parents and Citizens Association, North Australian Eisteddfod Council, National Council of Women NT, Darwin Hospital Advisory Board, Arts Council NT, Museums and Art Galleries boards of the NT, board of the Darwin Performing Arts Centre, and several post-secondary educational advisory bodies.

Nancy was appointed a Member of the Order of the British

Empire (MBE) in 1971, an Officer of the Order of the British Empire (OBE) in 1977, and an Officer of the Order of Australia (AO) in 1997. When she retired, she was made Chancellor Emeritus of Charles Darwin University. Given their social and educational backgrounds, both Austen Asche and Nancy Giese were perfect appointments for the Northern Territory University.

Northern Territory University, 1995–1999

Professor Nairn retired in 1995 and Professor Roger Holmes took on the role of vice-chancellor for 12 months prior to Professor Ron McKay, who had been effectively the Provost of Northern Territory University, becoming vice-chancellor. During this period there were major changes to federal funding for higher education and these changes depended significantly on each university's educational profile. The Department of Employment, Education & Training's (DEET) estimates of growth were enshrined in Equivalent Full Time Student Units (EFTSU) targets. DEET visited the university on a yearly basis to check its performance and was often critical in its judgement of the institution.

Funding from the Federal and Northern Territory Governments was circa $96 million in 1995. This fell to $87 million in the 1996 Budget, and $69 million in 1998. In December 1998 the Commonwealth Minister for Education, John Dawkins, promised NTU funding for all higher education places at DIT and University College of NT at the national average funding rate of $8,344 per EFTSU. This decision was in defiance of the earlier agreement that in small institutions the cost per EFTSU would naturally have to be higher than the national average. As a result, the Northern Territory Government was left with no alternative but to finance the shortfall using its own 'gap funding'.

From the beginning the university had to accommodate growth

while dealing with difficult budgetary shortfalls; the period from 1997 to 1999 would be even worse.

In its campaign for the March 1996 Federal election, the Liberal–National Coalition promised that both operational and research funding for higher education would be maintained and that it would expand provision for integrated further education and training. On 13 May of that year, however, Senator Amanda Vanstone told the meeting of vice-chancellors that funding for tertiary education would be cut by up to 12% in 1997, with further cuts to take place in 1998 and 1999.

The Northern Territory University, now facing more funding dramas, was obliged to seek a three-year special funding package of $3 million to enable it to adjust to lower levels of funding. This was agreed to, but only as an advance on the budget for 1998.

The university also had other costs to meet – the 1.3% per year indexed increases in salaries in 1999, the one-off cost of redesigning enrolment procedures, and the costs of voluntary early retirements and compulsory redundancies that were not fully allowed for in the budget. The challenge thrown to the Northern Territory University by DEET, coupled as it was with a deteriorating financial position, did not help the university at all.

The Commonwealth Government also contemporaneously proposed reductions in triannual funding, which exacerbated the problems.

With the position of the university precarious, the Federal Government unofficially threatened to cut off all funding unless a major review was conducted. In fact, the university's financial position was so bad that on at least two occasions Professor McKay and I had to see the Chief Minister in order to obtain funds so that salaries could be paid. The university had no financial reserves, and simply had managed its finances on a day-to-day basis.

In August 2001, following further representation from the Federal Government, KPMG was engaged to prepare a report covering Strategic Positioning for the Future for the Northern Territory University. A steering committee was set up for this purpose. The committee comprised:

Professor Ron McKay – Vice-Chancellor and Chair
Nancy Giese – Chancellor
Richard Ryan – Deputy Chancellor & Chair of Menzies School of Health Research
Justice Sally Thomas – Council Member
Ken Clarke – Under Treasurer – Council Member
Paul Tyrell – Secretary Department of the Chief Minister
Peter Plummer – CEO of Department of Education & Member of Menzies School of Health Research

In a transcript of a CDU Archives interview with Peter Plummer, who was CEO of Health at the time, he said:

> I first came to the Territory from Papua New Guinea in 1980. The reason I came was to take up a position as the first principal of Batchelor College.
>
> My memory is a little vague about the exact time when I got involved with NTU. I'm pretty sure it was about the time I was CEO of Health; I was on the Menzies Board. And that was also the time when the University appeared to be having severe budgetary problems. From a Government perspective, I, and several other CEOs, were involved in trying to assess – we were formally asked by the government – to try to assess the University's bid for new monies. It was clear also at that time that the Commonwealth was starting to be pretty clear it wasn't going to put out additional funds towards the NTU –

as the NT Government was also clear – unless they could be really persuaded.

Ultimately, in some discussions we had with the Commonwealth, we became aware that it was their firm view – and it was ours as well – that a really solid review of the University needed to be done. The question was, who would do it? And Commonwealth bureaucrats said to me – 'We just can't identify someone who we would really trust to just come in and do this. We just can't sort out who's available'.

Richard and I had been talking about it and I had said maybe Ken McKinnon would do it. I knew Ken because he was my boss in Papua New Guinea. I knew his standing in the academic world. I knew he was retired. The real question was would he take up the job. When I spoke to Mike Gallagher (a Commonwealth senior bureaucrat for higher ed.) – he and Bill Burmester said, 'Do you think you can get him?' And I said, 'Well can you pay?' So that was really the discussion that Richard and I had with Gallagher, that's the essence of it. And then from Canberra we went to Sydney and arranged to meet Ken, he agreed to consider undertaking the review, and it didn't take him long to say, 'I'll take it up.'

So really, I was in a position to pull back and let things happen because Richard was the more appropriate council member to liaise with Ken and Ron McKay and everybody else here.

A series of meetings were held with Federal Minister for Education (Nelson) and Commonwealth officials and after many difficulties a review by KMPG was undertaken.

I have a very strong belief that the Federal Government would have stopped all funding for the Northern Territory University if it hadn't been for the care, skill, and acumen of Peter Plummer, Under Treasurer Jennifer Prince, Ken Clarke, and several other members of the Northern Territory bureaucracy, all of whom used their contacts within the Federal Government to help control significant threats. The KPMG report was funded by the Federal and Territory Governments. Released in late August 2001, it said:

> When one considers financial comparisons between NTU and the 11 other 'smaller universities without medical schools', the starting base for the comparison is the Commonwealth Operating Grant and its comparison with Commonwealth-funded students. The overall conclusion to be drawn from the figures is that NTU has the highest Commonwealth Operating Grant per EFTSU of the 12 universities in the comparison. The NTU operating grant reflects the results negotiated between NTU and the Commonwealth in 1991/92 which meant that the operating grant for NTU would be 20% above the amount determined by the relative funding formula.
>
> It should also be noted that despite the projected reduction in the NTU Commonwealth Operating Grant from 1999 to 2002, the NTU still maintains the highest grant per EFTSU but, in 2002, this will be only 14.6% above the average compared with the 20% negotiated in 1991/92. On the other hand, it represents a relative increase over the 13.9% 'premium' that NTU received in 1999.
>
> It is an indication of the financial problem the NTU has that even with its high level of Commonwealth Operating grant per Commonwealth Funded ETFSU it suffered a $6.4 m reduction in its higher education operating result between 1998 and 1999 and moved into operating deficit . . . Even when the 1998 loss on its TAFE side is taken into account, NTU had

an operating surplus that was nearly double the average for the 12. One year later NTU was in operating deficit.

- Comparative figures for key financial measures. This data is only published on a sector-wide basis, but the table shows that:
- NTU was one of only five institutions to record a negative safety margin for 1999, although it showed a significant improvement in 2000
- NTU had a 1999 current ratio of only 0.68, significantly below the sector average of 1.82 and, although it showed an improvement in 2000, it was still below the 1999 sector average at the end of 1999 NTU had cash and investments equal to only 1.2 months revenue, significantly below the sector average of 5.8 months and, whilst the position improved in 2000 to 2.0 months revenue, this was still significantly below the 1999 sector average.

The KPMG report stated specifically that the Northern Territory University had faced a serious financial situation at the end of 1999. While the results for the year 2000 appeared to show some improvement, the university's ongoing financial viability would remain problematic without longer-term reform.

A change of government occurred while the KPMG review was being undertaken.

The new Labor government, while it had some different views on the management and roles of the Northern Territory University from the previous CLP government, was very supportive of the review. It is fair to say, however, that there were some strong negatives relating to some council members, staff and courses. (The report, a portion of which is included as Appendix F, details why it was imperative there be a change.)

While the review was underway, Vice-Chancellor McKay became seriously ill and sadly died. Professor Charles Webb (deputy vice-chancellor) then became acting vice-chancellor awaiting Professor McKinnon, who had agreed to the appointment as interim vice-chancellor. Professor McKinnon had held many roles that made him well suited for the interim appointment, including vice-chancellor of the University of Wollongong and Director of Education in Papua New Guinea.

On appointment, Professor McKinnon undertook further examinations of the university and suggested that as it was to become a new institution, Northern Territory University should change its name.

Professor McKinnon's confidential report, *The Present Situation of the Northern Territory University*, stated that the original impetus to establish a university in the Territory had been on the understanding of the importance of providing both local tertiary education and training, and regionally significant world-class research that would underpin the Territory's development:

> Fly-in Fly-out experts have been the norm for too long. The new University represents an invigorated focus on building a University that will bring international academic skills to the NT while at the same time participating as a partner in Territory development across all aspects of its social, cultural, and economic development. The NTU community and Centralian College Council and senior staff have been essential to the crucial early steps towards realisation of a new University better able to serve the needs of the Northern Territory.

Professor McKinnon also concluded that greater devolution to schools within the university was needed. The project to empower the schools was needed for two reasons: the faculties were too much like impermeable silos, which had resulted in the university's course and unit offerings becoming fragmented and duplicatory, which in turn resulted in less accountability than was desirable; and there was a strong perception in the community that the university was not student- or employer-focused enough, and that it was unresponsive to changing needs, whether in education, training or research. He therefore undertook a further review of the university and identified a number of practical issues that needed to be addressed. Overall, he concluded that:

> The strong management achievements of the University are not fully appreciated by the Government partners, with the consequent perception taking root that the University may be a bad risk, or at best not a good investment. (This tends to be reinforced by the University's practice of emphasising in pride of place its claims for special funding entitlements, thus fostering a sacred cow image.)

McKinnon considered these achievements to include the following:

1. Around 120 redundancies, reducing costs and allowing new blood.
2. Enterprise Bargaining Agreement with real productivity gains, maintaining VET load at 20 hours per week.
3. ISO accreditation of the Facilities Management group (very hard to achieve in universities)
4. The solution in 3–4 years' time of its electrical cost problems.
5. The reduction of VET teaching hours costs by around 28%.
6. The introduction of an accelerated third semester, with entry and exits planned for each of the three semesters.

Lack of Private Revenue

Private revenue is important because it is supplementary, and is not therefore tied. McKinnon suggested a way forward, at least with regard to international students. In addition to Asian students, he argued that the university should concentrate on attracting Americans and North Europeans. He argued that there was a growing market for short products – the replacement products being generated by the new market conditions. The VET wing of the university was identified as the most useful for this because it could package up a joint TAFE/university arrangement for those with weaker entry qualifications, an option often wanted in Hong Kong, for example.

Professor McKinnon identified Business Studies as the main drawcard for TAFE international enrolments and argued that VET funding in the Northern Territory was 'far too high per unit cost', being '(on 1995 figures reflected in the 1997 annual report) 100% higher than some'. Fundamentally, McKinnon was of the opinion that DEETYA considered the university to be exposed, heavily reliant on VET funding, lacking in private revenue and prone to want to do everything itself – the 'not invented here' syndrome. He maintained that 'taking the distance education products of others' was a way to both save costs and counteract the 'not invented here' syndrome.

Finally, Professor McKinnon recommended again that the university change its name to Charles Darwin University and look at extending its boundaries so that while it operated in the Northern Territory, it also enrolled students in other states and territories. This included opening a campus in Sydney, effectively both creating a new university and representing a reinvigorated focus on building a university that would bring international academic skills to the Northern Territory and participate as a partner in its development across all aspects of social, cultural, and economic development. The formation of the new university was also aimed at remediating the existing fragmentation of education training and research over a number of institutions and realising desired economies of scale and sustainability.

Despite vociferous disagreement from a number of parties, including two politicians, one local and one federal, who argued that it was inappropriate because of its origin, the name Charles Darwin University was chosen. It was distinctive and aspirational. The new university was established as part of the community of scholars and researchers in November 2003 through a merger of Northern Territory University, Centralian College in Alice Springs, and the Northern Territory Rural College in Katherine, which also included its adult education offering in Alice Springs and Tenant Creek. Batchelor College was not seriously considered at the time of the merger, as it too was undergoing a review.

A partnership was also created with Menzies School of Health Research, which became a controlled entity and formed part of the newly established Institute of Advanced Studies along with the School of Social Policy and Research and the Research Institute of Environment and Livelihoods. An advantage to being a controlled entity for the Menzies School was that the university's competitive research funding attracted additional funding via Block Grant Funding from the Australian Government to support infrastructure costs and postgraduate scholarships, which it had not been eligible for prior to the change.

At its inception, Charles Darwin University had a large spread of activities, with around 15,000 students, four main campuses in the Northern Territory, and dozens of other delivery sites both across the Territory and interstate. It was established at a time when the Australian Government was progressing a reform agenda outlined in the *Our Universities: Backing Australia's Future* report, which focused on sustainability, quality, equity and diversity in the university sector and regional institutions. Mindful of the Commonwealth Government's intentions for the university sector, the vision for Charles Darwin University at the time of its establishment was of a thriving university that dared to be different and take advantage of its unique geography and demography to benefit the whole community through education, research and community service.

The creation of Charles Darwin University on 5 November 2002 did result in a number of significant changes to staff and operations. A partnership agreement between the Northern Territory Government and Charles Darwin University was created. Perhaps the comments from an interview with Peter Plummer (stored in the University Archives) worked best to sum up the situation at the time.

> Ken McKinnon turned this University around. No question about it. In the language of people who live in Papua New Guinea, Ken McKinnon was a 'one talk' – I'll go and talk to him.
>
> So from my perspective, whilst it was not pleasant – it was in fact a very difficult period – the outcome has been, for this University, a very good one, I believe.
>
> The feedback from my contacts is, from my perspective, very reassuring. I remember last time I was here – back in May. I walked out of the University one evening thinking, Wow! I'm really impressed with what I'm seeing and what I'm hearing.

A new council was appointed, along with a new vice-chancellor, Professor Helen Garnett, while Kevin Davis AM became registrar and pro vice-chancellor. The council members were:

- Mr Richard Ryan AO, Chancellor
- Justice Sally Thomas AC, Deputy Chancellor
- Mr Barry Ford
- Ms E.A. (Janie) Mason
- Mr John McBride
- Ms Jennifer Prince
- Mr David Ross
- Professor Judith Whitworth AC
- Mr Mark Dunn
- Dr Steve Shanahan
- Mr Trevor LeLievre
- Mr Ippei Okazaki

Strategic Positioning Project

The implementation of the recommendations of the Strategic Positioning Project, jointly funded by the Commonwealth and Northern Territory Governments, began in 2002. The Commonwealth Government significantly assisted with this project by providing $3 million over two years to facilitate change. While some project recommendations were superseded by events later in the year, significant reform was brought about through the following developments.

First the Higher Education and Training Taskforce was established, with a brief to significantly reduce the number of course and unit offerings to levels commensurate with the university's capacity to deliver quality. Duplication and areas of low demand were particularly targeted. A reduction in excess of 25% was achieved.

Second, the University Council established a Working Party on University Governance, which made several recommendations to enhance effective governance to the Northern Territory

Government. These recommendations were influential in developing the governance arrangements for the new Charles Darwin University. Third, the Development Unit was established in March 2002 to act as the key facilitator in increasing the university's external revenue.

Progress following formal change to Charles Darwin University

Professor Helen Garnett, the first Vice-Chancellor of Charles Darwin University, was appointed in late 2003. The 2003 financial year was the beginning of a major period of change that would run for several years. The most notable of these changes in 2003 was the formal establishment in November 2003 of the University. This amalgamation of several Territory tertiary educational institutions aimed to establish the economies of scale so critical to the sustainability of a modern university.

Equally important in the formation of the new university was a formal partnership agreement with the Northern Territory Government, which paved the way for the expansion and streamlining of collaboration towards the shared goal of improvement in the quality of life of the people living in the region. Interim Vice-Chancellor Ken McKinnon signed the Partnership Agreement with the Northern Territory Government on 1 July 2003, saying the agreement signalled a new level of interaction between the university and its community. This agreement included 25 schedules based around four themes:

- Increasing resident professional capacity to address Territory opportunities.
- Meeting government needs.
- Recognising the University to better meet Territory needs.
- Enabling Indigenous social and economic development.

Examples of projects that were developed as a result of the agreement included:

- the exploration of a joint DNA facility – i.e., a virtual collection of scientists and infrastructure to collaborate on bioprospecting in the Territory. The facility would see the university, government, Menzies School of Health Research and a number of Australian Government agencies share infrastructure and resources. It would also host biologists and biochemists with interests in conservation biology, natural resource management and tropical environmental science, bioprospecting, health and diagnostics.
- the establishment of a Centre for Remote Telecommunications Solutions to explore the delivery of interactive distance learning to remote areas. The training would be aimed at school students, university students and professionals in communities. A feasibility study on this project has been completed and negotiations for private industry funding are well advanced.
- the development of new courses and programs to prepare graduates to work as health professionals in remote communities in the Territory. The courses will be developed with the help of government health professionals already working in remote communities with the specific needs of the Territory in mind.
- The development of postgraduate courses specifically designed for community development officers working in government.

A review of the university undertakings to 31 December 2005 indicated the progress that had been made in the first two years of Professor Garnett's tenure. Over the course of 2005, the university had continued to expand activities with the local Indigenous population. By 2004, student numbers had increased to the highest total on record, and in terms of total number of students studying at the university there was an increase on previous years, with the highest number of students attending VET studies. These numbers increased to 18,749 in 2006, comprising 6397 students in higher education and 12,352 in VET. Considerable work was also conducted on the university's balance sheet.

Charles Darwin University balance sheet, 31 December 2005, which includes comparisons for 2003 and 2004 annual reports, shows how equity increased by $65 million (from a base $201 million), or approximately 30%. In 2008, at the time of Professor Garnett's retirement, equity was in the vicinity of $369 million, a stunning achievement.

CHARLES DARWIN UNIVERSITY AND ITS CONTROLLED ENTITIES			
BALANCE SHEET AS AT 31 DECEMBER 2005			
	2005	**2004**	**2003**
	$,000	**$,000**	**$,000**
Current Assets			
Cash and Cash Equivalents	7,222	3,466	2,280
Receivables	5,140	5,310	3,121
Inventories	483	572	554
Other Financial Assets	51,044	45,913	22,532
Other Non-Financial Assets	7,082	5,057	427
Total Current Assets	**70,971**	**60,318**	**28,914**
Non-Current Assets			
Inventories	2,658	2,474	2,450
Property, Plant and Equipment	219,958	216,440	188,929
Other Financial Assets	226	225	11
		297	596
Total Non-Current Assets	**222,842**	**219,436**	**191,986**
TOTAL ASSETS	**293,813**	**279,754**	**220,900**

Current Liabilities			
Payable	9,246	6,702	5,643
Interest Bearing Liabilities	521	396	373
Provisions	9,360	8,724	8,408
Other Liabilities	4,715	3,570	971
Total Current Liabilities	**23,842**	**19,392**	**15,395**
Non-Current Liabilities			
Payables	866		
Interest Bearing Liabilities	797	1,217	1,612
Provisions	2,100	2,378	2,325
Total Non-Current Liabilities	**3,763**	**3,595**	**3,937**
TOTAL LIABILITIES	**27,605**	**22,987**	**19,332**
NET ASSETS	**266,208**	**256,767**	**201,568**
Reserves	60,834	59,040	29,444
Restricted Funds	8,331	10,731	5,917
Retained Surplus	197,043	186,996	166,207
TOTAL EQUITY	**266,208**	**256,767**	**201,568**

The transition from Northern Territory University to Charles Darwin University was incredibly difficult. Factors that contributed to the problems were:

1. the appointment of three vice-chancellors during the period of transition, a situation further exacerbated by Professor McKay's terminal illness,
2. the Federal Government's, and in particular the relevant Minister's, insistence on change, irrespective of local issues, the genuine shortage of working capital within Northern Territory University, which resulted in a severe shortage of liquid funds (cash) for wages and immediate debts,
3. the election resulting in change in the Northern Territory Government, and the political issues that it raised around certain staff members and courses,

4. the significant lack of general community confidence in the university and subsequent poor staff morale.

(For the interview conducted with me after I retired as chancellor in 2009, from the CDU Archives, refer to Appendix G.)

My successor as Chancellor was Sally Thomas AC – a perfect choice, and Charles Darwin University is now one of the engines of Northern Territory development, underpinning the employment and personal aspirations of the Territory's people. It provides about 85% of all tertiary education in the Northern Territory, working across both the VET and higher education sectors.

However, I have no doubts that the university would not be in existence today if it were not for the skill and advice provided by senior bureaucrats in the Northern Territory Public Service, coupled with the strong support of the University Council and the initial leadership from Interim Vice-Chancellor Ken McKinnon.

Chapter 15

Northern Territory Economy

The Northern Territory has a total area of 1,349,129 square kms, which accounts for around 17.5% of Australia's total land mass, and a coastline that extends more than 13,500 kms. However, at the end of June 2022, with the population of the Northern Territory having reached only 252,770, it is one of the least populated states in the world. Its population density was 0.16 people per square kilometre in 2021, making it the least populated state of Australia and only a fraction that of the ACT. Darwin has an estimated population of over 120,000 people. Aboriginal and Torres Strait Islander people account for 26.8% of the Territory's population.

Population density of Australian states and territories, June 2022

Position	State	Population Density
1	Australian Capital Territory	151.49
2	Victoria	23.54
3	New South Wales	8.64
4	Tasmania	7.24
5	Queensland	2.50
6	South Australia	1.62
7	Western Australia	0.89
8	**Northern Territory**	**0.16**

Australian Bureau of Statistics, National, State and Territory Population Density

The Northern Territory's population average growth rate is the lowest of all Australian states and territories. According to the Australian Census, 51.7% of people in the Northern Territory were male and 48.3% female. The top five ancestries for people in the Northern Territory are Kriol, Diambarrpuyngu, Greek, Waripin and Murrinh Patha. The top six countries of birth for people in the Northern Territory are Australia, England, New Zealand, Philippines, India and the United States of America.

The population of Darwin in 2024 was thought to be circa 148,000, with the entire Northern Territory population being circa 254,000.

The young median age in the Northern Territory coupled with its high transient and Indigenous populations, plays a significant role in the Territory's ability to repay its debts.

All economies are subject to business cycles. The frequency, magnitude and duration of cycles are influenced by the underlying structure of the economy and exposure of key industries to external factors that influence demand, prices and exchange rates. Over the past 25 years the Territory has experienced business cycles that average four years, with a range from two to seven years. These cycles have been driven by major projects, where domestic conditions are affected by resource exploration, construction, and production cycles. Employment and population growth broadly follow GSP growth, although not to the same magnitude given the capital-intensive nature of investment in the Territory and the higher productivity per worker that results.

The major sources of funding for the Northern Territory Government are grants it receives from the Commonwealth Grants Commission. These funds originate from the Goods and Services Tax (GST) and it is argued that the quantum granted is inadequate. A significant task for governments is to undertake public works and provide services that may be uneconomic, too impractical, too risky, or too inequitable for the private sector. The creation or delivery of these products and services serve the common good but may not generate a direct revenue stream. Borrowing is the enabler of such creations and the funds are not provided and the Northern Territory Government, like every other government, has used debt to fund investment in assets and development.

Following changes to the Loan Council arrangements, and in line with other jurisdictions, on 1 July 1994 the Northern Territory established the Northern Territory Treasury Corporation (NTTC) under the *Northern Territory Treasury Corporation Act 1994* to serve as the Central Borrowing Authority (CBA) for government and undertake the management of the Territory's public finances.

The NTTC's mission and objectives were designed to advance the Territory's financial interests and development and to improve its market identification in both domestic and international capital markets. Department of Treasury's Annual Report states that its objective is to provide the Territory Government with cost-effective funding, effective financial management and reliable service and advice, its board and management are committed to achieving this objective while upholding high standards of corporate governance, transparency and accountability through controls, policies and frameworks.

Under Section 5 of the Corporation Act, the Under Treasurer of the Department of Treasury and Finance (DTF) is designated as the NTTC's sole person and is subject to the direction of the Treasurer of the Northern Territory. To assist in achieving these objectives, an Advisory Board and an Audit Committee have been established to assist the Under Treasurer with issues relating to the NTTC's operations.

Initial members of the Northern Territory Treasury Advisory Board of 1994 were Tony Cole – former secretary to the Federal Treasurer (Paul Keating) – and me. Michael Martin was to be General Manager, with Ken Clarke the Under-Treasurer and Barry Coulter Treasurer. The NTTC has had only three general managers in its first 27 years of operation; the other two have been John Montague and Alex Pollen. It is one of the premier CBAs in the country. Notwithstanding that, it has had five under-treasurers and at least nine ministers!

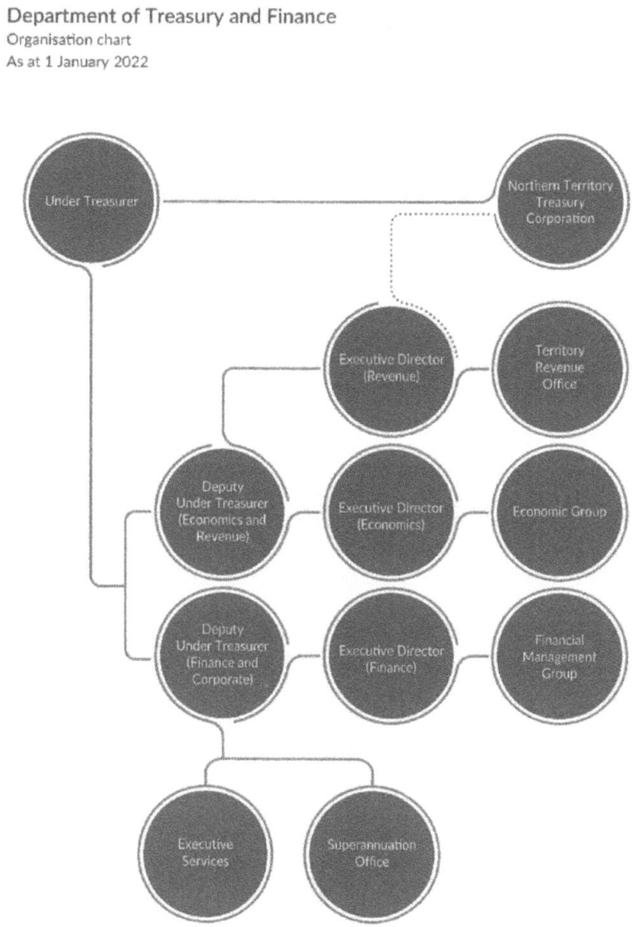

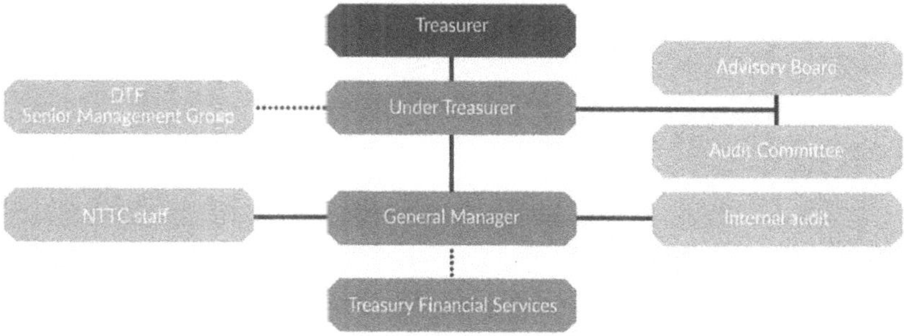

The Northern Territory Treasury Corporation reporting structure
Source: Northern Territory Treasury Corporation Report 2019–2020

How does the borrowing work?

The NTTC borrows funds and lends them to the Territory Government, government business divisions, government-owned corporations, local authorities, and other government organisations. Loans are issued in accordance with commercially based guidelines and practices.

All loans must be approved by the Treasurer of the Northern Territory in accordance with Section 13(2)(b) of the *Northern Territory Treasury Corporation Act 1994* and Section 31(1) of the *Financial Management Act 1995*. Loans are made via an entity called the Central Holding Authority (CHA).

Central Holding Authority or the CHA is the 'parent body' within the DTF that represents the government's interest in government-controlled entities.

On behalf of the Territory Government, the CHA looks after:

- assets and liabilities controlled by the government and managed by agencies on behalf of the government;
- revenue collected by CHA and regarded as Territory revenue in the form of taxation, untied grants (e.g., GST revenue) and fines;
- expenses where the main expense is the payment of

> appropriation to agencies, along with Territory borrowings, interest on cash balances of government business divisions and government-owned corporations, and the centrally managed employee costs of superannuation and long service leave.

General government agencies are funded through the CHA via appropriations, some of which are funded by loans provided by the NTTC. The CHA is the 'parent body' that represents the Territory Government's ownership interest in government-controlled entities. The funds are used to finance general government activities and the Territory's major infrastructure projects. As of 30 June 2023, loans to the general government sector totalled $7.8 billion, a decrease of about $281 million from the previous financial year.

Government business divisions

Loans to government business divisions represent borrowings by Territory government-owned entities that operate on a commercial basis. The funds are used to finance capital and operating expenditure requirements. At 30 June 2023, loans to this sector totalled approximately $148 million.

Government-owned corporations

Loans to government-owned corporations represent borrowings by Territory government-owned entities that operate on a commercial basis but are not guaranteed by the Crown, meaning that the Territory is not liable for their debts, liabilities, or obligations. The funds are used to finance capital and operating expenditure requirements. As of 30 June 2023, loans to this sector totalled about $1.4 billion.

Local government councils and other government organisations

Loans to local government councils and other government organisations represent borrowings. As of 30 June 2023, there were no loans outstanding to any such organisation.

Investment portfolio

The Territory Government's investment portfolio is formed by pooling the surplus cash balances of its bank accounts and investing them in a variety of secure short-, medium-, and long-term debt securities issued in the Australian financial markets. The broad objectives of NTTC in managing the Territory's investment portfolio are to ensure sufficient liquidity is maintained in the government's cash balances to meet all financial obligations as they fall due, and to obtain a return on the government's cash balances in line with the benchmark, while adhering to the investment guidelines approved by the Treasurer.

The investment portfolio comprises a range of secure investments, of which a significant proportion are short-term instruments including term deposits, bank accepted bills, promissory notes, and negotiable certificates of deposit. A core amount of the investment portfolio is available for investment for longer-term instruments such as floating rate notes and fixed term securities. As of 30 June 2023, the investment portfolio totalled $45 million.

Conditions of Service Reserve

The Conditions of Service Reserve (COSR) is a segregated pool of investments held within CHA at the discretion of the Treasurer and is intended for purposes such as meeting the Territory Government's unfunded superannuation liabilities.

NTTC is responsible for monitoring and reporting on the fund's performance and managing the relationship with the fund managers. The fund's investment performance is benchmarked against the performance results of the 'growth' product category as published in the monthly Morningstar Market Index Performance. This is consistent with the asset allocation mix applied to COSR. As of 30 June 2023, the market valuation of COSR was thought to be about $450 million.

Historically, the CBA's access to capital markets and the use of public–private partnerships provided states with the flexibility to raise funds for projects on which they placed a high priority. However, the system of federation still links the states to the Commonwealth in terms of credit assessment and rating. In other words, the Commonwealth is still seen implicitly as an underwriter of the obligations of the states and territories, even while the larger jurisdictions promote their ratings as a reflection of their fiscal skills and management capability.

As states and territories gained access to financial markets through their CBAs, the rigorous process for allocating funding to the most worthy national infrastructure projects became a competition between jurisdictions and local interests. Impartiality and technical scrutiny were afflicted by a parochial lens, with similar road, rail, port, and utility projects being undertaken simultaneously in two or more states. This had the effect of bidding-up the cost of scarce skills and resources and creating inefficiencies, which was reminiscent of the issues that had led to the establishment of the original Loan Council. Interestingly, throughout this period discussion between state representatives regularly turned to the common agreed benefit of borrowing through the most highly rated entity (i.e. the Commonwealth) and creating very large liquid bond series which each state could access. Such coordination was considered possible but politically unacceptable. It would require the consent of all parties, which they were highly unlikely to give as doing so would mean ceding effective control to the Commonwealth. The prospect of gaining access to the lowest borrowing cost was not a sufficient incentive to overcome these political barriers.

The Northern Territory uses its own CBA to gain independence from the Commonwealth and the Federal Department of Treasury. Having the ability to manage its own budget meant it could proceed with projects that might have failed to gain federal support; however, the cost of these projects still had to be met. Responsible budget practices are followed, but any deficits are generally funded through borrowings.

The Australian Loan Council began in the 1920s when the states and the Commonwealth raised funds separately through capital markets. This process created competitive pressure for major infrastructure and an uncoordinated rivalry. Consequently, in order to improve efficiency and timing of fundraising, the premiers agreed to a voluntary Loan Council arrangement in 1923. These arrangements were formalised in 1927 and included in the Commonwealth *Financial Agreement Act 1928*.

Under the Act:

- the Loan Council would regulate borrowing by the Commonwealth and states;
- the Commonwealth would borrow on behalf of the states;
- the states' ability to borrow would be limited;
- the Commonwealth and states would contribute to a National Debt Sinking Fund to redeem debt;
- the Commonwealth would provide grants to states to assist in meeting interest payments and sinking fund contributions.

By the 1950s the Loan Council's arrangements extended to the effective underwriting of state borrowings, which reduced the cost of borrowing but was offset by increased Commonwealth influence in state fiscal matters. This influence created tension as the Commonwealth fiscal agenda impacted on state-based budgeting. Soon the states were seeking alternative financing products and financial independence that avoided the Loan Council limits, and this eventually undermined the Council's power and purpose.

During the period of rapid expansion in the Australian financial markets in the mid-1980s, each Australian state and territory established a CBA. There was a strong demand for government-backed securities and increased trading activity in state government (semi-government) bonds. This contributed to a significant change in inter-governmental financial relations, as the states were able to move away from the previous Loan Council arrangements and enjoy an independent, positive financial environment for borrowing and investing. The Northern Territory Government generally receives the bulk of its funding from the GST, Northern Territory taxes and similar borrowing in markets.

However, when the Northern Territory gained self-government under the *Northern Territory (Self-Government) Act 1978*, significant rights such as Indigenous Land Rights and uranium mining were excluded from this. There was also provision for the Governor-General to disallow laws passed by the Northern Territory Assembly and for the acquisition of Territory land by the Commonwealth without compensation. These exclusions do not apply to the states.

Northern Territory economy and borrowing implications

The structure of the Northern Territory's economy is markedly different from those of the other Australian states, reflecting the small population base, the composition of its natural resource base, its comparatively large public sector, and the small size of its tax-paying sector. These points of difference partly explain its inability to generate self-sustaining growth.

Following self-government there were the inevitable demands to develop the Northern Territory economy so that it could become more self-supporting in terms of Gross Domestic Product (GDP), jobs and revenue.

The following Table, derived from Transport and Works Budget Paper 5 and Treasury Records 1993, illustrates how more than 50% of the Northern Territory's total assets were constructed in the 1980s after self-government, during a period of high inflation and high interest rates.

ESTIMATED REPLACEMENT VALUE OF ASSETS CREATED BEFORE AND AFTER SELF GOVERNMENT			
	Transferred in 1978 $m	Constructed Post 1978 $m	Total $m
Transport and communications	1746	1011	2757
Housing and community amenities	338	1233	1571
Fuel and energy	185	712	897
Education	138	443	581
Health	310	111	421
Public order and safety	53	197	250
Other	499	415	914
TOTAL	**3267**	**4123**	**7390**

Whereas Transport and Communications (mostly roads) comprised 50% of the Northern Territory's assets prior to self-government, it comprised only 25% of the assets created after self-government; and the major emphasis on asset creation after self-government was on Fuel and Energy (mostly electricity), Housing and Community Amenities (mostly housing and water and sewerage assets) and Education.

Plainly, these issues developed from the obvious difficulties caused by trying to develop an economy over a very large area with a very small population, limited infrastructure and other supports. They have been compounded over the last 20 years or so, and exacerbated by the COVID pandemic, which required massive government expenditure by almost every Australian state and territory. In some respects, this levelled the playing field between jurisdictions, as each had to undertake large borrowing programs. However, the fact that each jurisdiction was grappling with the problem of debt partially masked the Territory's financial difficulties. In addition, this ongoing expenditure coincided with a period of exceptionally low interest rates and substantial quantitative easing. Interest rates have now changed, and the Reserve Bank of Australia has indicated they could continue to do so.

Normally, one would expect investor demand for government debt to be low. However, while interest rates are in the low single figures the weight of money seeking investment opportunity remains high. This is mainly attributed to the scarcity of prudent investments that meet historical measures of good value. In this environment, government bonds are not bought purely on the basis of their yield, but for the protection and diversification that they bring to a portfolio, given their low risk of default.

Investors have always sought out innovations to improve their returns. However, the relatively easy conditions for borrowing are the amalgamation of a number of exceptional factors and do not represent a new ongoing paradigm. Refinancing ever-increasing amounts of debt will mean adapting to these conditions and chasing investors, and offering attractive solutions which inevitably increase the risk that funding inefficiencies could materially increase borrowing costs and exacerbate tensions. This is most evident and adverse for the weaker and smaller jurisdictions. It is therefore a significant factor for the future in terms of the Northern Territory's markets and borrowings.

Commonwealth Grants Commission

Funding for the Northern Territory comes from borrowings, Commonwealth Grants Commission (CGC) allocation and internal taxes, the most important of these being the CGC.

The CGC operates as an independent statutory authority responsible for measuring the relative fiscal capacities of the states and territories. Under the *Commonwealth Grants Commission Act 1973* it makes decisions on how to measure those fiscal capacities. The measuring of capabilities and disabilities attempts to recognise the differences between jurisdictions, and such measures have far-reaching financial implications, as they can encourage or discourage activities that would otherwise be taken or avoided.

The costs of providing government services such as health, education, housing and law and order are not uniform across states or even regions. They are essentially a function of underlying conditions in communities. Factors such as geography, climate, distance, population density, work opportunities and proportion of the population speaking English as a second language cannot be easily compared using a financial disability such as a multiple of an average, and these matters are cumulative and not mutually exclusive.

They also do not always lend themselves to financial solutions in the short to medium term, so expenditure directed towards them may not change them in a measured timeframe. There is a school of thought that allocations made by the CGC should take disadvantaged groups into greater account.

I believe that the CGC's importance to the Northern Territory has not received the attention it warrants from the Grants Commission. Its work is important for two reasons. First, the Territory is dependent on its GST share to a far greater extent than any other jurisdiction in Australia. Second, this dependence means the Territory too is vulnerable to the political pressures applied by the states to its processes and conclusions.

This was demonstrated with Western Australia's success in changing the system through the imposition of a floor to its relativity, irrespective of what the numbers showed. Western Australia, with a population of circa 10% of the national population, complained loudly that it generates more GST revenue than the meagre share it receives since it has had its allocation increased significantly.

Conversely, WA's Treasury reaps more than 50% in mining royalties, linked to the state's massive iron ore mines. South Australia, which has long been trying to foster its mining industry and grow its resources sector, still collects a much smaller percentage of the royalties than WA. Previous South Australian Treasurer Stephen Mulligan, speaking at a State Budget function in 2022, argued strongly that equitable GST distribution was 'the number one concern that state and territory treasuries have'.

There have been a number of articles, particularly in the Murdoch papers, all of which question the proceeds that WA receives and the need for greater transparency and how certain states and territories need greater assistance.

The use of Indigenous population statistics as a proxy measure for funding does not adequately recognise the wide range of circumstances and challenges experienced by Indigenous people in the Northern Territory. Since 1999 the Indigenous population of the Northern Territory has increased by 70%. Overall the proportion of the national population that now identifies as being of Indigenous heritage has also significantly increased. This has resulted in some institutions such as the University of Sydney demanding proof of Indigeneity on enrolment. It has also seen a significant reallocation of Indigenous funding to states in which a majority of Indigenous people reside in the major cities and who do not live in a traditional lifestyle. This in turn has reduced the share of funding available to the Northern Territory.

While a true needs-based model would seem more appropriate and yes more funding would assist, the solution to this issue needs to be based on a clear understanding of what is trying to be achieved; whether this is what the community wants and requires, and whether it is appropriate for the circumstances.

The use of GST relativities to the population of each jurisdiction in order to manage the allocation of the GST funding pool is also complex and volatile. There is volatility from year to year and the potential for major changes to be compounded in the years when population growth is below the national average.

The 2021 census data highlighted the changing pattern of Indigenous identification across Australia and the significant swing in 'unexplainable changes' also adds to the difficulty in the Budget construction, and in making and delivering long-term plans.

Plainly there is a need to recognise that Indigenous people who live in rural and remote areas are disadvantaged in terms of their ability to obtain such services as health and education. Menzies

School of Health Research continues to cater as widely as it can for Indigenous people in remote areas, but increased federal funding is required in order to service all the Indigenous needs.

The Census of 2021 recorded that there were circa 167 Aboriginal and Torres Strait Islander languages used at home by 76,978 Aboriginal and Torres Strait Islander peoples. The most widely reported language groups used were Arnhem Land and Daly River Region languages (14.5%) and Torres Strait Island languages (12.0%)

	2016	2021
New South Wales	216,176	278,043
Victoria	47,788	65,646
Queensland	186,482	237,303
South Australia	34,184	42,562
Western Australia	75,978	88,693
Tasmania	23,572	30,186
Northern Territory	58,248	61,115
Australian Capital Territory	6508	8949
Australia (b)	649,171	812,721

Australian Bureau of Statistics: Aboriginal and Torres Strait Islander People Census 2016 and 2021

As we have seen there have been significant increases in the number of people identifying as having Aboriginal and/or Torres Strait Island origin between the censuses. Increases in the population are influenced both by demographic factors such as births, deaths and migration, and by non-demographic factors including changes in whether a person identifies as Aboriginal and/or Torres Strait Islander in each census, the identification of children or others who have previously had forms completed by their parents or others on their behalf, and the impact of communications and collection procedures.

Research suggested that the Territory population should have reached 252,770 by the end 2022. This calculation was based on an average growth rate since 2011. In 2016 the Indigenous population was circa 75,000, or approximately 30% of the total population of 244,000. In the last eight years, the Territory's population growth rate has been low and in the last few years it recorded negative growth. Its average growth rate is the lowest in Australia.

It is interesting to note the NT population in 2024 as per the census was estimated to be 254,263.

Meantime the GSP growth rate is highly volatile. A large proportion of the Territory's population consists of Indigenous Australians and the population growth rate among Indigenous Australians is relatively high. However, despite an increase in money being allocated for Indigenous health and welfare by successive Federal and Territory governments, the standard of living remains low.

Changes in Indigenous status are collected through self-identification, and any change in how a person chooses to identify! Demographers say that it seems that only 45% of the change is due to natural increase and/or deaths.

The result seems to be that about one-tenth of the Indigenous population or circa 100,000 people were not included in the census prior to 2021. It is interesting that about 85–89% of the increase occurs in New South Wales, Tasmania, Queensland and Victoria!

Significantly the result of this is that the Northern Territory Indigenous population share has dropped by 1.5% to 7.5%. The Northern Territory Government consequently has to have continuous negotiations with the Commonwealth Grants Commission to ensure that changes in self-identification do not disadvantage the Northern Territory.

The remaining component of Aboriginal population growth

is identification change, in which people report their Aboriginal or non-Aboriginal status differently over time as recorded in the quinquennial Census of Population and Housing. In terms of official statistics, this refers to people identifying as Aboriginal in the latest Australian Census but as non-Aboriginal in the previous census five years earlier, or vice versa. In addition to the Bureau of Statistics census data from the Australian Census Longitudinal Dataset (ACLD), a 5% sample of linked census records suggests that the Aboriginal population of Australia experienced a net gain of about 80,000 from identification change during 2011 to 2016. Net identification gains have been high in New South Wales, Melbourne, Hobart and the Australian Capital Territory, but low or non-existent in much of remote Australia.

Delivering health, education and the like to a small, scattered population is difficult and has significant additional costs unfortunately, the current system does not take into account remote and isolated communities as it should.

Another category of funding for all states and territories comes from the Commonwealth Specific Purpose Payments. These are designed to help in addressing some of the entrenched disadvantages faced by Indigenous people but remain inadequate for the Northern Territory.

It must be remembered that the Northern Territory is heavily reliant on GST funding, as are all states, particularly the smaller/weaker states. The Northern Territory's GST share is theoretically determined by an independent process under which the needs of all jurisdictions are assessed on the same basis and the Northern Territory's GST share is reflective of its particular geographic and demographic circumstances – isolation, indigeneity with a small and dispersed population. Significantly the Northern Territory's share is not designed to address long-term issues of entrenched disadvantage, nor can it reduce the additional costs facing the Territory by virtue of distance and entrenched disadvantage.

Overall, despite the Territory receiving a multiple per capita compared to the rest of Australia in GST funding, this only represents its expenditure disabilities, i.e. the cost of providing services in a vast, sparsely populated area where social disadvantage is common. The funding is based on the current parameters for major high-cost new projects on initiatives that will divert money away from critical services, which are lagging behind the commonly accepted standard.

This exacerbates the poor social outcome and fuels claims of the gross underfunding of necessary services in the Northern Territory.

Debt

For the Northern Territory, debt has predominantly arisen because of pre-government neglect and the need for the Territory to change its structure so that it can ultimately become self-funding.

For Territory governments and commentators alike, concerns about appropriate levels of debt have rarely been matched by a reluctance on the part of investors to invest. As previously noted, normally one would expect investor demand for government debt to be low. However, while interest rates remain in the low single figures, the weight of money seeking investment opportunity remains high. This is mainly attributed to a lack of prudent investments that meet historical measures of good value; in this environment, government bonds are not being bought purely on the basis of their yield but for the protection and diversification that they bring to a portfolio given their low risk of default.

Historically, the market in semi-government debt grew rapidly, supported by rating agency assessments that identified innate economic strength in some state budgets, and by a Commonwealth guarantee that, while not explicit, was strongly implied through the Constitution. The precedent of the 1932 NSW Constitutional Crisis has often been referred to in such considerations; however, it is unlikely to be a relevant source of comfort for investors today, as it is more likely to be the reason that the Commonwealth would intervene to support confidence in the entire financial system and prevent systemic failure.

Recently the enormous level of global demand for good quality investments has also had a ripple effect that supports lesser quality investments as fund managers worked to allocate their portfolios, and this was partly offset by the demand for government-backed issues.

From a credit rating perspective reference, the Territory is seen as a commodity-based economy that regularly experiences booms and busts. However, this is also commonly seen as a mitigating factor for investment, as is the Territory's relationship with the Commonwealth.

Debt as a proportion of revenue reached a low of approximately 15% in 2016. This ratio has pushed out to approximately 100% in 2021 following the impact of changes to GST and the COVID response. This has not occurred before and is more than twice the long-term average ratio. The speed with which this ratio has increased is particularly concerning, as there has not been evident improvement in the economy. Current budget estimates could indicate a peak of approximately 160% in 2025.

The Territory has been in fiscal deficit since 2000. This includes the period of extended boom. As one would expect, the cumulative impact of this corresponds with the historical path of gross and net debt. However, the current revenues show the Territory's has an inability to address this deficit. And while such deterioration in debt in such a short period of time may be put down to the boom-and-bust nature of the Territory, failure to address this problem puts both the Commonwealth and the Northern Territory Government at risk of needing intervention and remedial action by the Commonwealth.

The following graph shows the current levels of Northern Territory gross and net debt. They are significantly higher than previously experienced and have been on a steepening trajectory since 2000. At some point the size of the debt must reach a level at which concerns about sustainability must arise.

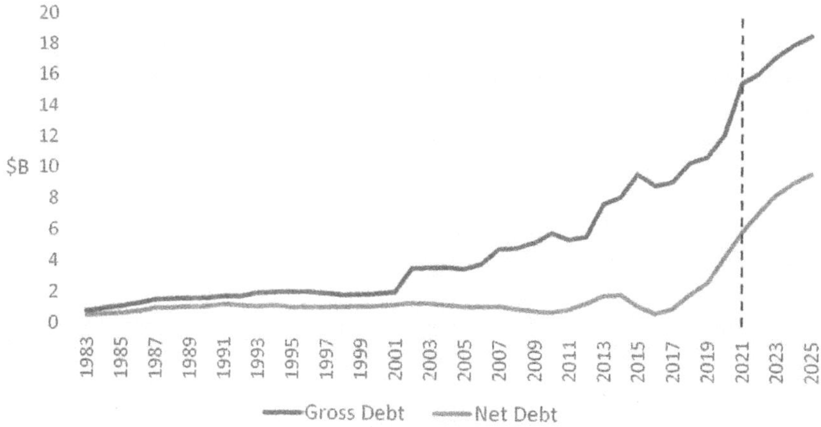

Source: Northern Territory Budget Papers BPS UPF General Government Sector 2000–2021

The implication of these figures is that debt has reached a level where budget restraint will only be able to contribute to managing the Territory's financial position, but not to fixing it. Some additional degree of direct external support will be required. While the statistics can change quite quickly when the economy improves, the Northern Territory Government needs to ensure that such opportunities are not squandered and improving financial ratios should be a high priority.

Specific challenges in debt reduction

Thomas Mann said that 'Everything is politics', and for public servants, who are trying to influence those with power for the greater good, it is a constant challenge. While power is conferred via the ballot box, competing ideas and philosophies dictate the timing and delivery of the policies. Consequently, budgetary discipline is a soft concept and is often most needed when it is politically expedient.

The long-term planning necessary to deliver change has not been a strong characteristic of Australian politics. Where it has occurred, such as with the superannuation reforms of the 1990s, its success is not universally admired, and the analysis of that success has often been clouded by other issues such as the immediate needs of the community, primarily in terms of housing affordability. The conflation of two separate policy issues (superannuation and housing) demonstrates the difficulty in getting and maintaining commitment to long-term economic strategies.

This table shows the level of the Northern Territory Government net debt as a percentage of GDP/GSP when compared to the ACT and Tasmania.

	2022–23	**2023–24**	**2024–25**	**2025–26**
Tasmania	7.10	8.90	10.20	10.50
ACT	13.10	14.90	16.50	NA
NT	24.80	26.50	25.50	24.00
Commonwealth	31.10	32.60	33.10	33.10
Total	**11.80**	**13.60**	**14.60**	**NA**

Source: Australian, 25 July 2022

The level of indebtedness has been a constant problem for the Territory and was part of the reason for its push for self- government. Ambitious ideas and the desire to realise perceived potential justified taking on debt, but regrettably few of the major projects it was to finance appear to have delivered the desired results. At the same time, the Territory's sources of income have failed to match the increased cost of delivering government services and the demands of the community. While it may be argued that such infrastructure is needed to attract the businesses and people needed to create these opportunities, there is little evidence of this occurring within the useful life of the projects.

It could also be argued that the development of the Yulara/Uluru resort justified the debt required to build it, as it has resulted in increased tourist numbers, increased employment, and increased taxable income for the Northern Territory. However, the debt write-off at the time of transfer to private equity was thought to be circa $200 million, and it is unclear when or ever it will be recouped through other Northern Territory Government revenue.

Competition, volatile markets, climate change and environmental concerns related to mining, have all put the Territory economy in a vulnerable position. Despite several attempts to create one, the Territory has no manufacturing centre, and its markets – even those within Australia – are thousands of kilometres away. Its prospects with economic policies need to be considered in this light.

The Territory's areas of comparative advantage lie in its strategic location as part of a country with a strong legal system and developed economy. However, these advantages have not been developed, largely because they would require the relocation of resources away from the more populous states. This is resisted by those states because they would lose out from such moves and it is politically unacceptable in a parliamentary system where population density determines the number of representatives in Canberra.

While the Territory climate is often cited as an impediment to any increase in population, many hotter, more humid, and more dangerous environments have much higher population densities. The government's commitment to increasing the Territory's population is essential but in spite of that, the vast majority of permanent overseas migrants to Australia (140,366 in 2019/20, plus 2,029,721 temporary visa holders) move to, or live in cities in the major states.

Then there is the debate relating to funding in terms of population density. (very low in NT at 1.6 people per square kilometre), and while trying to deliver services to remote areas is costly, it is also essential for the future of Australia.

This is a reality, not an *inefficiency*, in a democratic country and must be appreciated by every Australian.

Darwin also has a very active Australian Naval and Army base, and the RAAF has aircraft stationed at Tindal (Katherine). The Northern Territory is also the home of the North West Mobile Force or 'Norforce'. This force is unique – the Australian Defence Force's most critical surveillance, reconnaissance and military intelligence gathering squad. Norforce performs on an almost endless 365-days-per-year contract and patrols the north from Western Australia to Queensland in a 1.8-million-square-kilometre area of operations. Between the four Regional Force Surveillance Group squadrons – Darwin, Kimberley, Arnhem, and Centre – its area of operations effectively covers 52% of Australia's land and seas, the largest area of operations for any military unit in the world. Its strength is in its Indigenous soldiers' bush and survival craft, which enables it to operate in the most inhospitable parts of Australia's northern approaches, as well as their connection to remote communities.

In addition, not only are there approximately 2500 US troops stationed in Darwin on a rotational basis, there is no major schooling of Service trainees or Armed Forces in the Territory! The Australian Defence Force Academy and the Royal Military

College are based in the ACT. Apprentice training takes place predominantly in South Australia, and the service education field is dominated by the University of New South Wales.

Nothing of substance in education and training exists in the Northern Territory for the armed services.

The Northern Territory Government has demonstrated a complete inability to apply political pressure to change this. In addition to this, the bulk of the repair work arising from the Services, such as maintenance of aircraft engines, goes predominantly to the southern states with little consideration for the economies and communities of Darwin and Katherine. The Northern Territory has been ignored despite repeated requests for a fair portion of the cake.

The further development and the support of the armed services must therefore include a portion of the federal spend being directed to the Northern Territory instead of distribution being based predominately on the most populous states and used to promote training facilities.

This matter now appears to be under consideration based on Federal Government announcements in mid-2023 regarding the Australia Defence troop relocations. The Northern Territory Government engaged an economic advisory firm to investigate the effect of the proposed changes and the NT Government Media Release of the 'analysis' was distributed on 9 October 2023:

> ***Defence Industry to create 7600 New Territory Jobs***
> New independent economic analysis has revealed that the Northern Territory's thriving defence industry is poised to significantly contribute to the region's economy, generating over 7600 local job opportunities in the next four years.
>
> In particular, the government has partnered with Master Builders NT to release the 'Economic Impact of Defence Infrastructure Projects in the Northern Territory' report.

To assess the impact of defence infrastructure investments in the NT, Master Builders NT commissioned the services of ACIL Allen, an economic advisory firm.

The analysis also found that the defence sector is expected to invest up to $6.2 billion in the NT between 2023 and 2027, adding an average of $800 million annually to the existing construction activity levels in the Top End.

Specifically, this investment is projected to create an additional 7600 jobs, with 4300 directly in construction and another 3300 across various sectors.

It could also potentially contribute nearly five per cent to the Gross State Product in 2025/26, contingent on the Territory's ability to sustain high levels of local involvement.

The NT construction sector has a track record of scaling up as required, and this additional investment aligns with the industry's long-term average activity levels. In addition to the ongoing work at the Larrakeyah Defence Precinct, RAAF Base Darwin, and Crowley US Fuel storage, new defence projects are set to commence shortly.

The report confirms that the NT has the capacity to fulfil the expected Defence work and adjacent sector projects. Over the past years, the NT has witnessed an $8 billion decade-long defence infrastructure program, placing significant demands on the local building and construction sector.

Industry Capability Network NT has reported that 69 per cent of defence contracts over the last seven years has been awarded to local companies. Consequently, nearly $800 million, out of a total expenditure of $1.15 billion, has circulated through the NT economy.

The then Chief Minister and Minister for Defence, Natasha Fyles, emphasised the significant progress made in

> demonstrating the Northern Territory's industrial capabilities to undertake crucial defence projects.
>
> 'Over this last seven years we have seen $8 billion defence infrastructure economy enter our construction market,' Fyles said.
>
> The minister added, 'Local participation across these defence infrastructure programs has increased significantly and this is a testament to the work done by Master Builders NT in ensuring Commonwealth procurement processes are adjusted to the northern market.'

It remains to be seen, of course, if this will ever really happen. A discussion paper that I wrote could be considered for further development of the Armed Services in the NT, and indeed Australia. However, there are no votes nor finances to be gained. (See Appendix L.)

There is no level playing field for the Northern Territory at any time

The Territory must survive and develop by doing things that cannot be done elsewhere, and by doing them better. This could include more focused tourism, mining, and new industries in which it is on a level playing field or to create international joint ventures and to develop a brand that is keenly sought after. However, these sorts of activities are all, by definition, riskier and the Northern Territory does not yet have a track record of managing commercial risk.

Fundraising methods that have been employed (including the state-based Central Borrowing Authorities (CBAs)) were set up against a backdrop of major financial upheaval, that encompassed Paul Keating's 'Banana Republic' comment in May 1986 and the Black Friday stock market crash in October 1987. The demand for easily traded and strongly rated securities as both investments in their own right, and as speculative tools in fixed interest rate trading, was embraced. The Buy and Hold strategy for state bonds declined as major banks and financial institutions actively traded these markets. Over time the trading range contracted, the liquidity and turnover of these securities increased, and domestic bond issuance became a quick and effective way to raise funds. Offshore borrowing followed a similar path, creating a more diversified investor base and access to lower cost sources of funds.

Bonds issued to the public and guaranteed by the states ('retail bonds') were a popular investment until the late 1980s, not the least because of their perceived safety during a period of market volatility and high interest rates. However, as state borrowing requirements increased in size this source became less efficient and the increased regulatory burden of dealing with non-professional investors made this source of funding less attractive.

The Territory Bond series, which spread across maturities over 20 years, has been the main source of funds for the Territory since 2000. These bonds are part of the semi-government sector and are benchmarked against the bond yield curve derived from the major state bond series. The margin to this benchmark and to the Commonwealth represents the standard measure for pricing new bond series with good liquidity. However, liquidity is not guaranteed and is usually unavailable during times of market disruption. Consequently, derivatives (futures, swaps, and options) are commonly used to adjust bond exposure, particularly where large portfolio positions are held.

The Northern Territory Government has persisted with a retail bond offering every year since 1979. However, the cost of communication, registry expenses and administration of unpresented cheques has been an ongoing issue, particularly as the

Territory does not have relevant unclaimed monies legislation to deal with mature payables. The Advisory Board of the NTTC has made repeated requests to change the legislation, but this has been resisted by governments of both persuasions.

The government's main argument for retaining Territory Bonds has been the diversification that this retail branch brings to its sources of funding. However, as commercial bond issuance and the overall level of debt have reduced total Territory Bonds to less than 1% of outstanding borrowings, this benefit has become marginal. Lack of liquidity and misalignment with loans to counterparties also makes this product less attractive.

In the early 1990s the NTTC and other Central Banking Authorities used Yen Loans to secure larger tranches of long- term funding from Japanese investors, as at this time Japanese interest rates were lower than Australian rates. Such loans were useful for raising large funds, but were constrained by their heavy documentation, lengthy negotiation periods, large fees, and one- off nature.

The embedded covenants and lack of standardisation soon made this funding source impractical for all but the largest CBAs, as did the costs of FX hedging.

The Euro Medium Term Note (EMTN) program used by the NTTC was another platform for raising funds using standardised documentation and terms and conditions. It allowed issuance across various products both in terms and of time periods.

It was often used for overseas fundraising in Europe and Asia and proved to be a valuable tool, but it required hedging of currency exposure, and eventually the fundraising capability of the Australian domestic fixed interest rates market strengthened to a point where the Territory's annual borrowing requirement could be easily and cost effectively accommodated, making the EMTN program redundant.

State government (semi-government) debt had its origin in the government utility debt market, from issuers such as Vicfin, State Electoral Commission of Victoria (SECVIC) and Telecom. The inefficiencies of Yen Loans and the increasing size of state borrowing requirements encouraged state issuers to develop their own bond series and to promote trading activity. By the early 1990s most states no longer had a Commonwealth guarantee supporting their bond issues, and in September 1990 Paul Keating informed the Northern Territory Government that the Commonwealth's guarantee on its debt would be withdrawn on any new issuance after July 1991.

The ratio of state net public sector debt to GSP can be used as an indicator of the ability of state and territory governments to ensure future payments on their debts. The Northern Territory had the highest net public sector debt to GSP ratio at 15.4%, followed by Victoria (8.5%) and South Australia (8.3%), while the Australian Capital Territory had the lowest (-3.9%), followed by Tasmania.

Ratings

Rating agencies provide assessments of the credit risk associated with an issuer. This is a convenient alternative to the investment committees of potential investors undertaking their own analysis in-house and it has become an accepted process for recognising and setting measurable limits for risk exposure.

In the 1990s the Northern Territory Treasury was approached by Moody's Investor Service and Standard & Poor's, two of the world's leading rating agencies, to provide a rating assessment of the Northern Territory. Treasury saw little value in this exercise, given that its borrowing programs were relatively modest. However, as Moody's was not asking for payment, the Territory agreed to cooperate with the assessment process and granted access to Treasury staff and relevant data. This relationship has continued since then, although the Territory has conceded that there is some financial benefit in holding a rating and so now pays for it.

The Territory's debt level will continue to be a burden on the Budget for the foreseeable future. While this is far beyond what would be accepted in a commercial environment, in the government context it is not unique, although it is arguably reaching the limit of sustainable debt level.

Moody's has explicitly recognised the support provided by the Commonwealth Government in its assessment. While this dependency may be less of a factor in other states, the Commonwealth's tax collection powers still link the two groups together, regardless of the efforts of CBAs to present themselves and their jurisdictions as independent entities. There are some international precedents for this, such as the 1976 UK sterling crisis, which forced the Callaghan Government to borrow $3.9 billion from the International Monetary Fund. While the latter was a currency/balance payments crisis, it demonstrated the impact of a lack of confidence on financial markets and shows that in this case strategies will need to be adopted (with bipartisan support) to reduce volatility and carry the benefits of stronger years forward to protect the Northern Territory economy in weaker years.

The self-government movement that culminated in the *Northern Territory (Self-Government) Act 1978* mirrors many of the issues that led the states to seek more financial autonomy and independence in their financial activities. Whether the freedom it has given has been matched by benefits is debatable, not least because the most efficient way to borrow depends on satisfying the preferences of financial markets at a particular point in time. Another method of fundraising used by the Northern Territory Government is therefore public–private partnerships (PPPs). As the name implies, these are partnerships between the public and private sectors for the delivery of a project or service usually provided by the public sector. Their aim is to leverage the skills of the private sector in the timely and cost-effective delivery of major infrastructure. Additionally, they may also offer off-balance-sheet funding for a project that would otherwise be recorded as a liability, which can have political advantage. The Adelaide to Darwin Railway Project ($1.2 billion, 2004), the Darwin Waterfront Convention Centre ($1.1 billion, 2008), and the Darwin Correctional Precinct ($300 million, 2014) are examples of PPPs that have been undertaken in the Territory. While the financing risk was spread, however, these projects have still been costly and have not yet delivered the anticipated benefits.

Too much debt?

There is a vast difference between government debt and corporate entity debt. The question of how much debt is too much and what the consequences are for this situation is relatively clear when dealing with a corporate entity. In general, a corporation has too much debt as soon as it is unable to repay its debts when they fall due. If a business becomes financially unsustainable it may enter into administration and seek to protect itself from its creditors, as it pays off its debts, in order to avoid being placed into liquidation. It can also go straight into receivership. Under a receivership, the aim is to sell off the assets of the company to maximise the benefit for secured creditors.

For governments, however, the position isn't as clear. The tax-raising capabilities available to them mean that they can always claim to be able to raise funds to pay debts as they become due, and this can effectively extend their existence in perpetuity. However, the ability to tax/print money has not always been enough, for example countries with major dramas, such as Argentina in 2021 and Greece in 2012. When Britain's sterling crisis occurred in 1992 the UK Government was forced to withdraw the pound from the European Exchange Rate Mechanism (ERM) because of its failed attempt to keep it above the lower currency limit required by the ERM.

But where debt can be unsustainable for a corporation, in the government sphere such collapses can be avoided and justified by using powers that only governments hold. Since the early 2000s, quantitative easing as used in advanced economies has become an example of governments using such unconventional powers to allow their central banks to buy assets from financial institutions. This increases the value of the purchased asset while at the same time printing money, thus increasing the supply of money to fund the purchase. Such actions became necessary as official interest rates approached zero and conventional monetary policy became ineffective.

While falling interest rates have allowed governments to increase the amount of debt they hold, given the finite amounts of interest paid, this strategy relies on interest rates remaining low and defers the problem of when, and how, the debt will be repaid. Using debt to fund new assets that will contribute to productive and positive economic activity can be justified. However, using debt to pay for debt and to meet operational expenses is problematic, unless it is a temporary situation, and due to exceptional circumstances, that are expected to return to normal.

The problem is that the Territory is experiencing difficulties due to its primary revenue source from GST falling in relative terms annually. The Territory's specific GST relativity at the time of writing is currently 10% lower than it was in 2016/17, but the cost of services to meet the needs and expectations of the community has continued to rise.

The cost of providing services to a national standard is further complicated by the disabilities and cultural challenges innate to the Northern Territory. This needs to be addressed with a strategic plan and in coordination with the Commonwealth. The plan will need to incorporate a stronger economy with higher levels of each state and the Territory's own source revenue. In theory, a strong economy will in turn strengthen the economy, attract migrants, and increase the permanent population. However, this will be hard to achieve unless the Territory can find a unique resource or comparative advantage that it is allowed and encouraged to exploit. This proposition relies on the cooperation of other states that may otherwise see themselves as competitors, or as being disadvantaged through this process. In most cases, Australia's system of federation doesn't encourage states to recognise the benefits of sacrifice for the greater good of the nation. Similarly, parochial politics and bickering between states are two of the biggest barriers against national improvement. The Commonwealth Grants Commission's 2020 Review noted:

> The Northern Territory is the State with the weakest fiscal capacity largely due to its relatively large Indigenous and remote populations that are costly to service. Therefore, it has the highest GST requirement and relativity. In 2020/21, it's recommended relativity is 4.77, which is lower than its average relativity since 2009/10 of 5.08 (-0.31).

Structural change in the Territory is also difficult to achieve because of its small electorates. In a commercial enterprise the board represents shareholders and board members are legally bound to act in the shareholders' interests, because they can be held personally liable for breaching that duty. However, a government's decision to take on debt does not come with such penalties. The objectives and outcomes are only assessed at elections and sustainability is presented in terms of the policies of the next government.

Another measure of debt and its sustainability can be examined in relation to the trajectory of gross debt relative to GDP. The Parliamentary Budget Office's paper on 'Fiscal Sustainability – Long-term budget scenarios' Report No. 1, 01/2021 looked at this relationship and identified that the budget balance depends on the economy and the setting of government policy. If the debt to GDP ratio is stable, a surplus means the debt can be paid down, while a deficit will lead to an increase in debt.

However, the difference between the interest rate on debt and the rate of economic growth is fundamental to understanding how debt increases or decreases over time. Even in a balanced budget situation the debt to GDP ratio will increase when the interest rate on debt exceeds the economic growth rate, and it will fall when the interest rate is less than the growth rate. Consequently, it is possible for the debt to GDP ratio to decline even when there are budget deficits. At a national level the debt to GDP ratio peaked at the end of the Second World War. Over the following ten years the amount of debt was relatively steady. Nominal GDP growth averaged 14%, which compared favourably to interest payments on the debt of approximately 3.5%. Consequently, even though budgets run through this period were generally balanced, the debt to GDP ratio fell significantly.

In the 1990s the GDP growth rate was relatively low, and there was a period in which the interest paid by the government regularly exceeded the growth rate in the economy. Even though interest rates were falling, the amount of interest paid remained relatively unchanged because outstanding government debt was mostly on long-term fixed-rate bonds. The benefit of falling interest rates was reduced because of the legacy of high interest debt and the economy continued to be impacted by that legacy problem.

For the Territory's debt situation to improve it needs to aim for balanced budgets in an environment of strong growth. In other words, the growth rate has to be higher than the interest rate on its debt. The long duration and fixed-rate and low nature of much of the Territory's current debt could allow this to improve the debt ratios, but this will depend on sustained growth and fiscal responsibility.

Contributions to GSP, 2020/21 (source NT Government)

These percentages give an indication of the difficulty in reducing the Territory's debt, because the majority of working people are either in the public service or involved in the delivery of social services, rather than creating value directed into the Northern Territory from other economies.

At self-government, the Territory was allocated debt through the Commonwealth State Housing Agreement (CSHA). This long-term housing debt is still being carried by the Territory and the fixed interest rate on these credit foncier loans is now relatively high. Whether the Territory was burdened with too much debt at that point is a reasonable question, especially as its long-term obligations were not offset and it had assets it did not choose. However, as shown, its levels of gross and net debt were fairly consistent until the year 2000, since when they have taken a different trajectory.

Housing is accepted as being critical to improving Indigenous outcomes, as overcrowded housing feeds into poor health and education outcomes and exacerbates other community social problems leading to long-term issues.

Housing debt owed to the Commonwealth through CSHA and the Loan Council stood at $174 million in 2018. Provided it was not offset by measures that impacted on the Territory's ongoing allocation for social housing, the waiving of this debt would be beneficial.

In 2019 Senator Jacqui Lambie successfully campaigned for the Commonwealth to waive Tasmania's $150-million housing debt. The cost of servicing this debt represented almost half the Commonwealth's contribution to public housing ($15 million) in the state, with the effect that the debt led to the underfunding of housing. The same situation exists in the Territory, but the Commonwealth has not agreed to waive the Territory's debt as it should, illustrating the lack of significant voter power!

The Territory's current level of debt also substantively reflects the borrowings undertaken since 2000. The aim of those borrowings was to provide services at an equivalent national standard without consideration being given to the higher costs of supplying and maintaining these services and assets. This has added to the debt burden.

The Territory's services and systems have also been augmented each year rather than being replaced, leading to substantial costs for maintaining legacy systems. To create real efficiency, improvement must be measured as a net outcome. Some degree of pragmatic trade-off is required, and minor changes to services should be accepted rather than being used to justify persisting with legacy systems. For this to happen the benefits must be measurable and must outweigh the costs.

The Northern Territory Government has conducted two reviews of the Territory's budget prospects with the objective of creating a collective path. The first, under a Country Liberal Government, was led by Dr Neil Conn, and the second, under a Labor Government, was led by John Langoulant. The Conn review was moderately effective, but political pressures resulted in some of its major recommendations being bypassed. At the time of writing, one can't comment on the Langoulant review other than to say that a major recommendation – the sale of certain government assets – has been rejected by the current government.

Northern Territory business investment

The small size of the local market also creates difficulties for value adding and it is likely to remain small for some time. Given its isolation and harsh climate, Darwin is unlikely to expand into a major population centre in the near future, without significant economic stimulus.

The Territory's credit strengths include GST distributions and continuous assistance from the Federal Government and a stable government system. The flip side of these is that if agreement cannot be reached with the Federal Government, the Territory will have severe financial difficulties. Its small economy will force its debt to continue to rise unless there are significant changes. However, part of the solution to the problem may be solved by primary industry, which is currently in an economic uptrend.

Primary industry

The Northern Territory covers a vast area, loosely comprising four ecological regions:

- The semi-tropical 'Top End', with a distinct wet season (December–April) and dry for the remainder of the year;
- Barkley Tableland grasslands to the south-east, through to Queensland;
- Central Australian semi-arid region;
- the rugged Kimberley to the north-west.

Each region has a role to play in the grazing of beef cattle.

The search for grazing land initially was driven by the need for meat in the growing cities, and also by the prospect of land sales by the South Australian Government. The Northern Territory was opening up as a result of the Overland Telegraph, mineral prospects and the vision of Darwin Port as a gateway to Asian trade.

The explorers of the north were extraordinary men: the likes of Stuart, Sturt, Burke and Wills, Giles and Gregory to name a few. Gregory, for example, was engaged by the Western Australian Government to survey the Victoria River region for suitable grazing land; he and his small band roamed a vast area over 1854 to 1856, as a result of which Wave Hill and VRD were stocked. Equally intrepid were the 'boss drovers', who brought the herds into the Northern Territory from other states. Among them was a fair-skinned Scot, Nat Buchanan, who often rode with a parasol aloft; when the local natives asked, 'Where are you going?' he would scan the horizon and reply, 'Far away,' thus becoming known and respected as 'Paraway'.

Buchanan settled on Wave Hill in 1883, until it was auctioned to the Vestey Group in 1914. Buchanan also stocked Victoria River Downs (spanning WA and NT and initially covering 41,000 sq km). Heytesbury acquired VRD in 2012.

In 1882 the South Australian Government was awarded the first Northern Territory pastoral lease, to the initial settlers on Undoolya Station, bordering Alice Springs. The Hayes family bought the Undoolya lease in 1902, and the first cattle station has remained in the same family to this day. The station produces not only beef cattle, but table grapes and melons for southern markets.

The second pastoral lease was Wollogorang Station in the far north, bordering the Arafura Sea, populated by Indigenous people, and stocked with feral bulls, water buffalo, Indonesian banteng cattle and crocodiles. It was a challenging environment that led to much hardship and ownership changes. Alexandra Station in the Barkley was the third lease to be issued. This pastoral lease is still held by the original lease, North Australian Pastoral Co.

Currently there are 232 Northern Territory pastoral leases, with a unified voice in the form of the Northern Territory Cattleman's Association.

The massive holding of Wave Hill Station was held by the Vestey family from 1914 until 1992. Lord Vestey became notorious for breeding low-grade cattle in large numbers, with little in the way of property improvement, primarily for the purpose of exporting protein (in the form of chilled meat and Bovril) to England.

As stated earlier, the Gurindji tribe had strong traditional ties to the Wave Hill region, and after many years of fruitless efforts to improve wages and conditions, but more importantly, to restore their traditional land rights, they staged a strike and decamped to a site 20 km away from the homestead. Ultimately, the Australian Government granted them an excision over part of Wave Hill, with the excised area being further extended in 1974. This was closely followed by a decree that all Australians be paid a minimum award wage.

Current lease holders

The largest pastoral lease holders in the Northern Territory currently comprise:

- AACo Ltd (ASX Listed) – Burnette Downs, Montejinni, Delemere, Camfield
- Consolidated Pastoral Co – Newcastle Waters
- North Australian Pastoral Co – Alexandria, Mittiebah
- Heytesbury (Rhinehart) – Birrindudu, Mt Sanford, Victoria River Downs, Moolooloo
- Crown Pastoral (Oldfield & Costello) – Lila Creek, Crown Point, Andado, Mt Doreen and others
- Jumbuck and MacLachlan family – Wave Hill, Killarney

- Weir Family – Ammaroo Aggregation
- Hewitt Cattle – PSP Investments (Canada) – Narwietooma Aggregation, Numery

The cattle industry is now becoming a major contributor to the Northern Territory economy, with a significant multiplier effect. Buntine Roadways, Road Trains of Australia and many others operate hundreds of specialised triple-trailer road-trains over beef roads that are steadily being upgraded from rough road tracks to all-weather routes. These articulated trailers were originally designed by Kurt Johansen, an Alice Springs truck operator. Long-distance trucking is particularly important due to the lack of abattoirs in the Northern Territory. Most have failed, including an AACo Ltd abattoir built in Darwin in 2015 and mothballed in 2018 due to seasonal variability of through output and high labour costs. It remains the case that Northern Territory cattle are either trucked interstate for slaughter as package meat, exported live, or increasingly finished on interstate pastures or feedlots as organic certified.

The Northern Territory pastoral industry, until fairly recent times, was characterised by hardship and poverty. Extreme climate, lack of capital for property improvements, poor genetics, vast distances to market, exotic diseases, paucity of trace elements, the list of challenges goes on. The industry was focused on breeding store cattle for trucking south to fatten up on better pastures or feedlots. Family operators often struggled financially, while corporate enterprises with much greater resources were able to aggregate properties in the Northern Territory and interstate, develop scale and mitigate exposure to drought. Several of the corporates established in the late 1800s and early 1900s are still in existence today as agricultural powerhouses. More recent corporate entrants into the Northern Territory are Heytesbury,

Forrest, and an increasing number of foreign investment houses. Amid these huge corporates are the born-and-bred locals, such as the Oldfield/Costello interests owning well over 15,000 sq km of Northern Territory pastoral land (plus interstate holdings) and running in excess of 50,000 head of cattle.

In the past two decades there has been greater recognition of the returns that can be generated from beef growing in the Northern Territory in particular. The influx of overseas capital, receptive finance sources and increased scale of operations, have all contributed to investment in property improvements, genetics, technology and management skills. Stations now do bore runs using remote monitors, drones, and helicopters. Fences now exist where open range used to require exhaustive musters. There are big profits to be made. Another driver of what may turn out to be over-enthusiastic property valuations, is the availability of carbon sequestration subsidies.

An illustration of increased values seen in the estimated successive sales of one particular Top End lease:

2000	approx.	A$8m
2011	approx.	A$40m
2022	approx.	A$65m
2024	offered at	A$100m

These values are inclusive of capital improvements and variable cattle numbers, and most recently influenced by the lure of carbon credits for revegetation programs. Regardless, they indicate a growing international interest in land and water resources.

There is also an emerging recognition of the potential of other crops, whereas attempts in the past have tended to be dismal failures.

Rice, sugar and peanuts were an early prospect in the north, but encountered too many obstacles (birds, insects, variable wet season) leading to poor yields.

Sorghum and broadacre fodder crops are now successful supplements for the beef industry.

Cotton is becoming a significant Top End crop, dryland or irrigated, and supported by a cotton gin installed in Katherine.

Table grapes and melons have long been commercially cultivated at several locations in Central Australia where aquifers have ample irrigation water. (Undoolya Station produces many tonnes annually for southern markets.)

Mangoes and tropical fruits are well-established in areas from Darwin to Katherine and have the advantage of reaching markets earlier than other growing regions.

Aquaculture is now a popular contributor, hundreds of tonnes of prawns, barramundi and other emerging fish species being profitably exported annually, and not to forget the business of crocodile meat and skins, heavily invested by international fashion houses.

The Northern Territory Government is fostering this production diversity by allowing Northern Territory pastoral leases to apply for special licences for the cultivation of crops on areas that would otherwise be restricted to grazing.

To sum up: the future for Northern Territory agribusiness has never looked so promising.

Debt levels in various states – Northern Territory Finances

An analysis of the ABS public debt sector 2019/2020 showed that the Northern Territory's net debt was projected to grow to a deficit of approximately $9 billion in 2021/2022 and $12 billion by 2023/2024, creating a debt to revenue ratio of 179%. By comparison, Tasmanian net debt by 2023/2024 would be circa $4.13 billion.

The following graphs show that the net debt per capita in the Northern Territory being significantly higher than any of the states or territories.

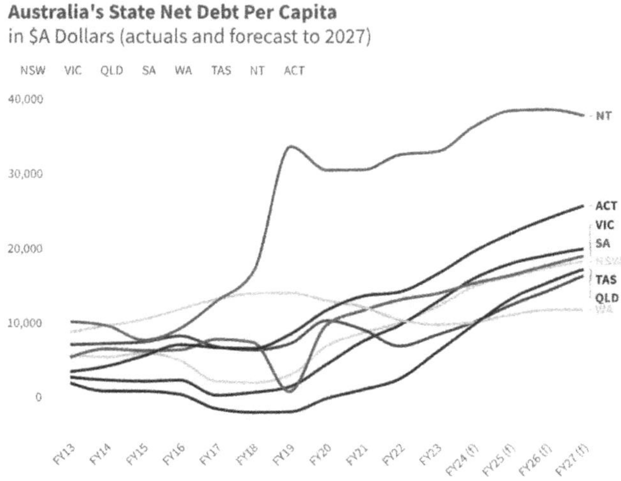

Australia's state net debt per capita
Source: EY Australia

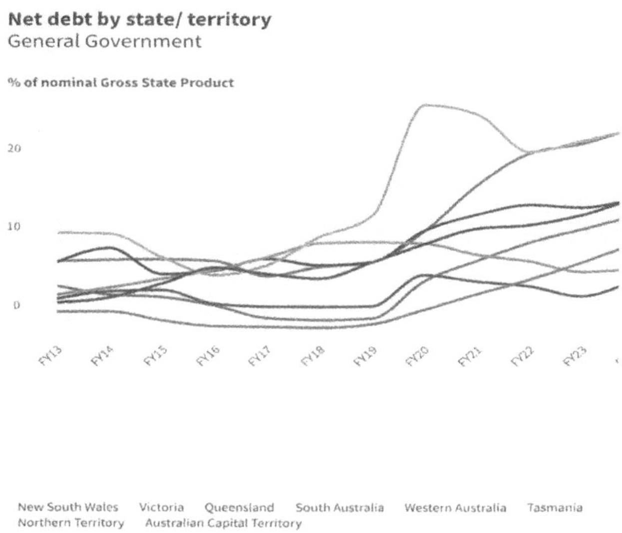

Net debt by state and territory as a
percentage of Gross State Product
Source: EY Australia

In 2022/23 there was an operating surplus of $146 million achieved, however this will have to be continued for many years to achieve a significant reduction in debt levels.

The figures in the tables below are taken from the relevant years' forecast budgets for the states:

- The debt levels of state and federal are thought to be around $1.3 trillion by 2024.
- Victoria's net debt by 2024 could reach $155 billion.
- New South Wales $53.2 billion by 2024 rising to about $104 billion three years beyond.
- Queensland $25.5 billion rising to $51 billion by 2024.
- Western Australia $24.5 billion rising to $25.5 billion by 2024.
- South Australia $25.5 billion by 2024.
- ACT nearly $8 billion by 2024.
- Northern Territory $12 billion by 2024.
- Tasmania $1.9 billion to be $4.4 billion by 2024.
- It is thought that federal debt will be in excess of $950 billion by 2024.

Northern Territory finances, 2022/23

Non-Financial Public Sector		General Government Sector
	2022/23	2022/23
	($000)	($000)
Borrowings	11,035	9,140
Total Assets	27,678	25,740
Total Liabilities	17,262	15,324
Net Debt	8291	6600

Northern Territory finances, 2021/22

Non-Financial Public Sector		General Government Sector
	2021/22	**2021/22**
	($000)	($000)
Borrowings	11,200	9,366
Total Assets	27,656	25,804
Total Liabilities	17,550	15,697
Net Debt	7702	6078

Northern Territory finances, 2020/21

Non-Financial Public Sector		General Government Sector
	2020/21	**2020/21**
	($000)	($000)
Borrowings	10,427	8,632
Total Assets	27,277	25,487
Total Liabilities	17,523	15,734
Net Debt	7662	6077

Source: NT Budget Papers 2023/24

A Commonwealth-related paper issued on 29 October 2023 stated that 'collectively States and Territories were facing an operating budget deficit in FY2023 of $4.6 billion and FY 2024 $11 billion respectively'.

This does not auger well for us as a country unless there is forward planning to reduce this.

Subsequent events, November 2024

It is interesting to note that Alex Treacy in the *Northern Territory News* reported that the Territory's Auditor-General published a damning report into government finances for the last fiscal period, with ballooning public sector wage and interest bills dragging the budget down. The article reported that the combined deficits exceeded $11 billion and the interest bill paid in 2023/2024 was $403.8 million.

Public sector wages over the last twelve months increased by $276.9 million to $3.1 billion, and an additional 539 full-time equivalent public servants were hired, taking the overall number to 21,455 FTEs.

Northern Territory Budget paper, 2024 update

A review of the Budget papers published in May 2024 shows some of the key features which are detailed in Appendix H. While there are some areas of improvement, it's often in a relative rather than absolute sense, as state debt levels increased to deal with COVID. The debt ceiling is approaching and the economic issues remain largely unchanged with no formal plan to rectify the underlying problems and attention on the social issues without connecting them to a solution. All these numbers show is that the tin has been kicked down the road.

The prudent management of debt and liabilities for the Northern Territory is very important with the ongoing objective to maintain or improve the Territory's credit rating.

The target: Territory's credit rating is Aa2 (negative) or better. Excessive debt can lead to restrictions on government's capacity to maintain levels of service through increased borrowing costs and can impact investor confidence resulting in negative effects on the Territory's economy.

The Territory's credit rating, assessed by Moody's in July 2024, showed an unchanged credit rating Aa3 with a stable outlook. Therefore, this fiscal strategy target has not been met.

The net debt to revenue ratio for the non-financial public sector 2023/24 outcome was 108%, five percentage points lower than the 113% projected in the original 2023/24 Budget. The improvement largely reflects higher revenue, mainly GST and taxation revenues, as a proportion of the increase in net debt. Despite the improvement, this fiscal strategy target has not been met.

(For more detail please refer to Appendix H.)

What to do?

It is clear from the figures presented that the Territory is in a very poor financial position. This can be put in context by noting that the Territory has problems and these will continue with its small population. Darwin is 3600 kms away from Canberra and faces issues of indigeneity, health, housing, climate, and remoteness that are all unfamiliar to most Australians.

The funding contributions made by the Commonwealth and states that help with supposedly disadvantaged sectors must be re-examined and restructured so that their potential serves the government better, as they could be much better utilised elsewhere, particularly within the Northern Territory. Having said that, some Northern Territory Government decisions could be challenged as to how appropriate they are for the groups they claim to serve.

It must always be remembered that it is impossible for the NT representment to repay debt by raising funds internally. The NT is totally dependent on large financial transfers through the Commonwealth Grant Commission and the only other source of income is the Federal Government itself.

The external influence of a system of federation that allows equal representation but in reality does not actually apply due to the imbalances of power and politics between jurisdictions, means that the Northern Territory's economic potential will continue to be impeded in favour of that of states with larger populations and economies.

Simplistically, money talks and votes count, and the Territory has few of either.

While the Northern Territory's debt position is very weak, it would be inappropriate to blame only the Northern Territory Government for this, or to expect the Northern Territory Government alone to resolve it. This should be a national effort, but this would of course bring the Territory and every other jurisdiction back full circle to their relationships with Canberra and each other.

Decisions need to be made on the basis of what is best for the country as a whole, and the sooner this is addressed the better, as eventually the Northern Territory will need fiscal help because it will be unable to resolve its debt issues.

In the current fiscal climate, and with interest rates varying, one day the Federal Government will have to help the Northern Territory Government with its debt control. Under current economic and population conditions it is impossible for the debt to be resolved.

State and Territory merger

Having spent most of my life living in the Northern Territory, I find the discussion in the media about South Australia and the Northern Territory merging to create one central state very interesting. This issue, raised by the former Deputy Premier of SA Vicki Chapman and the former Minister of Justice in the Northern Territory John Elferink, makes for entertaining reading, but it's difficult to see the matter being advanced in the Territory.

(Please refer to Appendix I.)

Stop Press: Debt pile grows

Debt Debacle

The Northern Territory debt situation has experienced significant activity since my 2024 analysis.

The treasurer for the Northern Territory has stated in a major announcement that net debt will reach more than $12 billion in 2025; it could reach $13 to $14 billion by 2029. The interest bill to secure this debt would be in the vicinity of $680 million in 2025/26, and more than $900 million by 2029, giving the Northern Territory the highest per capital debt in the country. It is believed the interest bill could be partly offset by an increase in Commonwealth grants in the period 2024/25 to 2028/29. The Northern Territory faces the challenge of a small population, circa 250,000, and an inability to raise funds internally like the States. So where will it end up?

It is interesting to read what sources such as the *Financial Review* and *S&P Global* say given that most States will have difficulties servicing the debts they carry. According to the media, the gross state debt has already increased by $329 billion in the period 2019 to 2024. These sources indicate that if the present trend continues the gross debt of all the States and Federal Government could exceed $3 trillion.

There are huge ramifications from here, such as AAA credit rating, ability to repay and more. Both Federal and State governments seem to have ignored the compounding factor of their spend together with the interest rates and the like, raising significant questions about the country's future for coming generations.

Conclusion

My career would not have developed as it did over the last half-century were it not for two beloved NT-based uncles. Or for that matter, the devastating cyclone that struck Darwin in December 1974, and the two young blokes who came to the Territory to make a quid on the roads and ended up helping with the big post-cyclone clean-up.

The Northern Territory is a long way from Duntroon where I started my life after school, but bizarrely there are connections. During the Second World War, Darwin was the forward defence zone for the country and my Henry Walker Eltin colleagues and I ended up with 4500 'soldiers in our battalion' and a billion-dollar business onshore and offshore. HWE, the first industrial company in the NT to list on the Australian Stock Exchange, had other major successes; it was the first company to have an Indigenous director and the first to form an Indigenous joint venture company employing and training Indigenous people.

There were the tough times too; it wasn't always an easy road. There were ill-chosen projects and damaging events relating to workers in remote places, to where I had to fly and deal with the employees and their families . . . it stretched us all.

Then there was the sadness of Neville Walker's death. And dealing with the dramas that came with the new government that, among other things, created two casinos and fostered a tourism industry.

But my special pleasure, my career highlight, is how, as a small group, the government, along with my colleagues, managed to create an educational institution that was to grow into a recognised fully resourced Australian university . . . and we succeeded. Though not a research-intensive university included in Australia's Group of 8, Charles Darwin University operates today as a successful well-regarded Australian university.

And no, I don't have instant solutions for the complexities that contribute to the challenging financial state in the Northern Territory. I do know that during the last decades of the 20th century the country witnessed significant changes that emerged post-cyclone and with the new self-government, allowing the Territory to change and grow.

However, for the Territory to further develop it must be remembered that federally votes count and the Territory has few of those. There needs to be changes in the country's priorities!

And if you asked me if I would do it all over again, the answer is a resounding yes . . . although perhaps I would do some of it slightly differently.

Darwin
September 2025

Acknowledgements

I would sincerely like to thank two work colleagues, Paula Nagel and Helen Robinson, for their help, guidance and assistance.

Others who have given their advice and support which has been invaluable were John Gamble, Peter Plummer, Alan Morris, Frazer Henry, Ross Springolo, John Montague, John Leake, Sharon Mulholland, Hamish Gidley-Baird, Ken Davies and Pat Jean. I would also like to thank my family Trish, Tim, Kathrine, and Victoria.

Wakefield Press editor Julia Beaven, typesetter Jesse Pollard and owner Michael Bollen have been wonderful in guiding me through the intricacies of producing the finished product.

I would also like to sincerely thank my two supervisors Don Zoellner and Rolf Gerritsen from Charles Darwin University, as this paper was originally designed to be part of a PhD, but I got lazy – it was not an ego trip!

Again, thank you to everyone for your patience and tolerance.

Appendix A

Henry Walker Eltin board members, 1994

Mr Neville Walker A.M.
Chairman
Mr Walker joined the board in 1981 and was appointed Chairman in 1987. He was formerly Joint Managing Director of Henry Walker Group Limited. He is an Executive Director who is a member of the Audit Committee with over 30 years experience in civil engineering, together with practical on-line management. He was formerly a member of the Rural Land Use Advisory Committee of the Northern Territory.

Mr Richard Ryan A.M.
Managing Director
Mr Ryan joined the board as Managing Director in 1988. He is a Fellow of the Institute of Chartered Accountants in Australia, a Companion of The Institution of Engineers. He is a Companion of the Institute of Management (U.K.), Chairman of Camberwell Coal Pty Ltd. and also Deputy Chancellor of the Northern Territory University and Deputy Chair of the Menzies School of Health Research.

Mr Akio Suzuki
Non-executive Director
Mr Suzuki joined the board in 1994. He is Managing Director of Toyota Tsusho (Australasia) Pty Ltd and Chief Representative of Toyota Tsusho Corporation. He joined Toyota Tsusho Corporation in Japan in 1964 and served in the Hamburg (Germany) office for five years as Chief Representative. He also held the position of General Manager of the Overseas Parts Department and Overseas Operation Department in Tokyo and Nagoya before being posted to Australia in September 1993.

Mr Malcolm Fricker A.M.
Deputy Chairman
Mr Fricker joined the board in 1981. He is the senior partner in a long established Adelaide law firm, Chairman of the Audit Committee and a non-executive Director, and was also formerly Chairman of the South Australian Jockey Club.

Mr Frazer Henry A.M.
Executive Director
Mr Henry joined the board in 1981. He was formerly Joint Managing Director of Henry Walker. He is the Executive Director in charge of contracting and mining, responsible for the overview of administration and operations of the Contracting division with 30 years experience in all facets of civil engineering and contract mining.

Mr Gatjil Djerrkura O.A.M.
Non-executive Director
Mr Djerrkura joined the board in 1994. He is General Manager of Yirrkala Business Enterprises, Chairperson of Miwatj Aboriginal Health Corporation and Chairperson of North Australian Investment Corporation and Chairperson of Batchelor College.

Mr Edmund Bailey
Executive Officer
Marketing
Mr Bailey joined the board in 1981. He is Alternate Director for Mr. Henry and Mr. Walker and has extensive experience in management of motor vehicle, truck and machinery dealerships and was a foundation member of the Australian Dealer Council. His responsibilities include an overview of the operations of Bridge Autos and Agserv Industries.

Appendix B

Henry Walker Eltin submission to government re joint ventures in remote areas and with Indigenous people & communities

41 – THE AUSTRALIAN Tuesday August 3 1993 – 41

BUSINESS & COMPANY NEWS

Aborigines buy into mining contractor

Landmark alliance points to future

By Bina Brown

Community involvement: Mr Djerrkura, left, and Mr Ryan are talking about developing a mine together

ABOUT the same time the High Court made its historic Mabo decision which recognised native title, Mr Richard Ryan and Mr Gatjil Djerrkura were talking about doing a mining development together.

In normal circumstances there would be nothing extraordinary about a white mining executive negotiating a multi-million-dollar deal with an Aboriginal investor.

But, with tension mounting between mining companies and Aborigines over land rights, the relationship is looking increasingly unusual.

To Mr Ryan, the Adelaide-based managing director of mining contractor Henry Walker Group Ltd, there is still nothing special about the Aboriginal and Torres Strait Islander Commercial Development Corp becoming its fourth-largest shareholder.

"It is just commonsense," he says of the arrangement designed to increase the company's chances of winning projects in remote locations. "I don't think we're anything special."

Mr Djerrkura doesn't agree. "We have achieved a landmark in as far as Aboriginal involvement in the mining industry and that is something that has never been seen before," he said.

"It is an alliance that will enable Aborigines, in partnership with a leading outback contract miner, to achieve a strategic position to target projects on Aboriginal land."

The deal, signed in July after nine months of negotiations, has already paid off.

Henry Walker, the corporation and the Jawoyn Aboriginal people in the Northern Territory, have already formed a joint venture to provide contract mining services to Zapopan NL, the developer and contractor of the Mt Todd gold mine north of Katherine.

Henry Walker has half of the $23 million joint venture with the rest shared equally between the Jawoyn Association and the corporation.

All the parties involved agree unequivocally that the joint venture illustrates quite clearly how the mining industry and Aboriginal interests can work closely together on a strictly commercial basis.

"This arrangement provides a possible model for future economic co-operation where mining activities impact significantly on Aboriginal people," Mr Djerrkura said.

Mr Ryan and Mr Djerrkura first began talking last year when their separate companies were bidding for the same job in Western Australia and decided to make it a joint venture.

The bid was unsuccessful because "we were getting to know each other", Mr Ryan recalled.

"What we then did was we got to know each other a bit better."

But joint venturing wasn't always going to work. "It started getting too complicated. The problem was we (Henry Walker) had the expertise and the basic equipment but it wasn't a paying proposition to put the groups together," Mr Ryan said.

"The corporation is not really in the mining business itself, but being in joint ventures it is really the Aboriginal group they represent such as the Jawoyn people that had to be in there.

"So we came to the conclusion that the best way to put it together was to make them an offer to take convertible notes in the company.

"Convertible notes is a bit like a trial marriage in the sense that you get to know each other before you tie the knot."

The corporation, a federal statutory authority with a range of commercial ventures worth about $20 million, last month agreed to buy seven $500,000 convertible notes which it can convert into shares in two years.

"Funnily enough, at the same time we were doing this, we started talking to the Jawoyn people in the Northern Territory who, in turn, were talking to the corporation in Canberra," Mr Ryan said.

Once known as the Northern Territory's only listed company, Henry Walker, which now has its corporate headquarters in Adelaide and contracting head office in Perth, is keen to be involved with the locals.

The Australian, Tuesday August 3rd 1993, pg. 41

Henry Walker

Submission No. 23

RECEIVED
13 MAR 1998

12 March 1998

The Committee Secretary
House of Representatives Standing Committee
on Aboriginal and Torres Strait Islander Affairs
Parliament House
CANBERRA ACT 2600

Dear Sir,

Attached for you information is Henry Walker's submission to the Inquiry into Indigenous Businesses. For the purpose of full disclosure, I advise that I currently am a member of the Board of Directors of the Aboriginal and Torres Strait Islander Commercial Development Corporation,

Henry Walker would be happy to answer any questions arising from the submission, or requests for further information, from the Committee. These should be directed in the first instance to Don Murchland. Manager, Corporate and Investor Relations,

Yours sincerely,

D Murchland

PP Richard Ryan AO
Managing Director

SUBMISSION

INQUIRY INTO INDIGENOUS BUSINESSES

Henry Walker Group Ltd

March 1998

EXECUTIVE SUMMARY

As one of Australia's major contractors to the minerals sector, Henry Walker has experience, and an ongoing interest, in the development of Indigenous business enterprises.

Our experience has shown that the formation and conduct of successful joint ventures with interests is not only possible but holds the potential for mutual benefit.

Notwithstanding this, the cultural differences and disparities in financial, commercial, and vocational resources present an intimidating barrier to economic co-operation between and mainstream enterprises. The result is that developing a joint venture with interests can sometimes be seen as being 'too hard'.

In this environment, the role played by the Aboriginal and Torres Strait Islander Commercial Development Corporation (CDC) has, in Henry Walker's experience, proven beneficial. The CDC's provision of commercial, financial, and managerial resources has enabled the formation of joint ventures in which Aboriginal interests were able to assume an equal partnership with Henry Walker.

Accordingly, it is essential that the activities undertaken by the CDC continue to be the province of an organisation dedicated to the economic development of Aboriginal and Torres Strait Islander people.

Upgrading of commercial resources would improve the organisation's effectiveness further. From a business perspective, the 'one-stop-shop' has attraction in its simplicity. Making the organisation responsible for the bundling and packaging of the array of relevant assistance programs, grants, and initiatives available from various government departments and agencies, on a project by project basis, could improve the efficiency of delivery of these services and significantly simplify the process for those seeking to develop the skill, financial and other resources of businesses.

At a local level, the CDEP program administered by the Aboriginal and Torres Strait Islander Commission has also enabled Henry Walker to join with community interests in the conduct of civil engineering projects.

Finally, Henry Walker is conscious that this submission may read as being especially supportive of the CDC. This is not by the intent of the company's representations, nor should this support be construed as enthusiastic support for the Commission *per se*.

Instead, we would hope that this submission be accepted evidence of the real need for an independent, appropriately resourced, commercially focused organisation that will help organisations and mainstream companies overcome the barriers that would otherwise mitigate against joint business success.

SUBMISSION OUTLINE

Section 1 Henry Walker's interest in business

The company has a history of co-operative relationships with organisations, including a number of successful joint ventures. Henry Walker anticipates entering into further joint ventures with organisations in the future.

Section 2 Opening comments

provides some opening comments on the pre-requisites for business, which Henry Walker submits should provide the context for discussion of how to encourage business.

Section 3 Experience in joint ventures
outlines four case studies summarising Henry Walker's experience in joint ventures with Indigenous organisations. The experiences of the company in these joint ventures are the basis for this submission.

Section 4 Importance of joint ventures
discusses joint ventures as an avenue for business development for Indigenous organisations and companies. Henry Walker anticipates that opportunities for joint ventures between Indigenous organisations and companies servicing the Australian minerals sector will grow.

Section 5 Barriers to development of JVs with Indigenous business
discusses potential obstacles to the development of joint ventures involving aboriginal interests and companies. Henry Walker's experience with factors which obviated or ameliorated these obstacles are reported.

Section 6 Specific comments on the CDC and other recommendations
discusses the role performed by the CDC and some avenues for encouraging the development of joint ventures involving Indigenous organisations and companies.

1. Henry Walker's interest in indigenous business

Henry Walker is an Australian owned mining and engineering company listed on the Australian Stock Exchange. The company conducts operations in most states of Australia.

Henry Walker has a long record of commercial co-operation with Aboriginal communities and organisations.

Henry Walker derives approximately half of its revenue from contract mining. A further 17% is generated from civil engineering with a significant share of this being revenue generated from the mining industry.

Our involvement in mining, and extensive operations in northern and remote Australian locations, has given the company an ongoing interest in participating with Aboriginal and Torres Strait Islander organisations.

Apart from the desire to be able to utilise capable joint venture partners and employees in remote operations, our clients in the resource sector are, increasingly, expecting our tenders to provide opportunities for indigenous persons and communities to participate in the employment and revenue created by projects developed within their locality.

The company's business ventures with Aboriginal interests are summarised and appear below under the title '3. Successful joint ventures by indigenous organisations and Henry Walker'.

In 1994, Henry Walker benefited from investment in the company by the Aboriginal and Torres Strait Islander Commercial Development Corporation. The Corporation has retained an investment of over 1 million shares in Henry Walker and is represented on the company's Board of Directors.

In 1996, the company committed to a 5 year, $1 million Aboriginal Employment Strategy. The Strategy, which is jointly funded by the company and the Department of Employment, Education.

Training and Youth Affairs, is aimed at increasing Aboriginal employment across the company's operations.

The Strategy has seen, with the assistance of the Department of Employment, Education, Training and Youth Affairs, the development of accredited traineeships and skill acquisition certificates to assist indigenous people acquire skills relevant to commercial activities conducted within their community's area of interest.

With a large proportion of the company's business being conducted in remote locations and involving mining projects, Henry Walker expects to be involved in further joint ventures with Aboriginal organisations.

Henry Walker is currently involved in over 40 mining and engineering contracts in Australia and anticipates revenue of approximately $700 million in the year to 30 June 1998.

2. Opening comments

Preamble

Henry Walker submits that the most meaningful starting point for a discussion about encouragement and support for indigenous business is with an analysis of the pre-requisites for commercial enterprise.

The challenges indigenous people and organisations face in establishing sustainable businesses can be particularly difficult. However, while these challenges may be greater for indigenous businesses, the basic pre-requisites for a sustainable business are common for all enterprises.

Conducting the discussion on indigenous business within the context of these prerequisites will direct the Inquiry to:

- identify why successful indigenous businesses have flourished;
- identify the hurdles to be overcome for indigenous businesses to achieve further success;
- identify initiatives and recommendations capable of supporting long term business development and prosperity.

Basic pre-requisites for business

The minimum conditions for the establishment and ongoing existence of any commercial enterprise are:

- the existence or, reasonable prospect, of a market of sufficient size to justify investment and financial backing;
- access to the necessary resources (financial, skilled, professional, etc.) to enable a business entity to be constructed and operate; access to customers/business partners and the securing of agreements with customers, joint venture partners etc.
- the achievement of sufficient sales and profits to enable the business to meet financing obligations, any necessary re investment, and provide an economic rate of return;
- finally, perhaps most importantly, the least tangible ingredient is the "human factor".

Notwithstanding how readily all of the preceding pre-conditions can be met, the business is unlikely to continue to exist unless the key people involved have vision of the commercial opportunities that can be won, and the will to negotiate, work and "do what it takes" for those opportunities to be realised.

For a joint venture, there is the added pre-requisite that the enterprise be a 'true' joint venture, in that both parties contribute both financially and intellectually to the venture's success. Joint ventures will simply not 'get off the ground' without potential participants respecting the ability of other potential partners to make the appropriate contribution.

It is acknowledged that Aboriginal and Torres Strait Islander businesses may have other additional social and cultural pre requisites for success. Their omission from the list is solely attributable to the fact that Henry Walker is not able to make any meaningful comment or observation on the subject, and is not intended to diminish their significance.

3. Successful joint ventures by Indigenous organisations and Henry Walker

Case study 1: Civil engineering joint venture at Gove

Since 1985, Henry Walker has participated in two multi-million dollar commercial joint ventures with the Yirrkala people of Gove through the community's contracting company, Yirrkala Business Enterprises Pty Ltd.

The joint venture completed civil engineering contracts for the Nabalco bauxite project.

In Henry Walker's view, the joint ventures were successful. Apart from providing profits for both partners, the success of the joint ventures has created a strong relationship of mutual respect between both parties. This is likely to encourage the formation of new joint ventures involving Henry Walker and Yirrkala Business Enterprises for future civil engineering projects in the East Arnhem Land region.

Case Study 2: Mirrkworlk Joint Venture

The Mirrkworlk Joint Venture (MJV) was created in 1993 when the Jawoyn Association and the Aboriginal and Torres Strait Islander Commercial Development Corporation entered into a joint venture with Henry Walker to conduct contract mining at the Mt Todd Gold mine.

The MJV has provided exclusive contract mining services to Mt Todd since 1993. In 1996, MJV was awarded the contract for mining under the Stage 2 development of Mt Todd for the 8 years to year-end 2004. The $160 million contract involved a substantial expansion to operations at the mine. The mining contract terminated early in November 1997 following the client's suspension of operations at the mine due to unprofitable gold prices.

It is Henry Walker's view this project was extremely successful and that the Aboriginal and Torres Strait Islander Commercial Development Corporation played an essential role in the creation of the MJV. The financial, legal, and general managerial input provided by the CDC enabled Aboriginal interests to commit to a 50% interest in the joint venture.

Case Study 3: Umbakumba Joint Venture

Henry Walker entered into a joint venture with the Umbakumba Community Council on Groote Eylandt in the second half of 1996, to undertake roadworks for the Department of Transport & Works.

Using labour and plant jointly contributed by the community and Henry Walker, the Umbakumba Joint Venture completed approximately 40km of roadworks on Groote Eylandt.

Henry Walker understands that the Umbakumba Community Council was funded under the CDEP program. The availability of funds made available by the program gave the council the financial footing to join Henry Walker as an equal partner in the joint venture.

A highlight of the joint venture was the high participation rate of Aboriginal people in the project; at times the construction crew, including supervisory staff, was entirely comprised of Aboriginal people. The contract was successfully completed with profits distributed equally between the joint venture partners.

Case Study 4: Murrin Murrin mining contract

In January 1998, Henry Walker was awarded a $180 million mining contract at the Murrin Murrin nickel project in Western Australia. The company's final tender included an offer to conduct the contract at the mine in joint venture with Aboriginal interests.

The company was able to propose a joint venture as a result of successful negotiations with the CDC. The result of the negotiations was an agreement by the CDC to join Henry Walker in a joint venture to conduct the contract, and to divest a portion of its equity in the joint venture to local aboriginal interests.

The joint venture is still in the process of being finalised. The involvement by the CDC provided a conduit for rapid commitment by Henry Walker to a joint venture with Aboriginal interests, on the understanding that local Aboriginal communities would also be involved.

4. What is the relevance of joint ventures for the development of indigenous business

Henry Walker's experience and interest in indigenous business lies in the formation for joint ventures with indigenous organisations.

It is our belief that joint ventures provide significant benefits for established companies and their indigenous joint venture participants.

Through joint ventures with Aboriginal organisations, Henry Walker has:

- been able to participate in commercial ventures which attract business by virtue of their indigenous shareholders;
- been able to participate in business ventures in regions where the company would not, ordinarily, expect to be involved, eg: Umbakumba, Gove;
- benefited from the capital risk sharing with organisations that are accustomed to, and have an interest in, remote regions;
- had improved access to employees accustomed to working and living in remote regions, and who do not have to be flown to and from capital cities at the commencement and conclusion of rosters.

In turn, Henry Walker believes these joint ventures have provided Aboriginal interests with:

- the opportunity to participate commercially in projects which might otherwise have presented capital, technical or managerial demands beyond their present resources;
- the benefits from the transfer of business and technical skills and employment experience;
- participation in accredited vocational training programs, some

of which have been especially structured to also address local community interests as well.

Given these advantages for both parties, joint ventures offer the opportunity for nurturing indigenous businesses and increasing the profile and understanding of indigenous business within the Australian business community.

Henry Walker anticipates that opportunities for joint ventures between indigenous and non-indigenous businesses will increase as a result of:

- the desire for greater economic participation by Aboriginal and Torres Strait Islander people from mining economic activity within their communities:
- the ongoing development of new minerals projects;
- the aforementioned (refer page 4) trend to require the inclusion in tender documents of an outline of avenues for indigenous involvement in employment and revenue streams created by the project.

Measures which encourage the formation of joint ventures will encourage the development of indigenous business. Conversely, barriers to the formation of joint ventures between established Australian companies and indigenous people and organisations represent barriers to the development of indigenous business.

5. Potential challenges and obstacles to joint ventures involving indigenous people and organisations

In our experience, the formation or success of joint ventures involving indigenous people can be inhibited or threatened by a number of common hurdles which prevent the achievement of the pre-requisites for business, summarised at the opening of this submission.

Equally, our experience demonstrates that joint ventures involving Aboriginal interests and companies is possible, and holds the potential for mutual benefit.

A summary of the typical obstacles to the formation of joint ventures with Aboriginal interests, and our experience in dealing with those obstacles, follows.

1. *Non-continuity or breaking up of work*

Contract mining and civil engineering is a capital intensive business. Without the assurance of adequate ongoing work it is difficult to finance capital equipment purchases. Civil engineering projects are often broken up into small discretionary projects, tendered separately. Conversely, where projects are tendered on a turnkey basis (ie: as a package to a single contractor}, organisations can approach financiers with more viable propositions.

As Henry Walker experienced at Umbakumba, the COEP program can provide the financial resources with which indigenous people can acquire vocational and business experience and skills by addressing opportunities within their community. As at Umbakumba, where significant projects can be identified, the program can enable the community to attract companies to enter into joint ventures, in which vocational training and technical and supervisory skills can be transferred.

2. *Inability to contribute resources commensurate with meaningful participation*

Probably the greatest hurdle for indigenous communities and organisations seeking to participate in joint ventures, is the difficulty in mustering the resources for a significant level of participation.

Apart from the capital requirements (a 5 year open cut mining contract can require $10 million to over $20 million of mobile equipment in the initial year), a meaningful contribution towards the creation of a joint venture carries demands in terms of commercial negotiation and analysis, legal work and management.

Difficulty in resourcing these demands carries a dual impact - not only are indigenous communities hamstrung in their ability to participate in joint ventures but their attractiveness to mainstream companies as a joint venture partner is diminished.

In Henry Walker's experience, the CDC has provided an invaluable focal point through which the company has been able to pursue Aboriginal involvement in large scale mining projects.

The Corporation's ability to fund significant capital investments and involve local Aboriginal interests has enabled indigenous interests to maintain a *50% share of the Mirrkworlk Joint Venture and, it is expected,* a *similar share of the joint venture to conduct the Murrin Murrin mining contract.*

At a *more local level, the funds provided by the CDEP program at Umbakumba, enabled the community to maintain* a *50% equity share in civil engineering projects in their region.*

3. *The "Too Hard" complex*

The political and social structures of indigenous organisations and communities are not well understood in non-indigenous circles.

Australian companies (including Henry Walker) are generally unfamiliar with Aboriginal and Torres Strait Islander values and customs. The task of negotiating with different organisations such as land councils, community associations and tribal factions, often via lawyers, is "too hard" for most business people.

The involvement of a multiplicity of government representatives who are delivering programs and/or agencies designed to assist indigenous people can add further to the perceived complexity getting joint ventures with indigenous persons 'off the ground'.

Once again, it has been Henry Walker's experience that the involvement of the CDC has facilitated the formation of joint ventures with indigenous businesses. Most individual companies do not have the time or resources to be involved in brokering agreements with various indigenous interests or the confidence in dealing with community issues and factions at a *local level.*

4. Skills and employment issues

The comparatively low level of vocational experience and skills typically found amongst most remote indigenous communities does not encourage consideration of local Aboriginal people for employment on projects.

There are various state and federal government funded training programs and initiatives that can overcome help indigenous people acquire the skills and experience to participate in projects.

However, the identification, access, co-ordination and integration of these various initiatives with the development of joint ventures or business enterprises is rarely simple, and can prove intimidating for those unfamiliar with sorting through the various program names, funding sources, committees and advisory bodies.

5. The human factor is non-existent: the main players are not given the scope to do business

Finally, the very preponderance of external advisors, lawyers, accountants, and consultants *(some of whom have their own vested interests)* employed by indigenous organisations to provide managerial and professional advice, can mitigate against companies and indigenous organisations 'doing business'.

Business requires a shared view of commercial opportunity and the will to find a commercial solution upon which a business can be based. In our experience, this rarely results from gatherings of hired lawyers, consultants or accountants but rather, from a meeting of parties who demonstrate "goodwill" toward achieving the desired goal.

The formation of joint ventures and other commercial arrangements between indigenous organisations and companies, will work best when companies are able to negotiate directly with commercially-capable representatives with a direct interest in agreeing a business solution that benefits that indigenous organisation.

It is Henry Walker's experience that this role was well performed by the CDC in respect of the joint ventures to conduct mining at the Murrin Murrin and Mt Todd mines. At Umbakumba, the CDEP Co *ordinator also performed* a *similar function. In both instances, the ability to deal directly with* a *person with authority, who shared our desire to do business and who possessed commercial understanding, enabled the creation of viable joint-ventures.*

6. The encouragement of joint ventures involving indigenous business

As the preceding discussion indicates, Henry Walker's experience with the CDC has been positive. It is improbable that the company would have been able to enter into the large joint venture at Mt Todd, and that being prepared for Murrin Murrin, without the conduit and financial and commercial resources provided by the Corporation or a similar organisation.

We are conscious that the this submission may read as being especially supportive of the CDC. This is not by the intent of the company's representations, nor should this support be construed as enthusiastic support for the Corporation *per se.*

Instead, this submission should be accepted as evidence for the real need for an independent, appropriately resourced, commercially focused organisation that will help indigenous organisations and mainstream companies overcome the barriers that would otherwise mitigate against joint business success.

The CDC has, from Henry Walker's perspective, been able to perform that role – providing the links and involvement with Aboriginal and Torres Strait Islander interests in a way that a bank could not aspire to, while also providing the commercial focus and approach that enabled business to be done.

Accordingly, it is essential that the activities undertaken by the CDC continue to be the province of an organisation dedicated to the *economic* development of Aboriginal and Torres Strait Islander people.

Re-allocation of the Corporation's financing and investment roles into a general (ie: without links to Aboriginal and Torres Strait

Islander people) investment banking organisation would result in an organisation without the capacity to offer itself to business as a credible interface with Aboriginal interests.

Our experience at Umbakumba has convinced the company of the value of programs such as the CDEP program, supported by competent locally based co-ordinators, as a means of providing communities with the financial resources with which they can develop businesses and attract joint venture partners.

This submission has already noted that the potential for increasing involvement for Aboriginal and Torres Strait Islander people in joint ventures as a result of:

- the desires by traditional land holders to achieve improved employment outcomes and more direct economic involvement in projects; and
- the ongoing development of new minerals projects.

The extent to which this potential is translated into increases in indigenous business will obviously be enhanced by measures which further reduce the hurdles that make the formation of joint ventures difficult, and assist the organisations to achieve the pre requisites for business sustainability.

With this in mind, Henry Walker makes the following specific suggestions:

- as noted earlier, one of the assets that the CDC has brought is *(apart from a capability to act as a conduit to capital for indigenous organisations and a focal point for companies to target indigenous organisations)* commercial experience and understanding.

Henry Walker believes the CDC's effectiveness could be improved with an upgrading of its commercial **resources.**

- the formation of joint ventures involving indigenous organisations can only be enhanced by simplifying the process to a "one stop shop' operation.

Under this concept the CDC, or a successor organisation, would deliver and co-ordinate all government programs and initiatives that relate to indigenous business and be responsible for packaging and delivering of all other programs

that maybe relevant to the formation of joint venture involving indigenous business (eg: labour market programs, skill acquisition programs) for a particular project on an as-required basis.

Henry Walker also recommends that Federal and State Government examine the structuring of public works tenders and contracts to be let in Northern and remote Australia with a view to ensuring that the tender structure encourages participation by indigenous businesses and the formation of joint ventures comprising indigenous businesses and established companies.

This could be achieved through letting projects on a turnkey basis, or bundling several years work together to provide a project which will increase the probability of indigenous businesses attracting finance.

For example, significant capital amounts are allocated for expenditure in Northern Australia under the Health Improvement Priority Program.

Under the current system, administration of the entire contract amount is usually allocated to a single consultant who then issues a number of tenders for the various locations, or various items, for which the infrastructure expenditure is intended.

Rather than adopting this piecemeal approach, the tendering of a number of contracts on a regional basis would provide tender packages of sufficient size for indigenous businesses to commit to equipment purchase and attract joint venture interest.

Supporting Documentation

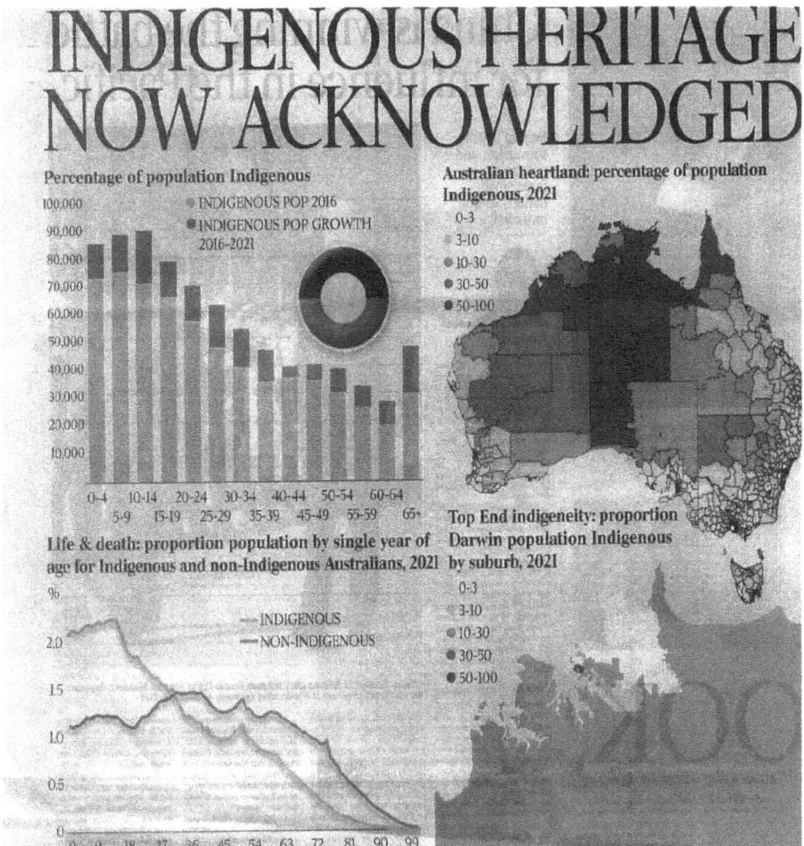

The Weekend Australian, October 12 2022

Yek Maninh Traditional Owners discuss lease and royalty issues with NLC representatives

In Many areas, a system of 'managers' and 'owners' operates. Land managers generally have maternal links to the land while landowners generally have paternal links to the land. Aboriginal landowners and managers have specific and complimentary land rights and obligations to ensure the spiritual and physical health of defined areas of land

Aboriginal land is private property owned under special freehold title. It is inalienable – in other words, it cannot be bought, acquired or forfeited.

The Aboriginal Land Rights (NT) Act 1976 has enabled Aboriginal people to gain inalienable freehold title to 50 per cent of the Northern Territory and, through the High Court's 2008 Blue Mud Bay decision, about 85 per cent of the NT coastline.

For the most part, Aboriginal landowners with inalienable Aboriginal freehold have the exclusive power to control the direction and pace of development on their lands. The public, in the form of Government at various levels, has only limited rights to impose external development or conservation direction or constraints.

Aboriginal land is not owned by individuals. It is granted as a communal title. Land is formally held by land trusts – groups of Aboriginal people who hold the title for the benefit of all the traditional owners and people with a traditional interest in the land.

Under the land Rights Act, decisions over the use of Aboriginal land must have the consent of the traditional owners as a group and ratified by the Land Council. Aboriginal land in the Northern Land Council area is held as inalienable Aboriginal freehold – the strongest form of title in Australia.

Appendix C

Administrator's report regarding liquidation of HWE in 2005

Attention ASX Company Announcements Platform
Lodgement of Open Briefing

HWE

Henry Walker Eltin

open briefing

corporatefile.com.au

Henry Walker Eltin Group Limited
33 Paul Street North
North Ryde, NSW 2113

Date of lodgement: 23-Feb-2004

Title: Open Briefing. Henry Walker Eltin. December 2003 Profit Result

Record of interview:

corporatefile.com.au
Henry Walker Eltin Group Limited recently announced a pre-tax profit of $6.9 million in the six months to December 31, 2003. In the same period last year you reported a pre-tax loss of $30.8 million. Where are you in the turnaround of this company?

CEO Bruce James
The company's track record over the last three to four years has clearly been poor. The last half year is the first profit result in line with management expectations for some time. We've definitely stabilised the ship.

But, there remain issues that have to be resolved if we're to generate acceptable returns. Plant is the obvious one. Improvements in plant management are essential if we're to see a steady improvement in margins.

New contracts and our strong order book give us the opportunity to achieve a far better outcome going forward and we think this latest result, although the margins on the surface are disappointing, is a first step towards achieving our longer-term goals.

One of the key issues we obviously face is getting the optimal funding mix to finance our new growth, and that's something we're going to be focused on in the next couple of quarters. Our capex program is going to rise and we will be reviewing all the options relating to operating leases, buying and the mix of debt and equity, with the aim of making sure we maximise shareholders' returns. I'm not going to go into the details on funding issues and I'm not making any specific profit forecasts, but what I will say is that we've put this company in a position to grow.

After a period of serious instability, I'm looking forward to the next few years of talking about growth rather than the issues of reorganisation, write-offs and bad contracts that were my focus in my first year as CEO.

corporatefile.com.au
Although the profit result was in line with your advice at the AGM in November why wasn't a stronger profit performance more evident in the last six months?

CEO Bruce James
Specific negatives included the under-budget performance of HWE Civil, the strength of the Australian dollar which impacted on the contribution from the Yandi iron ore contract, the lack of any contribution from the Cockatoo Island joint venture mine and the ongoing need to more efficiently manage our plant.

We have limited the impact of the Australian dollar's rise with productivity improvements at Yandi and the other negatives are likely to become positives in 2005.

HWE Civil recently won a new contract with Vopak and has another two contracts under final negotiation totaling $70 million. We've retained resources within HWE Civil and have the capacity to manage the growing order book. I've got a $200 million revenue target in mind for civil work in 2005 and that will certainly lift our returns. In relation to Cockatoo Island, I'd expect a positive contribution in 2005. We've overcome the operational problems and confirmed reserves.

Plant management is a major issue. Current under recoveries on plant are a legacy of past policy and we're actively managing for a better outcome. We are focusing on plant utilisation and availability on a site by site basis. Repairs and maintenance programs are under review and decision making has been moved closer to the work face. This means that clear accountability for cost has been pushed into each business.

corporatefile.com.au
Previously you've indicated a margin of 4 percent is an appropriate return for your contracting businesses. What needs to occur to achieve that margin and when do you consider it likely you'll achieve that margin across your contracting operations?

CEO Bruce James
We have to get our volume up whilst continuing to improve margins. I've mentioned the recovery in Civil and we've got strong work on hand in both HWE Mining and Simon Engineeering. In the last period our EBIT margin was 2.5 percent. If we strip out HWE Civil it was 3.0 percent. A target of 3.3 to 3.5 percent is embedded in our thinking for 2005. Beyond that, there's more scope.

I'm expecting our corporate and business unit overheads to remain stable during the growth phase. I believe we can manage at least $1.5 billion in revenue on our existing structure.

corporatefile.com.au
Your order book has risen to $2.2 billion from $1.1 billion at December 2002. What benchmark returns do you seek in the tendering process?

CFO Andrew Price
The returns required are dependent upon the nature and location of the contract and the type of equipment required to undertake the work. As a general rule of thumb we require at least 20 percent return on assets employed at the project level. We review this on a case by case basis, particularly where the equipment will be off balance sheet.

corporatefile.com.au
Why are you growing more rapidly in mining when you previously stated you'd grow the services stream of your business?

CEO Bruce James
Our desire to grow the services stream hasn't diminished but we need to manage that growth appropriately and balance it with higher than anticipated demand from the resources sector. Our strategy for a 50:25/25 mix between mining services and the other service streams remains in place. However, our strategy must also have the flexibility to react to changes in demand in the various marketplaces in which we operate.

The increase in mining work will, to some extent, mask the growth we anticipate in HWE Civil and Simon Engineering, but we are definitely seeing signs of growth emerging. Last year, Simon Engineering lifted its order book from approximately $140 million to $310 million and we need to execute that new business efficiently and profitably. The civil business is also securing new contracts as I mentioned previously and we're confident that these new contracts will result in solid returns for the business.

corporatefile.com.au
The cash flow statement notes that investment in plant, property and equipment was only $15.4 million versus $58.4 million in the previous corresponding period. Why was it low in the recent six months?

CFO Andrew Price
A combination of factors. Due to negotiations, the timetable for some of the new contracts has slipped a few months and that's pushed some capex into the second half. Also, with some of the new and existing work we've been able to redeploy some plant and reduce the amount of idle plant. For example, approximately 75 percent of the fleet required on one recently awarded underground contract was sourced from existing equipment, while 100 percent of the equipment on another underground job was supplied by the client.

corporatefile.com.au

What is the forward capex program?

CFO Andrew Price
Capex in 2003 was approximately $96 million and I expect this year to be in line with that in 2003 or a little higher. A lot will depend on the timing of new work commencements and our final decisions on capital structure. Obviously it will be heavily skewed to the second half year. Included in our forecast is an expectation on the commencement of projected contracts, the timing of which may fall into the 2005 year.

corporatefile.com.au
Net debt to shareholders' funds has improved recently to 58.1 percent from 73.5 percent as at June 2003. Are you now expecting the ratio to rise and what would you regard as an appropriate range for this measure?

CFO Andrew Price
From 2001 to 2003, gearing ranged from 65 to 90 percent and we think that range is too high. Our general objective would be to keep it below 65 percent with a long-term objective closer to 50 percent, but I accept we could rise above that level for a short period, especially as we bring on some new work. We're currently reviewing our plans in relation to debt levels and the mix of on balance sheet and off balance sheet funding required for the growth being experienced.

corporatefile.com.au
Is there any intention to boost funding from asset sales?

CFO Andrew Price
We have assets outside the core contracting business and we will sell those assets if we think we can get better returns elsewhere. Non-core assets are constantly reviewed.

corporatefile.com.au
You received a tax credit in the latest period that boosted net profit to $12.4 million. Will you return to normal tax rates in the second half?

CFO Andrew Price
Yes. The one-off benefits of the tax consolidation process have now been fully crystalised. We do not expect any major adjustments in the second half that will affect the tax expense calculations.

corporatefile.com.au
You've mentioned you won't give specific profit forecasts but what level of guidance can you provide?

CEO Bruce James
At the AGM in November we said we'd produce a second-half year modestly above the first-half year. We're talking pre-tax profit. That statement remains valid. We also said the 2005 year would more clearly reflect the improvements underway in the company and that statement also remains valid. We're laying a foundation to grow steadily over time.

corporatefile.com.au
Is it your intention to restore the dividend and what is your capability to frank a dividend payment?

CEO Bruce James
The directors wish to declare a final dividend this year so long as we meet our plan. We have plenty of surplus franking and should be able to fully frank any payment.

corporatefile.com.au
Thank you Bruce and Andrew.

For previous Open Briefings with Henry Walker Eltin Group Limited view www.corporatefile.com.au

For more information about Henry Walker Eltin Group Limited view www.hwe.biz

Administrators Report – General Comments

Reasons for companies' failure and appointment of Administrators –

MC GRATH NICOL AND PARTNERS

Having investigated the HWE Administration Group's business, financial affairs and assets, the Administrators consider that while many factors contributed to the company's failure, the key reason was the decision taken in May 2004 to execute the Indonesian coalmining (KPC contract) with PT Bumi Resources requiring funding of USD $130 million, without committed financing facilities in place.

By the time Administrators were appointed to the HWE Administration Group on 31 January 2005, USD$70.6 million had been invested in the project, with another USD$$84.4 million due by April 2005. This investment placed considerable pressure on the group's cash resources, even after accounting for a capital raising in mid-2004 which injected $42 million of equity into HWE.

Other contributing factors were:

- Poor internal planning, reporting and control procedures
- The development of strategy at management rather than Board level, and
- A lack of integration of newly acquired businesses.

The Administrator's Report shows that poor Internal Controls and Corporate Governance were the major factors causing the liquidity problems. These included entering into contracts without the appropriate financing in place and a lack of up-to-date financial reporting.

The comment is also made, that not all strategy and future planning were delivered adequately to the Board.

It is difficult to comment on the lack of integration of the newly acquired businesses as the Company's interests were so diverse, both nationally and internationally, but the end result, which was Liquidation, supports the Administrators "comments".

The Report resulted in an article in the Australian Financial Review by Yvonne Bell (June 29, 2005) which expands on and clarifies Henry Walker Eltin's problems. (Seen.24)

Discussions were held with several major Contracting Companies but unfortunately none of these came to fruition, due predominantly to the state of the market at the time.

Henry Walker Eltin then went into liquidation, which was the "Winding up of the Company."

Attached is an Administrators Chart of all Henry Walker Eltin entities together with a time bar of the administration/liquidation process. Attention is drawn to comments made on 04/04/2014 which support my comments concerning the liquidation and distribution to creditors and members.

Having realised this state, the company's assets were disposed of over a period of years and funds were distributed.

The company had a series of goals which it needed to meet to satisfy the market, but unfortunately it did not reach them as promised, as the report details (see Appendix C). Bruce James resigned in 2004 and was replaced as interim CEO by Robert Cleary. He in turn resigned on February 8, 2005.

This ground-breaking national engineering giant entered voluntary administration on January 31, 2005, during the peak of the mining boom, and this, in itself, generated enormous publicity in both the general and the financial press.[1]

The voluntary administration was implemented by a breach of the company's banking covenants with Westpac, which was caused by the PT Bumi Resources contract (Indonesia) and was not because the company was unable to pay its debts. HWE had adequate liquidity to meet its day-to-day commitments. Under the rules now in place this would therefore not have happened today despite the circumstances.

The company failure was investigated by the Administrators. Below (Figure 11) is an extract of their report followed by an extract from *Delisted Australia's* report (Figure 12). They point to three specific factors in the company's failure.

---

1 Yvonne Ball, "HWE slammed for poor financial planning," *Financial Review*, June 29, 2005, https://www.afr.com/companies/hwe-slammed-for-poor-financial-planning-20050629-jv77r

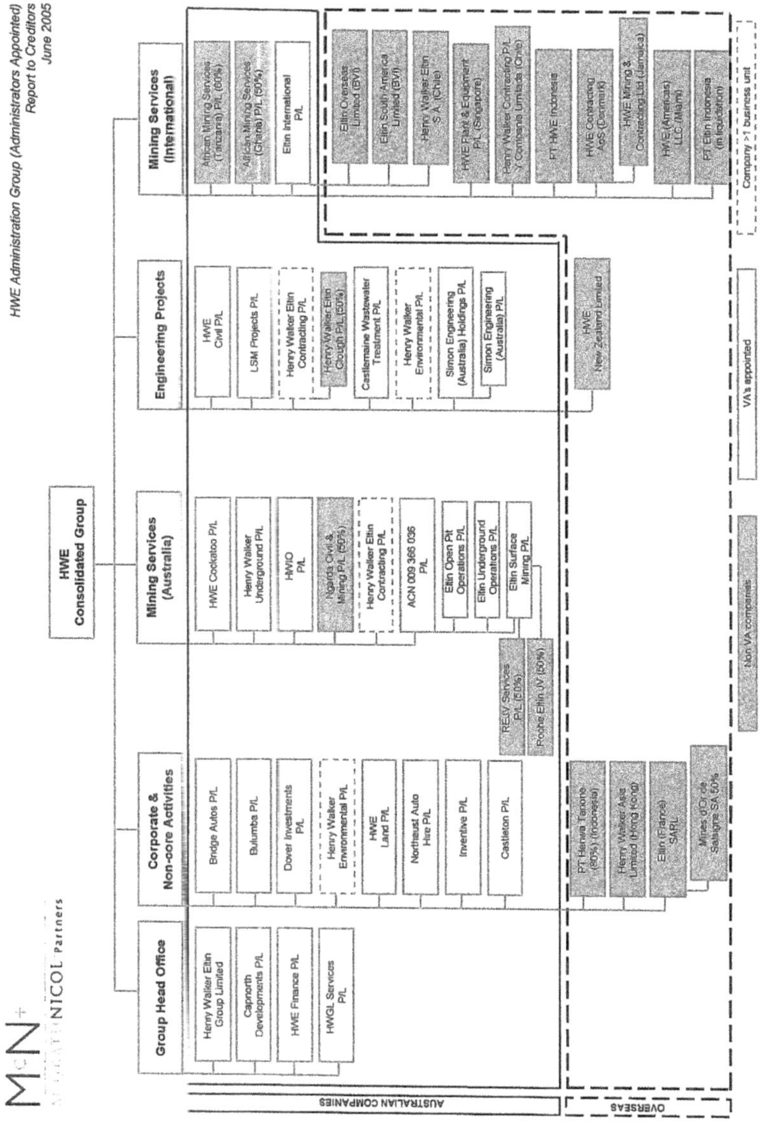

Figure 11: McNicol & Partners: HWE Administration Group (Administrators Appointed) Report to Creditors June 2005

In addition to the Australian companies HWE had subsidiaries registered in overseas jurisdictions, including New Zealand, France, British Virgin Islands, Hong Kong, Chile, Denmark, Jamaica, Singapore and Indonesia, which are not in Administration. The Administrators have undertaken independent reviews of those operations where appropriate.

Summary information for those entities to which Administrators have been appointed are detailed in **Appendix A**. More detailed statutory and financial information for companies under Administration on an entity-by-entity basis are outlined in **Appendices B to AA**.

4.3 Overseas operations

As at 31 January 2005, HWE's principal overseas trading operations were:

- HWE Mining and Contracting Limited ("HWE Jamaica") – providing mining and civil engineering services. Glencore is an equity partner in both joint ventures.
- Henry Walker Eltin SA ("HWE Chile") – an equipment hire business located in Santiago. Equipment is currently employed on short-term hire contracts to various mining interests within Chile.
- African Mining Services (Ghana) Pty Limited ("AMS") – a 50% JV with Ausdrill Limited, operating several mining services contracts in Ghana.
- PT HWE Indonesia and PT Henwa Tanone (principally "the Bengalon Project", or "the KPC Project") – a 10-year coal-mining contract with PT Bumi Resources.

Further information on these entities is provided in section 8 of this report.

4.4 Outstanding winding up applications

No winding up applications were filed against HWE or its Australian subsidiaries prior to our appointment.

HENRY WALKER ELTIN GROUP LIMITED

SPECIAL NOTE TO HWE SHAREHOLDERS: The administrators have made a distribution to shareholders, a somewhat unusual event. To our knowledge there has been no other distribution by administrators to shareholders of a listed or previously listed company in the past 20 years. Many of you sold your shares to deListed to crystallise your capital loss. Thank you to those who have offered the proceeds of the distribution to us. As the company did not emerge from administration, we were not able to register the transfers and the proceeds are yours to bank and keep. In our opinion this distribution is assessable income if you previously claimed your loss, but you should seek professional advice.	04/04/2014
delisted following non-payment of annual listing fees in respect of the year ending 30 June 2014	30/08/2013
we understand this company failed and has finally been delisted by ASX following non-payment of annual listing fees	30/08/2013
The company has not paid its annual fees in respect of the year ending 30 June 2014 but are already suspended from official quotation. In accordance with listing rule 16.5, entities that pay their annual listing fees on or after 23 August 2013must pay by bank cheque only. Under listing rule 17.15, any entity that has not paid its annual listing fees as required by listing rule 16.5 by 5.00 pm EST on Thursday 29 August 2013 will be removed from the official list with effect from the close of trading on Thursday 29 August 2013.	23/08/2013
The company has not paid its annual fees in respect of the year ending 30 June 2014 but are already suspended from official quotation. In accordance with listing rule 16.5, entities that pay their annual listing fees on or after 23 August 2013must pay by bank cheque only. Under listing rule 17.15, any entity that has not paid its annual listing fees as required by listing rule 16.5 by 5.00 pm EST on Thursday 29 August 2013 will be removed from the official list with effect from the close of trading on Thursday 29 August 2013.	23/08/2013
deed administrators provide a market update - shares may still be of value notwithstanding the earlier issue of a loss declaration - if you are still a shareholder, you should await developments	21/12/2012
deed administrators provide a market update	16/12/2009
administrators have paid 100 cents in the dollar on creditors claims admitted - a "significant" new claim is disputed and it is unlikely there will be further payments to creditors within the next 12 months	17/09/2009
deed administrators provide a market update	02/06/2009
deed administrators are still finalising a matter in relation to a creditor claim - this is subject to proceedings which will be heard soon	07/11/2008
deed administrators confirm that creditors whose claims have been admitted, have now been paid in full - they have recently received a substantial claim	31/03/2008

Figure 12: http://www.delisted.com.au/company/henry-walker-eltin-group (pages 1–5)

that may involve litigation	
the Deed Administrators have now paid a second dividend of 50c/$ distribution to admitted creditors in the Mining Pool Entities, bringing the total dividends to date to 100c/$ and paid a second dividend of 50c/$ distribution to admitted creditors in the Non Core Pool Entities, bringing the total dividend to date to 60c/$	15/08/2007
a first and interim dividend at the rate of 50 cents in the dollar was declared on 20 September 2006 for each of the Mining Pool companies - it is anticipated that unsecured creditors of the Mining Pool companies will ultimately receive total distributions of 100 cents in the dollar on admitted claims	20/09/2006
ASIC grants relief from financial reporting requirements and provides an extension of time to hold annual general meetings	12/04/2006
ASIC has accepted an enforceable undertaking from Shareholder Advocacy Pty Ltd (SAPL) in relation to their prohibited use of information on company registers - SAPL had sent unsolicited letters, offering to lodge proof of debts with the companies, ION, Sons of Gwalia and Henry Walker Eltin - SAPL has agreed to cease sending offers to shareholders, lodge proof of debts for those persons who accepted SAPL's offer with the Administrator of the relevant companies and also refund to shareholders "a pro-rata amount of the fee paid by shareholders to SAPL" - sorry we don't know how much you will get back!	16/03/2006
reports that the administrators have received some claims from shareholders asking to be treated as creditors - according to the administrators "none of these claims are in our view claims of any substance at this point in time" - this follows the declaration by the administrators (see note immediately below) that there will be no return to shareholders	03/03/2006
reports that a meeting of creditors has voted to place HWE group companies under a deed of company arrangement that will see financial creditors paid in full, major credit creditors paid around 65 cents in the dollar and small creditors paid about 20 cents in the dollar	03/03/2006
a **loss declaration** has been issued and the capital loss can therefore be claimed in the financial year the declaration is issued	03/03/2006
administrators advise that the sale of the contract mining business to Leightons is now completed - the next stage of the administration involves the convening of creditors meetings in March, at which creditors will vote on a Deed of Company Arrangement	01/02/2006
administrators announce they have executed a binding agreement with Leightons for the sale of HWE's contract mining business - while the sale is subject to a number of conditions, the administrators expect completion by mid-December 2005	01/12/2005
Leighton Contractors Pty Limited has entered into a Heads of Agreement with the Administrators of Henry Walker Eltin Group Limited (HWE), to purchase the Australian and New Zealand contract mining assets of the company for $215 million, subject to documentation and certain conditions including the approval of the Foreign Investment Review Board	10/11/2005

administrators indicate that it appears certain there will be no return to shareholders - they intend to make an Administrator's Declaration under section 104-145(1) of the Income Tax Assessment Act 1997 (allowing shareholders to claim their capital loss), but will withhold the Declaration until the conclusion of the HWE Mining business sale process - we will carry the declaration here as soon as we are aware it has been issued - deListed will therefore no longer buy HWE shares	25/10/2005
administrators refer to the recent court decision permitting a shareholder to lodge and have admitted a proof of debt for voting purposes at a meeting of creditors, notwithstanding his claim related to his acquisition of shares (this decision has been appealed by the way) - the administrators believe that any shareholders who consider they may have a provable claim in the administration of the HWE group will need to obtain their own legal advice	25/10/2005
it is our understanding some shareholders have received a Notice for Lodgement of Proof of Claim against Henry Walker Eltin from Shareholder Advocacy Pty Ltd - this follows the finding by Justice Ray Finklestein in the Sons of Gwalia case that shareholders who purchased shares where they have been misled and deceived are to be treated equally with unsecured creditors (this finding by the way is not necessarily in the best interests of shareholders as a group) - we do not recommend that shareholders participate in the Shareholder Advocacy action and suggest that for the moment they observe proceedings (if they are mounted) from the sidelines	06/10/2005
Louise Karen Hicks resigns as company secretary	16/09/2005
directors Frazer Henry and Andrew Price resign	13/09/2005
ASIC advises of relief from financial reporting requirements	12/09/2005
creditors vote in favour of a resolution to adjourn the second meeting of creditors to a date to be determined by the Administrators which is no more than 60 days after 8 July 2005 (in the event that the Administrators form the view, that the period within which the adjourned meeting must be held should be longer, Court approval will be sought to adjourn the meeting to a date not more than 120 days after 8 July 2005) - this is the meeting at which creditors are considering whether or not to enter a Deed of Company Arrangement	08/07/2005
New Zealand goldminer OceanaGold and the administrators announce the completion of arrangements for HWE's exit from the Fraser's Decline project at OceanaGold's Macraes gold field	01/07/2005
administrator releases his report, informing creditors of the financial position of the various entities, the reasons for HWE's failure and recommending the company enter a Deed of Company Arrangement - this to be considered at a creditors meeting on 8 July 2005 - administrator believes it is unlikely there will be any return to shareholders - but it is "necessary to progress the sale process before the Administrators can form a final view on that matter"	29/06/2005
Clough Limited (ASX:CLO) has completed the transaction with the Henry Walker Eltin Administrator to buy its Western Australian Civil construction business	02/06/2005

administrators announce the commencement of a sale process in relation to HWE's mining contracting and services business	19/05/2005
Clough Limited (ASX:CLO) yesterday executed a Heads of Agreement with the Henry Walker Eltin Administrator to buy part of its Western Australian civil construction business - the Parties are working towards finalising the acquisition within the next 10 days	18/05/2005
administrators of Bridge Autos Pty Limited (a part of the Henry Walker Eltin Group of companies) today announced the sale of the company to listed automotive retail group AP Eagers Limited	05/04/2005
administrators advise of the sale of HWE's Northern Territory-based civil engineering business to Macmahon Contractors Pty Limited, a subsidiary of Macmahon Holdings Limited - this is the latest in a series of satellite business disposals aiming to reduce trading risk and stabilise the operations of the group	16/03/2005
administrators of Simon Engineering (Australia) Pty Limited announce the sale of Simon to Abigroup Asset Services Pty Limited, a subsidiary of Abigroup Limited, securing almost 1100 jobs - Simon is part of the Henry Walker Eltin Group of companies (no mention of the sale price!)	03/03/2005
Ausdrill Limited reaches agreement to purchase HWE's 50% interest in African Mining Services (Ghana) Pty Limited (AMS) for $1.369m, to be satisfied by an issue of Ausdrill shares - a shareholder loan by HWE to AMS will also be repaid	28/02/2005
Justice Hely of the Federal Court of Australia grants an extension of the period within which the Administrators of HWE must convene the second meeting of creditors - the meetings must now be convened by Monday 23 May 2005	16/02/2005
administrators have been seeking to maintain and preserve operations, determine the claims of creditors and employees and conduct assessments of the businesses carried on by HWE to determine the profitability or otherwise of various contracts	15/02/2005
interim CEO, Robert Cleary, has resigned from the company effective immediately	08/02/2005
at first meeting of creditors today, creditors elected representatives to various committees of creditors	08/02/2005
company announces with regret that its Chairman and founder Neville Walker passed away suddenly earlier today (Mr Walker died when his car hit a tree at Weddell in rural Darwin)	07/02/2005
the HWE board announces that Messrs John Gibbons, Jack Crumlin and Keiran Hutchison of Ernst & Young, who were appointed administrators of the Company on 31 January 2005, have resigned as administrators by notice in writing given to the Company - the board advises that it has today appointed Messrs Anthony McGrath, Scott Kershaw, Joseph Hayes and Shaun Fraser of McGrathNicol+Partners as voluntary administrators - peculiar to say the least for administrators to last just one day in the job (subsequent reports	01/02/2005

suggest Ernst & Young pulled out after realising they had a potential conflict of interest - was it unpaid bills for professional work?)	
shares suspended from quotation	31/01/2005
appoints John Gibbons, Jack Crumlin and Keiran Hutchison of Ernst & Young as voluntary administrators to its operations - this follows the decision by Glencore Finance AG not to proceed with the proposed recapitalisation announced on 23 December 2004, and difficulties experienced by the company in securing long-term funding arrangements - administration never augurs well for shareholders, but it is too early to speculate on the possible outcomes	31/01/2005
name changed from Henry Walker Group Limited	01/12/1999

Appendix D

Henry & Walker miscellaneous papers

BUSINESS The Advertiser, Wednesday, August 7, 1996 35

Contract miner on record roll

By KATE ASKEW

The Henry Walker Group has recorded its ninth consecutive record annual profit, lifting profit by 14 per cent to $17.7 million, from total group revenues of $440.9 million.

The managing director of Henry Walker, Mr Richard Ryan, has predicted a solid year ahead for the Adelaide-based group, with work on hand amounting to $829 million.

It will seek to pick up two additional contracts in Indonesia and in South America to add to its highly successful contracting division, which was the chief force behind the jump in revenues.

The contracting division contributed $314 million to annual revenues which was a 68 per cent increase from the previous financial year.

The company attributed the increase in contracting revenue to new contracts won during the year – including the $300 million BHP Yandi iron ore contract and two new Western Australian underground development contracts at the Blendevale zinc project and the Mt Morgans gold mine – as well as a change in the "mix" of revenue and a full-year contribution from its underground mining arm.

"Traditionally the money has come from contract mining and road construction and land. This time we've earnt a bit of money through things like project management," Mr Ryan said.

Earnings per share was 17.6c compared to 17.3c in 1994-95 and it hopes to lift it by 10 per cent in 1996-97.

The company has declared a six-month fully franked dividend of 4.5c a share – payable on November 1 – giving shareholders a 18 per cent increase in total annual dividend to 8.25c a share.

Although the group's Chilean operations recorded a small loss on revenue of $1.5 million it was "exactly on budget" because it was its first year of operation in South America and was still establishing its presence there.

Its only contract in Chile is a $52 million five-year mining contract for Companie Minera Carmen de Andacollo at the Andacollo copper mine in northern Chile.

"We're going to be looking for another major job there but it won't be for at least six months because want to keep bedding down the Andacollo contract," Mr Ryan said.

Profits from its Indonesian operations at $3.48 million were high at 10 per cent of the total revenue.

"They're mature contracts which means a couple of them we've been working for some years which means we just know better how to do the job," Mr Ryan said.

It has also undertaken its largest civil contract in Indonesia, a $28.5 million job to undertake a diversion of the Kelian River around the proposed extension of CRA's Kelian gold and copper mine in East Kalimantan.

Kumagai who? Japan's third biggest construction company, Kumagai Gumi, has very quietly built a major presence in Australia in only three and a half years. TONI WHITMONT profiles a truly quiet achiever.

FIN/R 5/9/84

The silent invasion of Kumagai Gumi

ASK most people in the construction industry if they know much about Kumagai Gumi and you get a blank look and a short "no". Even those at chief executive level reply along the lines of "I don't know much about them but they are not the sort of outfit you'd walk away from".

What most people don't realise is that Japan's third largest construction company (in terms of market capitalisation) is very active in Australia; Kumagai (NSW) Pty Ltd, its Australian vehicle, is involved in projects and proposals worth $1.23 billion.

The nine Japanese businessmen and engineers that make up Kumagai Gumi's Australian subsidiary make sure that it keeps a low profile but they are very serious about Australia.

Of the $1.2 billion worth of projects, $420 million have already commenced or have secured building approvals – not bad for a company that has only been operating in the country for three and a half years.

Kumagai is involved in a broad cross-section of developments – from coal mines to casinos and from shopping centres to "ski tubes".

And if it gets the go-ahead on two proposals that are in the pipeline, it will have pulled off a huge coup. Those projects could more than double the size of its Australian business.

Kumagai and Sydney property developer Essington Ltd are on the short list for the redevelopment of the Museum Station site in Melbourne in a deal that could be worth $300 million.

At the same time, Kumagai has thrown its hat into the ring with Meekatharra Minerals Ltd for a proposed $300 coal mine in South Australia.

Kumagai sees itself primarily as a construction company but it has taken the role of a developer in its initial forays into the Australian market.

Its principal function so far has been to organise finance and provide technical assistance in construction. Where it does have the title of "contractor", it has usually sub-contracted the work to Australian companies.

Ken Bilston, whose company Bilston Welding Engineers Pty Ltd is involved with Kumagai in the underground passenger railway planned for the New South Wales ski fields, said recently that Kumagai is "really not much more than a banker yet but this will change".

"It recognises that it may have to be a banker for five years before it can start to be a serious builder," he said.

Kumagai is not linked with any of the major Japanese trading houses or banks. But its referees include the heavyweights – Sumitomo Mitsui and Yokohama – and those credentials are vital to its Australian operations.

"Kumagai generally does not put up its own finance . . . but it has the muscle and the background to arrange finance, introducing its partners to banks and institutions who then put up the funding," said Mr W. Heron, a partner in Price Waterhouse, the firm which handles Kumagai's approaches to the Foreign Investment Review Board.

A spokesman for one company working with Kumagai who preferred not to be named said that "one of the reasons that it has so much work in hand is that it seems to have an unlimited source of funds to get a project through its construction phase.

"They can drive a hard bargain but every time they want money for a project, they get it," he said.

While it has been relatively isolated from building so far, Kumagai's commitment to Australia is real.

Its Australian managing director, Mr Tony Mitani, explained last week that Kumagai Gumi wanted to do business in Australia because unlike a number of countries in which it already operates, Australia is economically and politically sound.

But behind his words of support for Australia is Tokyo's strategy to lessen its dependence on the flagging Japanese market and broaden its presence in the Middle East and the Pacific rim countries.

The slow down in their domestic market has forced a number of Japanese construction companies to look elsewhere for growth.

In a recent note on the Japanese construction industry, Nomura Securities said that "with residential construction declining and capital investment by private firms sluggish, the industry is now facing its most difficult time since the first oil crisis."

Mr Mitani. . . Australian visit

A survey of the 136 companies making up the Overseas Construction Association of Japan published in July showed that foreign construction topped ¥1,000 billion ($A5 billion) for the first time in the year to March 1983.

For the first time, Australian orders (¥54.6 billion or $A273 million) contributed to the 14 per cent rise.

On a reverse basis, Kumagai Gumi comes in at number five among the leading Japanese construction companies, following Kajima, Shimizu, Taisei and Obayashi Gumi. In terms of profits, it is number three.

But of the five, it is generally recognised as the most active overseas with up to 25 per cent of all sales sourced outside Japan.

Overseas business in 1983 contributed ¥89 billion ($A445 million) out of group revenue of ¥631.4 billion ($A3.16 billion). Kumagai Gumi made a net profit at ¥14.9 billion ($A74.5 million).

(This compares with two of the leading Australian contractors – Leighton Holdings Ltd's recently reported $11.5 million profit on sales of $620 million, while Jennings Industries Ltd turned in a profit last year of $14 million on turnover of $325 million).

CORPORATE FOCUS

While Kumagai's Australian operations are only just starting to make real contributions to group earnings (Mr Mitani would not release any sales or profit figures), it is clear that Australia has a high priority for Tokyo.

A fortnight ago, the 93-year-old chairman of Kumagai, Mr Jinichi Makita, arrived in Australia for the launch of the Adelaide Station and Environ Redevelopment Project, the $160 million joint venture between the SA Superannuation Fund Investment Trust and Kumagai.

"We get very strong direct support from head office," said Mr Mitani.

"Most Japanese companies take three months to come to a decision. If we wish to make a $20 million investment, head office will decide promptly," he said.

Because of its direct access to head office, Kumagai has been able to move decisively in Australia.

One of its partners in the Adelaide project commented that "Kumagai did a lot of homework before coming to Australia market – now that they've done that, they are very responsive to our approaches".

Asked about Kumagai's long-term objective in Australia, Mr Mitani replied "to be in a position to negotiate directly with the unions".

But Australianisation is still more than five years away, he said.

Mr Mitani ruled out the possibility of stock exchange listing.

When it does Australianise, it will follow the path of its US counterpart inviting in a key local shareholder.

"Every local partner now is a candidate," said Mr Mitani.

Wary of the building unions, Kumagai has taken care to structure its operations so that its local partners have the responsibility for direct union contact.

In many instances it has also taken care to pick projects where it does not compete directly with established Australian construction companies.

"We are not interested in straight tenders and we don't want to compete with local companies," said Mr Mitani.

"But if projects need funding, then we have a chance of participating without competition."

(Kumagai may have found it has little competition in some projects because they are relatively high risk.

For example, it stepped into the Wandering Star tourist resort on the north coast of NSW after the Malaysian group Ipoh Gardens withdrew.)

The ability to arrange funding has been a vital ingredient in Kumagai's strategy in Australia.

But the other key element is its reputation for technical excellence.

Kumagai Gumi recently completed the largest construction testing facility in Japan and has introduced a number of new construction techniques.

Its "Seikan Tunnel", the world's longest undersea tunnel linking Honshu and Hokkaido, has been recognised as breaking new ground in engineering.

The company is drawing on that reputation to establish itself in Australia.

It has technical service agreements for most of its projects and will be taking an active role in the provision of specialist equipment and design facilities in the construction of the "ski tube" and the Wintinna coal project if its proposal is approved.

Kumagai has used its reputation to secure its construction of a $12 million tunnel for a hydro-electric scheme near Port Moresby with Brisbane-based Watkins Ltd.

It is difficult to place Kumagai in the context of the Australian construction industry.

First, Kumagai refers to itself as a civil engineering and construction company but most of the construction work is done by its Australian partners.

For example, Concrete Constructions Pty Ltd is the builder of The Quay luxury apartments in Sydney which Kumagai stepped in to finance after the collapse of Trustees Executors and Agency Co Ltd.

Concrete Constructions is also building an office block in Canberra and the Sydney's Pitt Street and Chevron hotel projects (which are due to start by early next year), all of which Kumagai is financing.

Second, its main function

Continued page 37

From page 13

has been the arrangement or the provision of finance, so it may be more appropriate to compare Kumagai to a lending institution or a developer.

Third, while it has plans for more than $1 billion worth of projects, the figures mean little until the revenues start to flow in.

Those that do know the company point to the huge reserves of its parent and to its international standing before saying that it does not have an Australian counterpart.

Mr Ron Goodwin, general manager of Watkins Ltd, commented that "Kumagai has no competitor in Australia.

"It takes a high profile in the management role in projects and uses local know-how and local contractors to do the work for them. And it often puts in its own money."

Another of its Australian associates said that "Kumagai parallels Civil and Civic in terms of scope and operations – they both use in-house professionals. But Kumagai tends not to be a marketer in the traditional sense and it is much more low key than Australian companies."

Mr Mitani however dismissed observers' unfamiliarity with Kumagai.

And regardless of the vagaries of the industry in which it operates, he is convinced that Kumagai will continue on its current growth path and that its name will become more closely identified with the Australian construction industry.

Projects – commenced and planned

Name	Total cost of development	Other participants	Stage	Kumagai's participation
NSW				
The Quay	$48 million	Concrete Constructions	now selling	arrange finance
Chevron Hotel re-development	$50 million?	Essington Ltd, Concrete Constructions	building approved, start Jan	technical advice, arrange finance
Pitt Street Hotel	$120 million	Essington, Concrete Con	waiting final approval, start Jan	arrange finance, technical advice
Wandering Star resort	$35 million	Icanus Constructions Services Ltd	stage one completed	arrange finance, principal contractor
"Ski tube" railway	$30 million	Transfield Pty Ltd, Bilston Welding Engineers Pty Ltd	start early next year	49% equity, specialist construction
26 Northbourne Av, Canberra, office block	$10 million	Concrete Con	finish this year	arrange finance
Macquarie Field Old Age Home	$45 million	Essington	negotiating land lease	arrange finance
VICTORIA				
Sale shopping centre	$20 million	City council and Pak-Poy and Kneebone	finish this year	project management
Museum Station re-dev	up to $300m	Essington	on short list of developers	arrange finance, technical advice
SOUTH AUSTRALIA				
Adelaide Station re-dev	$150 million	Pak-Poy and Kneebone	construction started	60% equity, supply $80m finance
Wintinna coal mine	$300 million	Meekatharra Minerals	on short list	25 per cent equity, contractor and financier
QUEENSLAND				
Portside units	$14 million	Watkins Ltd	finish this year	arrange finance, 15% equity in Thiess Watkins, technical advice
Holiday Inn, Surfers Paradise	$65 million	BGH Pty Ltd	finish this year	arrange finance, technical advice
Townsville casino	$45 million	Sir Leslie Thiess, Sheraton group, Bartlett group	waiting final approval	15% equity

CONTACT

HENRY WALKER GROUP LIMITED

VOL. 4 No. 3 DECEMBER 1993

MJV BREAKS EARTH

First loads from Batman deposit at Mt Todd. Right foreground shows the crushing plant and left background are the leach pads.

The Mirrkworlk Joint Venture (MJV) has commenced mining the Mt Todd gold deposit for client Zapopan. The joint venture partners are Henry Walker Contracting Pty Ltd (50%), the Aboriginal and Torres Strait Islander (ATSIC) Commercial Development Corporation (25%) and the Jawoyn Association (25%). The MJV employs Henry Walker Contracting to manage the mining operations on its behalf.

Mt Todd is approx. 40kms from Katherine and all staff are being housed in the town. Mining operations at present are carried out on an 11 shifts per week basis over 6 days utilising a Liebherr 994 Excavator owned by the Joint Venture and 3 x 777 Dump Trucks hired from Henry Walker Contracting. Anciliary hired equipment is a Komatsu WA600 Loader, D275 Bulldozer and GD625 Grader.

The MJV has started hauling 2.5 million tonnes per annum of ore to the crusher in Phase 1 of the project which has an estimated 3 year life. Zapopan will then treat the crushed ore by the heap leach process and is expected to produce 100,000 ozs of gold per year.

The MJV at present employs 16 people and Henry Walker Contracting has 12 people at the site. Training programmes are being put into place to ensure the Jawoyn employees are fully trained in all aspects of mine site requirements. Phase 2 of the contract still to be let by Zapopan, will be an 8 year mining phase where an expected 4 million tonnes of harder ore will be mined each year.

STOCK EXCHANGE OPEN DAY
BRISBANE 23 October 1993

Henry Walker was one of thirty five of Australia's leading public companies and stockbrokers who took part in the Brisbane Stock Exchange's Open Day on Saturday, 23 October 1993.

The Open Day provided an excellent opportunity for the company to present a public face to potential investors, while also servicing current shareholders.

It was estimated that some 5,000 people attended the Open Day which aims to assist in breadening understanding about the workings of the stockmarket and equity investment amongst members of the public.

Richard Ryan and Karen Murray at the Group's stand in Brisbane.

THE BOARD OF DIRECTORS
of
HENRY WALKER GROUP LIMITED
wish all Staff
and their families a
HAPPY AND JOYFUL CHRISTMAS
and our best wishes are
extended to all for the
NEW YEAR

Page 2 CONTACT

DARWIN AIRPORT RELOCATION

Rossair has recently relocated its Darwin operations into a new facility on the northern side of Darwin Airport, in the general aviation area constructed by the FAC as part of the redevelopment of the airport. The new hangar is capable of accommodating aircraft as large as the de Havilland Dash 8 or the SAAB 340.

The new facility is equipped and staffed to provide a full range of engine, airframe, electrical and instrumentation services to commuter airlines, charter operators, government agencies and private operators. To complement these services, Rossair also retails a wide range of parts, engines, avionics equipment and exchange components from the new premises.

The new Darwin facility will also enable our Northern Territory customers to access other specialized Rossair services such as turbine engine maintenance, propellers, cylinder work, engine driven components plus repair and overhaul of instruments and radios.

This investment continues the company's focus on regional expansion and the provision of specialized maintenance services. In the longer term it is intended to use the facility as a base to extend Rossair's range of services to customers in eastern Indonesia and Papua New Guinea.

NEW DIRECTORS

The group has recently announced new Directors who have joined the Board.

Mr Gatjil Djerrkura OAM becomes a non-executive director. He is Chairman of the Aboriginal and Torres Strait Islander Commercial Development Corporation and General Manager of the Yirrkala Business Enterprise. **Mr Djerrkura** is also Chairman of the Miwatj Aboriginal Health Corporation and Deputy Chairman of North Australian Investment Corporation.

Mt Akio Suzuki becomes a non-executive director. He is the Chief Representative in Australia for the Toyota Tsusho Corporation.

Mr Brian Kimmings is an alternate director for **Mr Gatjil Djerrkura**. He is General Manager of the Aboriginal and Torres Strait Islander Commercial Development Corporation.

THE ANNUAL REPORT - WHAT A SHAREHOLDER THINKS!

The letter below is reproduced in its entirety and was received following the release of the Annual Report.

Subject commendation to the Henry Walker Group for the continued excellence with the company's presentation of the Annual Reports.

As a retired professional broadcasting engineer consultant and one of the early shareholders of the company (now in my wife's name) we have just received and perused the company's 1993 comprehensive annual report and my heart immediately warmed to the well presented notice of the A.G.M. But as a biased semi-professional photographer I was very impressed with the impeccable photography throughout the report which in itself was a masterpiece of presentation in every respect.

On behalf of my wife, the shareholder, I would like to highly commend the Henry Walker Group Limited management and staff for their successful dedication to the company over recent years and I believe such energy will generate even greater success in the future.

Jack Burgesson, M.I.E. Australia
Victoria

CONTACT Page 3

TOYOTA'S 25th BIRTHDAY

Twenty five years ago, in 1968, **Bridge Autos** were awarded the Toyota Franchise in Darwin. And, believe it or not, a Toyota Corona cost $1993.00.

The original business was Bridge Motors which developed in the 1940's in the Stuart Park area near the present site.

The name was changed in 1967 to Bridge Autos when businessman Royce Fitzgerald took over and he successfully won the Toyota franchise in 1968. In those days the company sold the popular Crown Deluxe, the Corolla 1100 Saloon and the Crown pick-up (utility) as well as the Corona.

Present Managing Director, **Tony Shaw** joined the business in 1974, eight weeks before Cyclone Tracy devastated Darwin. The Cyclone severely damaged the premises but it was business as usual a few days later after clearing away the debris.

Further developments took place over the years and by January 1988 Bridge Autos had become part of the Henry Walker Group.

Bridge Autos is now all set to take advantage of a new Toyota November '93 campaign which coincides with the 25th Anniversary

The Old Bridge Autos premises

Tony Shaw said that Bridge broke its long standing vehicle sales record in June this year when the company sold 199 vehicles. The previous best was 104 in May 1985.

"We would like to see a similar result following this Toyota campaign" **Tony** said "but we will wait and see".

The Current Stuart Highway premises

YANDI GOLF DAY

It was another lovely and hot Sunday in the Pilbara for the third Annual Yandi Golf Classic. The scorecard included many locals from Newman, several representatives from BHP Iron Ore and 10 starters up for the day from Perth office. They were in stark contrast to most of the Yandi crew who were just getting their second wind after a serious night's partying. There were few surprises on the day as the course was in fine condition and the normal copious amounts of amber fluid were consumed.

Nonetheless, it was a relief that someone other than **Rob Brierley** took home the winning prizes. This was guaranteed by **Rob's** absence. Congratulations also to **Bernie Rowan** who took out the title of Mens Longest Drive which meant that the Newman Golf Club did not get to clean up altogether.

Peter Claringbull, Bernie Rowan, Hans Kashull preparing (studying) for next award. Person accepting current award (speaking) is the President of the Newman Golf Club.

APIN CONTRACT

Henry Walker Contracting were recently awarded an $11 million contract to construct the services and roads for the next stage of the Waler Barracks development at Palmerston. The project is part of the Army Presence in the North initiative (APIN) undertaken by the Department of Defence.

The job involves installing deep sewer, water, stormwater and electrical and telecommunications services below ground and roads, street lighting and electrical sub stations, including an emergency power house, from ground level up.

The day to day activities in the field are co-ordinated and supervised by **Trevor Wilson**, **Tony Kruger** and **Henri Moulin. Henri** is assisted by **Rod Ward** who came across from WA to help with the substantial roadworks component of the job. On site Management is carried out by **Rob Wallwork**, Project Manager and **Darryl Turner**, Superintendent. **Bruce Jackson** is the Project Engineer, with responsibility for coordinating quality control. The sea of paperwork is calmly managed by Site Clerk **Janys Street**.

Progress has been good since work commenced on site in mid September this year. The total duration of the project is expected to be forty eight weeks, with completion in late July 1994, weather permitting.

VALE JIM HALLION

Jim Hallion or **"Hardrock"** as he was affectionately known, commenced with Henry Walker in 1973. He first started at the Edith River Road job near Katherine and then in subsequent years, followed the Henry Walker projects as a Dozer Operator. When **Jim's** days as a Dozer Operator closed, he moved into the role of a security caretaker for Henry Walker properties in Darwin which he carried out until his death.

Jim passed away on 24th November 1993 in Darwin.

The Management and Staff of Henry Walker Group extend their deepest sympathy to **Jim's** family.

RUSSELL NELLIGAN

"Russell The Bullet" is putting the Company slogan into effect "making the earth move under his feet".

Russell Nelligan, pictured above, is a Disabled Athlete who approached Henry Walker Contracting for sponsorship early in January 1993. He needed financial assistance towards training and costs associated with competitions in the Disabled Sports area, in his case athletics.

In 1992, **Russell** joined the Special Olympics and represented Western Australia at the IV National Games in Brisbane. On the track, **Russell** won one Gold and four Silver medals, one of which was for the five kilometre cross country race. He has participated in netball, cricket, roller-skating and horse riding. In 1992 **Russell** was voted "Netballer of the Year" by the WA Disabled Sports Association.

Currently, **Russell** receives a Disability Support Pension and also has a part-time job as a School Crossing Guard. The HW sponsorship has helped him successfully compete with the best. This is evidenced by his results in the 1993 State Games where he won two Gold, two Silver and one Bronze medal.

His record continues to be impressive in his chosen field and with the V National Games of the Special Olympics being held in Perth in December 1994 we are hoping that the sponsorship helps him to further achieve his goals.

GOOD LUCK RUSSELL !!!

LAND SALES INCREASE

Land developed by Henry Walker Contracting at Palmerston, Katherine and Alice Springs has sold well over the past few months. Land Development Manager, **Malcolm Rawson** said that increasing demand over the past 12 to 18 months has seen sales increase significantly.

"The land bank that the Group has held for many years in the three areas has been sold" **Malcolm** said "and we feel the first home buyer scheme introduced by the N.T. Government together with the concentration of defence facilities at Waler Barracks near Palmerston has had an effect on these increased sales".

In the past 18 months in the suburb of Gray in Palmerston, 160 lots have been made ready for sale and at last count, 143 have either been sold or under contract. Part of these sales took place at a recent auction where 49 blocks were put up and 45 fell under the hammer with the remaining 4 sold after the auction.

"A very pleasing result" commented **Malcolm** "as this was our first experience at such a large auction of land".

Continued development will take place over the next 5 years with some 300 blocks still to be developed in Palmerston, Katherine and Alice Springs.

Bridge Autos' **Leonie Wood** has taken over producing their regular staff newsletter which was renamed Bat News.

Leonie has put quite a lot of thought into the format and is picking up interesting bits and pieces for production. However, like all newsletters, **Leonie** has to chase staff for stories. So to all Bridge staff, give **Leonie** a call and pass on the information so that the newsletter continues successfully.

A piece from the latest Bat News:- Bridge Autos have formed a ladies volley ball team with an unusual name - Bridge Autos Toyota Sheilas! Must be a good outfit - the grading has gone from B grade to D grade.

Training in Indonesia took on a new meaning for Service Manager, **Trevor Kroemer**. For breakfast one morning, he feasted on chilli crab. A brief recess was called in the morning session when **Trevor** had to excuse himself.

The view over Darwin and the Harbour from a high point at Bayview Haven

BAYVIEW HAVEN CANAL ESTATE

The Bayview Haven Canal Estate is a land development project being undertaken by Dover Investments (60% HWG, 40% others) on an elevated area of land overlooking Darwin Harbour.

The site was originally developed during World War II as the Frances Bay Explosives Complex to hold ordnance for the Australian Army, Navy and Air Force and the United States Navy. The original facility was used up until Cyclone Tracy and then fell into disrepair with damage to the buildings by vandals and the weather.

Henry Walker Contracting is constructing the subdivision for Dover Investments and the first stage is expected to be completed toward the end of November.

The location and history of the site has resulted in additional work to that normally required, being carried out on planning, heritage, archaeological and engineering matters. Detailed heritage and archaeological reports were prepared and submitted to the government before any work could be carried out on the site. Several of the original buildings are being preserved as part of a heritage park confined within the site.

After five months work, 51 fully serviced allotments have been completed.

The project also has building lots with a marina frontage as well as the strategically placed elevated blocks with panoramic views. The subdivision is only a short distance to the centre of Darwin and by the time of its completion will take on the "beautiful suburb" description given to the area during the war years by the staff who inspected construction of the military structures.

CONTACT — Page 7

Site Office Wetar Island Indonesia Rainer Rasmussen, Sandra (standing) and Anita.

A happy group at the Newman Cup. Seated in the foreground from left are Peter Claringbull, Tom Holt, Roy Smith, Kathleen Smith and Vivenne Noffs.

Future issues will feature Bridge Autos, Agserv and Rossair

John Ponter, next to the conveyor at the Mount Todd Project.

Kevin Smith ready to go at Yandi.

Wetar Island Indonesia.
From Left: Mujiono, Chris Stephens, Rudy, Haji Arsyad, Herman Schulte, Norman Salanusa, Rainer Rasmussen.

Wetar Island Indonesia
Herman Schulte and
Norman Salanusa.

CONTRACTING COMPANY

Andy Dean (now at Yandi) filling up at the Leinster Project.

Chris Stephens giving directions at Wetar - or is he hitchhiking?

CONTACT Page 9

SAFETY

Safety Audits have been performed at many sites now with the goal of providing safe workplaces and safe methods of work.

Congratulations are in order for Tanami, Koolan and Woolwonga minesites for passing the threshold of 180 LTI free days. At the time of printing Tanami had achieved a record-breaking 210 LTI free days, Koolan had just passed 240 LTI free days and Woolwonga was standing at 277 LTI free days.

Nonetheless, for the 12 month period ending 31 October 1993, initial calculations reveal a rise in the LTI (Lost Time Injury) frequency rate to 17.0 for Contracting as a whole. This is up from the 13.6 LTI frequency rate reported for the 12 months ending 30 June 1993. While stressing that these findings are indeed only preliminary, due care is required if we are to reach our stated goal of a LTI frequency rate of 10.0 or below.

QUALITY ASSURANCE

The Contracting division survived its first "surveillance review" by Bureau Veritas International since having gained accreditation on 12 March 1993. Sites/offices chosen at random were Darwin office, Woolwonga, Bayview Haven and Perth office. Some very minor non-conformances were detected, but were quickly resolved by issuance of corrective actions. The next visit by Bureau Veritas will be in six months time when a full-scale audit will be undertaken.

AGSERV REBUILDS SUPER HAULER

Groote Eylandt Mining Company (GEMCO) has five purpose-built off-road, 850 WR Model Kenworths at its manganese mine off the coast of the Northern Territory.

The trucks have given exceptional service over the years, and even considering the costs of regular maintenance and rebuilds (at around 36,000 operating hours), the trucks are more economically viable than changing to a conveyer belt system.

Although there have been major rebuilds on the island, it is cheaper to ship the trucks to the mainland, than to bring in the parts to do the job.

Agserv Industries, the Group's Truck and Equipment Division in Darwin are currently working on the rebuild of the second Kenworth after being the successful tenderer for the task.

In their Darwin workshop, Agserv strip the trucks right to the ground and replace the engine and transmissions with equipment supplied by GEMCO, but then rebuild the trucks from the chassis up including all electrical and hydraulic gear.

Mudguards and walkways are purchased from local manufacturer, Tristar Engineering, and then bolted together by Agserv.

A 'W' Model cabin is placed on top of the giant and "looks like a pimple on a pumpkin", according to Agserv's **Col Berry** who oversees the project.

For the large truck enthusiast the 850 WR Model Kenworth pulls a lead trailer which is a quad axle with a payload of 60 tonne, then a triaxle also with a 60 tonne carrying load and finally a bogie with a 45 tonne payload.

Agserv has a good completion time with the entire rebuild taking eight to nine weeks.

NEWS BRIEFS

INDONESIA

Target Attained

The Group recently announced that it had reached the stated aim of generating 15% of its contracting turnover from the Indonesian operations.

Two new contracts recently signed by PT Darma Henwa (Contracting's 80% owned Indonesian company) should take the revenue for the Indonesian operations in 93/94 to approx. $19m.

The new contracts are the Kali Kuning roadworks at Wetar Island ($5 million, reported in Vol 4 No. 2) and an earthworks contract at the Petangis Coal project at Kalimantan ($1.6 million).

General Manager Indonesia, **Garret Dixon** said "the two new jobs will boost the employment number of PT Darma Henwa to approximately 200, which is becoming a sizeable work force!!"

Perth Visit

PT Darma Henwa Chief Accountant, **Afrizal** took in the sights of Perth recently when he visited the city with his wife **Santi**. During their stay, **Afrizal** took the time to meet the staff at the Perth office and catch up with **Roy Smith**. It is understood no accounting matters were discussed!!

The word from Jakarta is that **Afrizal** and family already have next years tickets to Adelaide booked!

* * *

RUSTLERS ROOST SOLD

The Groups gold exploration subsidiary Kintaro Gold Mines Pty Ltd has sold its 80% share in the Rustlers Roost Joint Venture. Gold Miner, Valdora Minerals exercised an option to purchase the interest in October 1993.

The sale of Rustlers Roost now leaves only the Driffied Joint Venture interest near Pine Creek as the last major exploration holding of the group.

Kintaro Gold Mines still holds a small number of exploration licences over tenements throughout the Northern Territory.

* * *

KATHERINE

The $900,000 Optech Project on the RAAF Base, Tindal, just outside Katherine is due for completion in late November.

This joint venture between Henry Walker and Concrete Constructions commenced in July and has included water and sewer services, earthworks and roadworks surrounding an Operational and Technical Facilities extension to the Base.

* * *

GROOTE EYLANDT

Minor civil works for BHP Gemco continue on Groote Eylandt including minor roadworks, gravel stockpiling and a recent crack patching programme in preparation for the wet season.

A crushing programme is planned for mid December to replenish stocks of sealing aggregate for the Highway rebuild in Mid '94.

In other news, keen golfers are invited to enter the gruelling "Henry Walker Summer Cup" to be held at the Alyangula Golf Club on December 12th. (For further information contact Groote Site office).

* * *

ROSSAIR'S CANBERRA OUTLET

On the 13th September, Rossair Product Support opened a new outlet at Canberra Airport. The outlet is able to retail a wide range of parts, engines, avionics equipment and exchange components, both in Canberra and the adjoining regions.

Canberra resident, **Michael Kent** has been appointed Manager of the new outlet. **Michael** has been involved in the Aviation industry in the Canberra region for the past five (5) years.

SPORTS AWARDS

Congratulations to **Steven Marshall** aged 10 years who was recently awarded the Schweppes Junior Sportsperson of the Week award. **Steven** is the son of Agserv Industries General Manager, **Peter Marshell.**

Steven's sport is Diving and in November he was named Male Diver of the Year by the N.T. Diving Association. The award came only a year after he took up the sport.

Steven was the Northern Territory's best performer at the Summer National Titles in Melbourne in April when he finished 11th in his age group in both the one metre and three metre springboard events.

Steven Marshall

CONTACT Page 11

McARTHUR RIVER MINE PROJECT

As announced in the September issue of Contact, Henry Walker Contracting were awarded the McArthur River Mine Siteworks Contract.

Work is progressing well with the minesite preparation and the company was recently awarded another contract to build 3.1km of Haul Road from the Minesite to the Carpentaria Highway.

Managing Consultants are Fluor Daniel Australia Limited, working on behalf of McArthur River Mines, a wholly owned subsidiary of Mt. Isa Mines Pty Ltd who are developing a 1.5m tonnes per annum underground lead/zinc/silver mine and processing plant at McArthur River Mine site.

The staff is Project Manager **Malcolm McMinn**; Supervisor **George Lavercombe**; Foreman **Jimmy Mann**, and Site Clerk **Janet Daws**. Heavy emphasis is placed on Safety by Fluor Daniel Aust Ltd and with a crew of approximately 34 employees we are pleased to announce we are a LTI free project to date.

The Mine Site preparation work involves several large hardstand areas and access roads, as well as initial excavations for the underground shafts (portals).

The site is located 720km south-east of Darwin and approximately 100km inland of the Gulf of Carpentaria. The famous fishing town of Borroloola is approximately 60kms west and an enjoyable day's fishing was had recently when **George Lavercombe** (Luv-A-Rum) and crew organised a fishing trip.

McArthur River Recreation
Jimmy Mann (background), Darryl Tinning (subcontractors), and Jeff Williams (subcontractors), holding the fish (and there is plenty of it!)

After a late start (**George** slept in) the crew headed to Batten Point where they boarded "Croc-Spot Tours" and spent the day reef fishing around West Island in the Sir Edward Pellew Group. As the photo shows the fish caught were slightly larger than Noel Dickinson's prize catch shown in the September Contact. The regular Saturday night BBQ at the mess featured grilled reef fish.

Current McArthur River contracts should be completed by mid December, but more on-going contracts may see the crew on a few more fishing trips before the job is completed.

Page 12 CONTACT

EXPORT AWARDS

"Dressed to the Hilt" at the Gala Dinner were from left Robbie Reid, Bernie Rowan, Viv Noffs Frazer Henry, Declan Hoban and Maree Hoban.

A significant achievement was attained by Henry Walker Contracting on 24 August 1993 when it was nominated a finalist in the 1993 West Australian Industry and Export Awards. The company became a finalist in two categories: firstly, for the "Services Export Award", and secondly, for the coveted "Quality Management Award". We were chosen as one of 46 finalists out of a field of 431 companies. Other finalists included companies both large and small, ranging from our clients BHP Iron Ore and CRA to such enterprises as Presbyterian Ladies College and Peters Ice Cream.

The Honourable Derrick Tomlinson (MLC), visited the Perth Office on Friday 1 October 1993 and formally presented the finalist plaques to deputy General Manager, **Kevin Kelly**.

All that was left was to attend the Gala Dinner and Presentation held at the Convention Centre at the Burswood Resort in Perth on Wednesday 13 October. **Frazer Henry** accompanied several employees and their partners to the event all "dressed to the Hilt" in black suits, bow ties and evening dresses. Attendees totalled about 500 as the tension built when the finalists were announced along with brief video descriptions of the companies' involved.

Disappointingly, Contracting missed out in the end as the winners were chosen. A sigh of relief was heard from **Kevin Kelly** as he was spared the ordeal of having to address the hundreds in the audience. Afterwards, over one or two drinks we all took consolation both in the fact that it was a strong first effort for the company, and with the knowledge that had there been a category for the loudest shirt, WA Manager **Bernie Rowan** would have won uncontested!!!

Happy 40th !!!

John Jones, General Manager of HW Contracting achieved another milestone as he turned 40 on 27 November. Thirteen of those years have been spent with Henry Walker at various remote sites and the "big smoke" offices.

"JJ" commenced in October 1979 at Jabiru as Project Manager where Henry Walker was performing earthworks around a new plant site. Thereafter, he was assigned to various civil projects near metropolis' such as Halls Creek and Mosquito Creek. In those days work hours were transmitted to payroll in Darwin by telex, where possible, or over the radio-phone when lucky.

In July 1986, John was appointed General Manager of Contracting. Since then he has helped guide the division from principally a NT-based roadworks contractor with an annual turnover of $28,000,000 to its current entity as a national and overseas competitor with an annual turnover of $125,000,000.

CONGRATULATIONS, JJ and we hope you are around for many years to come.

A young J.J.

The more recent version.

CONTACT Page 13

Who's Who

BARRY LEWIS
AGSERV INDUSTRIES DARWIN

TERRY CORNELIUS
P.T. DARMA HENWA JAKARTA

TODD PENNIFOLD
AIRCRAFT ACCESSORY SERVICES - ADELAIDE

BILL NEILSON
BRIDGE AUTOS NEW CARS - DARWIN

PETER VRUCAN
HW CONTRACTING - DARWIN WORKSHOP

KEN DEAN
HW CONTRACTING - TANAMI

BILL O'BRIEN
ROSSAIR GENERAL AVIATION - ADELAIDE

social chatter

NEW APPOINTMENTS

Bridge Autos

Tracey May
Detailer, New Cars
Appointed 7.9.93

Brendan O'Donnell
Driver, Spare Parts, Berrimah
Appointed 20.9.93

Julie Partridge
Detailer, Used Cars
Appointed 24.9.93

Linda Robb
Cashier, Administration
Appointed 7.9.93

Agserv

Thomas Mitchell
Mechanic, Service Dept
Appointed 16.8.93

Lyle Warden
Diesel Fitter, Service Dept
Appointed 27.9.93

Michael Ryan
Truck Sales Manager
Appointed 20.9.93

Henry Walker Contracting

Robert Wallwork
Project Manager, APIN
Appointed 7.9.93

Robert Buckland
Personnel Officer, Perth
Appointed 23.8.93

Julie Moyle
Site Clerk, Bayview Haven
Appointed 23.8.93

Dave McQuire
Accountant, Mt Todd/Darwin
Appointed 13.9.93

Warren Dumesney
Leibherr Technical Trainer
Appointed 2.10.93

Ian Sharp
Open Pit Superintendent,
Koolan
Appointed 11.10.93

Janys Street
Site Clerk, APIN
Appointed 13.9.93

Geoff Price
Executive Mining Specialist,
Perth
Appointed 11.10.93

Darlene Flockhart
Site Clerk,
Yandi
Appointed 1.11.93

Kevin Broxam
Operator Trainer
Appointed 1.11.93

Terence Early
Technical Superintendent,
Petangis
Appointed 13.9.93

Michael Trainor
Mine Superintendent,
Petangis
Appointed 1.10.93

Richard Hemmingway
Finance Manager,
Jakarta
Appointed 6.9.93

Rossair

Mathew Johnson
Storeman,
Canberra Branch
Appointed 6.9.93

Michael Kent
Manager,
Canberra Branch
Appointed 26.7.93

Christine Jones
Technical Record Officer,
Darwin
Appointed 4.10.93

Georgina Dawson
Receptionist Clerk,
Darwin
Appointed 13.9.93

FIVE YEAR SERVICE

Agserv

Ray McNeil
Parts Department
Commenced 3.8.88

Henry Walker Contracting

Roy Smith
Accounting Manager,
Perth
Commenced 14.11.88

Michelle Garling
Administration,
Darwin
Commenced 14.10.88

Phil McArthur
Project Supervisor
Commenced 20.7.88

Richard Seet
Management Accountant
Commenced 28.11.88

TEN YEARS SERVICE

Bridge Autos

Trevor Kroemer
Service Manager
Commenced 24.10.83

PROMOTIONS

Henry Walker Contracting

Trevor Curtis
Maintenance Supervisor,
Leinster
4.9.93

Brent Goodall
Maintenance Supervisor,
Tanami
18.9.93

Kevin Kruger
Project Supervisor,
Darwin Sites
30.10.93

Peter Derrington
Project Supervisor,
Darwin Sites
30.10.93

TRANSFERS

Henry Walker Contracting

Maurie Evans
Project Supervisor,
Kali Kunung, Indonesia
1.9.93

Herman Schulte
Project Supervisor,
Petangis, Indonesia
1.9.93

BIRTHS

Henry Walker Contracting

Phil & Sharon McArthur
Son Dean
Born 13.10.93

Garret & Blair Dixon
Son Harry
Born 27.9.93

21ST BIRTHDAY

Henry Walker Group

Tina Anthes
Darwin Office
7.11.93

Edward Larner
Adelaide Office
16.11.93

CONTACT Pc

TEAM SPIRITS

On Saturday 6 November, Henry Walker Contracting fielded two teams to compete in the annual Perth Wildcats Sports-a-thon. The venue was the Lords Recreational Sports Centre, the new practice home of the Wildcats. Each team played four sports during the afternoon: basketball, netball, soccer and volleyball.

Competition included teams from BHP Steel, Telecom and a celebrity team that featured Wildcats Steve Davis and Trevor Torrence.

A variety of talent was displayed among the Henry Walker teams including the basketball prowess of Estimator, **Graeme Tyler**. **Sue Strong** scored a lonely goal in the indoor soccer court in a thrashing at the hands of Union Steel. **Bernie Rowan** also scored a goal for the other Henry Walker team but most people remember the centre-court knee scraping gyrations of glee that followed which were meant to mimic Diego Maradona.

Despite minor injuries (with aches and pains still felt on Monday morning) and a couple of savage losses, Henry Walker teams did manage a few wins on the day. A great time was had by all and we all look forward to further competitions. None the less, it was unanimously agreed that we should all stick to Contracting as we would not make any money for Henry Walker in the sports arena!

AS

NEW

USED

CARS

Alistair Montgomery, Bridge Autos Used Car Manager has made many changes since he took over a year ago. "We have had people walking through thinking they are looking at new cars" he said "and that is because we are keen on quality and the better types of vehicles".

Most Bridge Autos used cars are priced between $10,000 and $18,000 with the great majority of them less than 10 years old and all are covered by a 3 month/5000km warranty.

So, if you are looking for good quality and value in a used car, give **Alistair** a call.

KALGOORLIE CONTRACT

Henry Walker Contracting has won a contract to mine gold deposits nea Kalgoorlie for the Poseidon Group.

The contract, worth $28 million involves mining the Jubilee Open Pit for 3 year and the Samphire Open Pit for 2 years. The work will commence in January 1994

Group Managing Director, **Richard Ryan** said the company was encouraged b the Kalgoorlie contract because it was the company's first move into the gol mining capital of the country.

HW Contracting General Manager, **John Jones** said that the Jubilee Mine ha been operating for 7 years and this contract which involves 6.1 million B.C.M (banked cubic metres) is to cut back the eastern wall and deepen the pit. Th Samphire Mine involves Henry Walker Contracting shifting 4.4 million B.C.M.

BLOOD DONORS

Responding to a widely published appeal about a dozen brave office staff from HW Contracting, Perth office made the difficult decision to attend the local St John's Ambulance in Perth to give blood. Even this seemingly uneventful exercise turned into something of an event. Accounts expert **Angie Rapana** was rejected on the spot, having given birth within the last 12 months. Payroll Officer, **Mary Jane Merchant** fainted, ensuring herself extra tea and biscuits. However, most notoriety was reserved for **Frank Ashe**, from whom the St John's staff could only extract half a litre of blood. Reinforcing age-old stereotypes, Plant Manager **Rick Shea** was heard to comment, "Now, I know accountants have only half a heart!"

Your Contact Liaison

Declan Hoban	-	Henry Walker Contracting
Peter Marshell	-	Agserv Darwin
Simon Robertson	-	Adelaide Office
Brian Hawken	-	Agserv Kadina
Leonie Wood	-	Bridge Autos
Trevor Lambert	-	Rossair

ZIP-PRINT DARWIN PH: 47 0179

Henry Walker
Contracting Pty Ltd
YBE
PTY.
LTD.
Joint venturing creates new construction culture
TERRITORY
CONSTRUCTION
ASSOCIATION
REGISTERED BY AUSTRALIA POST - PUBLICATION No. SBP 2338 - ISSN 8353
NORTHERN TERRITORY
CONSTRUCTION
Volume 15 No. 2
November/December 1994

Aboriginal work ethics

The Henry Walker Group is proud of its success in joint venturing with aboriginal groups in the Northern Territory.

Following the successful opening of the Mt Todd mine for which Henry Walker Group and the Jawoyn Association entered a joint venture together with the Aboriginal and Torres Strait Islanders Commercial Development Corporation, Henry Walker entered negotiations with Yirrkala Business Enterprises (YBE).

The result was a joint venture to rebuild a tailings dam for the red mud waste from the alumina refining process.

The dam was built to a new design developed by NABALCO which won the 1994 Engineering Excellence Award.

The award, presented by the Institute of Engineers, Australia was given for the thoroughness and excellence of the engineering design and research that went into changing the waste disposal method used over the last 20 years at the mine to a more environmentally

YBE-HWC joint venture office staff (from left) Rita Finn, Pat Banes, Leonie Westerland, Diane West, Vepessa Gambley, Louise Maymanu, Ledua Rika.

Workshop manager Rossco Ruslint (above left) and project supervisor Wally Dickson. Rossco finished the job with a surprise win on Tattslotto which he said could set him up for life! He would always remember the joint-venture job he said.

Page 14 *Northern Territory Construction* November-December 1994

ix with Henry Walker's

acceptable system. The system had been used in some other mines.

But the judges were impressed with the way that a relatively new and untried process was researched, modified and improved to suit the particular characteristics of the Gove plant red mud waste.

Yirrkala Business Enterprises contributed to the construction of this new disposal system called "dry stacking" introduced two years ago. NABALCO tackled the implementation with two project managers, one for "Ponds Area Earthworks" and one for "Dry Stacking Infrastructure".

Contracts were let to eight site-based contractors for $19.1 million.

The job was completed nearly three months early and $2 million under budget.

The latest YBE-HWC joint venture tackled another stage of the modification of NABALCO's tailings dams. It involved a range of earthworks and an extension to the main stormwater security drain.

The smooth running of the project confirmed both venturers' confidence in sharing the work on a construction project.

"About 15 people worked on the whole project, half Aborigine, half Caucasian Australian," contract manager Graham Cullen said. "It was a happy job — everyone was keen to jump on whatever machinery was needed at that moment.

"We had excellent cooperation from NABALCO through site superintendent Paul Francis of GH&D and NABALCO contracts administrator Chris Smith."

The joint venture worked with quality assurance systems which were supervised by site engineer Bruce Jackson.

On-site manager was Gatjil Djerrkura. Project manager was Graham Chester.

"Cooperation was tremendous," Graham Cullen said, echoing Gatjil Djerrkura's words. "YBE's administration was good, so was ours.

"All the machinery, owned and operated by YBE was well maintained.

"We contributed in the administration and tendering and on the quality assurance systems side."

The tailings dam and the expanse of earthworks

Henry Walker Group was recently highly commended by the Defence Department for its quality work on the subdivisional preparation for APIN infrastructure in the Litchfield Shire near Palmerston.

Henry Walker Group's interest in making joint venturing with aboriginal groups a success has been formulated into company policy this year.

It was recently distributed to all sites of the contracting division of the group.

Henry Walker Group Limited, it says, while wishing to make a profit from joint venture projects with aboriginal communities, as a matter of policy and philosophy, will remain sensitive to the cultural concerns of the local community.

The policy states that the Group will encourage and help develop an aboriginal employment, educational and training strategy wherever possible and this will apply particularly with joint venture projects between the company and Aborigines.

The Group has decided that field staff must have a firm understanding of Aboriginal and Torres Strait islander issues and will get suitable training to achieve this.

Senior executives have agreed to be conversant with these issues.

Henry Walker Group, as a matter of policy, recognises that cultural awareness of the two indigenous cultures must always be considered in management and training programs for Group staff.

Already the company has run training courses for Jawoyn plant operators in Katherine.

The business has been established to compete for substantial civil and mining contracts that have the capacity to offer training and employment to a significant number of Indigenous people in the area.

Although only recently commenced, Ngarda has already won two major contracts. The first was for Western Mining Corporation's Leinster Nickel Operations in the northern goldfields. The second, for Woodside Mines Train No. 4 projects at Karratha in conjunction with Ausco Building Systems.

Retail Trade

Peter Kittle Motor Company – Northern Territory

Peter Kittle Motor Company operates as a motor vehicle dealership in two locations in the Northern Territory: Alice Springs and Tennant Creek. It holds a number of vehicle franchises including Toyota, Mitsubishi, Diahatsu, Holden and Nissan. The company also deals in used cars, vehicle spare parts, car accessories and motor vehicle service operations and a car wash operation in Alice Springs.

The business also operated a dealership in Katherine - that business was sold during 2000-01.

The Peter Kittle Motor Company was established in 1992 as a trading name for the joint venture (Alice Car Centre Pty Ltd). The joint venture has three partners, Goldsack Nominees Pty Ltd (25%), Yaamba Pty Ltd (25%) and CAAMV Trust (50% representing the interests of IBA and Centrecorp Aboriginal Investment Corporation Pty Ltd). IBA's interest in CAAMV Trust represents a 17.7% equity in the joint venture.

At 30 June 2001, the joint venture had 107 employees in its two locations. There are nine Indigenous employees in the venture.

Appendix E

Assorted articles relating to casinos

And:

- NT Government Hansard papers recording 'Statement by the Northern Territory Chief Minister, Paul Everingham announcing the take-over of the management of the Casinos.
- Joint Press Release from NT Chief Minister Paul Everingham and Federal Hotel's John Haddad announcing reconciliation of their differences.
- Letter from NT Chief Minister Ian Tuxworth to Federal Treasurer Paul Keating re new international operators.

M-942-84

30 SEPTEMBER 1984

STATEMENT BY THE NORTHERN TERRITORY CHIEF MINISTER, PAUL EVERINGHAM

AN AGREEMENT SIGNED IN LONDON ON FRIDAY WILL ALLOW TWO OF THE WORLD'S BEST-KNOWN CASINO OPERATORS TO TAKE OVER THE MANAGEMENT OF THE NORTHERN TERRITORY'S CASINOS IN DARWIN AND ALICE SPRINGS.

THE CHIEF MINISTER, MR PAUL EVERINGHAM, ANNOUNCED THAT THE TWO CASINOS WILL BE OPERATED BY DIAMOND LEISURE PTY LTD, A COMPANY WHICH WOULD COMPRISE PRATTS OF THE UNITED STATES AND ASPINALLS OF LONDON, AS SOON AS FINAL APPROVAL IS RECEIVED FROM THE FOREIGN INVESTMENT REVIEW BOARD.

PENDING F.I.R.B. APPROVAL, DIAMOND LEISURE PTY LTD COMPRISES NORTHERN TERRITORY SHAREHOLDERS.

HE SAID THE CASINOS WOULD BE OWNED BY THE TERRITORY PROPERTY TRUST.

THE TRUST WILL COMPRISE HENRY AND WALKER LIMITED AS THE MAJORITY INTEREST, NORTHERN TERRITORY AND AUSTRALIAN EQUITY HOLDERS, THE OVERSEAS OPERATORS, AND A TOKYO-BASED CONSTRUCTION CONSORTIUM, KUMAGAI.

ADDITIONAL UNITS HAVE BEEN SET ASIDE FOR FURTHER PARTICIPATION BY TERRITORY AND AUSTRALIAN INTERESTS.

THE AGREEMENT APPOINTING DIAMOND LEISURE AS OPERATORS OF BOTH CASINOS WAS SIGNED IN LONDON ON FRIDAY BY NTDC CHAIRMAN, MR RAY MCHENRY, AND EXECUTIVES FROM PRATTS AND ASPINALLS.

2

THE SIGNING OF THE LONDON AGREEMENT AND THE ESTABLISHMENT OF THE TERRITORY PROPERTY TRUST AS OWNER OF THE CASINO PROPERTIES PAVES THE WAY FOR MULTI-MILLION DOLLAR HOTEL DEVELOPMENTS IN DARWIN AND ALICE SPRINGS.

THE CHAIRMAN OF THE BOARD OF THE NEW OPERATING COMPANY, DIAMOND LEISURE PTY LTD, IS MR RICHARD RYAN, A DARWIN CHARTERED ACCOUNTANT WHO IS A DIRECTOR OF HENRY AND WALKER LIMITED.

CHIEF MINISTER EVERINGHAM HANDED OVER THE NEW GAMING AND LIQUOR LICENCES TO MR RYAN DURING A PRESS CONFERENCE IN THE BOARD ROOM OF THE DARWIN CASINO SHORTLY AFTER 3:00AM TODAY. THE PRESS CONFERENCE WAS ATTENDED BY A SENIOR EXECUTIVE FROM DIAMOND LEISURE, MR CHRIS RAPHAEL, AS WELL AS MR NEVILLE WALKER, MR FRASER HENRY, MR TED BAILEY OF HENRY AND WALKER, AND MR T. MITANI REPRESENTING KUMAGAI.

MR WALKER SAID FULL DETAILS OF HIS FIRM'S PARTICIPATION IN THE TERRITORY PROPERTY TRUST ARE BEING DISCLOSED TODAY TO THE ADELAIDE STOCK EXCHANGE.

KUMAGAI IS ALREADY INVOLVED IN PROPOSALS FOR THE CONSTRUCTION OF A CASINO/HOTEL COMPLEX ON THE OLD ADELAIDE RAILWAY STATION AND OTHER LARGE DEVELOPMENTS IN AUSTRALIA.

MR EVERINGHAM SAID NEGOTIATIONS WOULD CONTINUE WITH ELDERS IXL AND TERRITORY INTERESTS TO BECOME INVOLVED IN THE PROPERTY TRUST, BUT EXTRA PARTICIPATION WAS NOT CRUCIAL TO THE SUCCESS OF THE CASINO DEVELOPMENTS AS CURRENT INDICATIONS WERE THAT THE FULL ALLOCATION OF TRUST UNITS WOULD BE TAKEN UP.

ENDS

M-994-84

13 OCTOBER 1984

JOINT PRESS RELEASE BY THE NORTHERN TERRITORY CHIEF MINISTER, PAUL EVERINGHAM AND MANAGING DIRECTOR OF FEDERAL HOTELS, MR JOHN HADDAD

THE NT'S CHIEF MINISTER PAUL EVERINGHAM AND FEDERAL HOTELS' JOHN HADDAD ANNOUNCED THAT THEY HAD RECONCILED THEIR DIFFERENCES FOLLOWING THE RECENT CHANGE OF OWNERSHIP OF THE DARWIN AND ALICE SPRINGS CASINOS.

MR EVERINGHAM SAID HE HAD SEEN FEDERAL HOTELS' MOST RECENT PRESS RELEASE AND REPORT TO THE STOCK EXCHANGES, AND WAS HAPPY TO ACCEPT FEDERALS ASSURANCES THAT THEIR GROUP ASSETS EXCEEDED THEIR LIABILITIES BY MORE THAN $30 MILLION.

"IT SEEMS LIKELY THAT THE DIFFICULTIES FEDERAL HOTELS HAD BEEN EXPERIENCING LAST YEAR ARE NOW BEHIND THEM," MR EVERINGHAM SAID.

MR HADDAD SAID FROM MELBOURNE, THAT HE WAS DELIGHTED TO ACCEPT THE CHIEF MINISTER'S ASSURANCES, AND IN THE SPIRIT OF GOOD WILL FEDERALS WOULD TAKE NO FURTHER ISSUE WITH PAST EVENTS. MR HADDAD ALSO SAID THAT THE LEGAL ACTION TAKEN AGAINST MR EVERINGHAM WOULD NOW BE DROPPED.

"WE ARE NOW LOOKING FORWARD TO AN EARLY FINALISATION OF THE VALUATION PROCESS AND PAYMENT. FEDERALS THEMSELVES WILL MOVE QUICKLY AND MR EVERINGHAM HAS ASSURED ME THAT THE NORTHERN TERRITORY GOVERNMENT WILL DO ITS BEST TO ENSURE A SPEEDY CONCLUSION TO THE MATTER," MR HADDAD SAID.

ENDS

ATTACHMENT C

41AP- * -11A08- .-019-N-1018-84
41BP- * -11A09- .- -

TO: THE HON. PAUL KEATING,
TREASURER.

ORIGINAL PAPER
No.
Laid upon the Table
27 / 2 / 85

FROM: THE HON. IAN TUXWORTH,
CHIEF MINISTER,
NORTHERN TERRITORY.

20 OCTOBER 1984

I WAS DISAPPOINTED AND PERPLEXED TO LEARN OF YOUR DECISION TO PROHIBIT FOR 90 DAYS, PROPOSALS BY INTERNATIONALLY RENOWNED OPERATORS TO LEASE AND OPERATE THE HOTEL CASINO COMPLEXES IN DARWIN AND ALICE SPRINGS.

IT WOULD APPEAR THAT THE MAIN GROUNDS FOR YOUR DECISION IS THAT THE PREVIOUS OPERATORS FEDERAL HOTELS, AN AUSTRALIAN COMPANY, STILL WISHES TO OPERATE THE TWO CASINOS.

THE N.T.GOVERNMENT HAS ALREADY MADE THE DECISION THAT FEDERAL HOTELS IS NOT A SUITABLE OPERATOR OF N.T. CASINOS. THEREFORE, THE FACT THAT FEDERAL HOTELS WISHES TO RETURN TO THE TERRITORY AS CASINO OPERATORS IS OF ACADEMIC INTEREST ONLY.

THE DECISION REGARDING FEDERALS WAS MADE AFTER CLOSELY OBSERVING FEDERALS' PERFORMANCE OVER THE LAST FIVE YEARS, AND DETAILS OF THIS HAVE ALREADY BEEN SUPPLIED TO FIRB OFFICERS. THIS INFORMATION IS HIGHLY CRITICAL OF FEDERALS AND I DO NOT WISH TO CANVAS IT FURTHER IN THIS TELEX.
THERE ARE NO AUSTRALIAN INTERESTS OTHER THAN FEDERALS WHO WOULD BE CAPABLE OF OPERATING A CASINO OF INTERNATIONAL STANDARD. THIS IS EVIDENCED BY THE FACT THAT CASINOS IN QUEENSLAND, SOUTH AUSTRALIA AND WESTERN AUSTRALIA ARE TO BE OPERATED BY FOREIGN OPERATORS. I UNDERSTAND YOU HAVE ALREADY GIVEN APPROVAL FOR THESE OPERATORS TO CONDUCT BUSINESS IN AUSTRALIA.
THE N.T.GOVERNMENT BELIEVES IT HAS SELECTED THE BEST POSSIBLE OPERATORS FOR ITS CASINOS AND STRONGLY BELIEVES THAT THEY WILL CONDUCT THE OPERATIONS IN THE WAY WHICH WE HAVE ALWAYS WISHED -- THAT IS, AS THE FOCAL POINT FOR INTERNATIONAL TOURISM TO THE NORTHERN TERRITORY.

THE TERRITORY PROPERTY TRUST, THE OWNER OF THE CASINO PROPERTIES, ADVISES ME THAT YOUR DECISION COULD WELL PUT IN JEOPARDY FINALISATION OF THEIR ARRANGEMENTS WITH THE NEW OPERATORS. I WOULD EXPECT THEY WILL CONTACT YOU TO EXPRESS THEIR CONCERNS.

I URGE YOU THEREFORE TO RECONSIDER YOUR DECISION AS SOON AS POSSIBLE. IF THERE IS ANY FURTHER INFORMATION THAT YOU REQUIRE, PLEASE HAVE YOUR OFFICERS CONTACT MY OFFICERS.

YOURS SINCERELY,
I.L.TUXWORTH,
CHIEF MINISTER.

ENDS

AAAA

NT expels owners of casinos

By BRIAN JOHNSTONE of AAP

FEDERAL Pacific Hotels was yesterday expelled by the Northern Territory Government as the owner-operator of the two casino-hotels it has built in Darwin and Alice Springs with no idea how much it will be paid for the properties.

The Territory's Liberal Country Government invoked compulsory acquisition legislation at 3am yesterday and handed the licence over to the new casino owners, the Territory Property Trust, which combines Australian, Japanese, American and British business interests.

Executives and key staff from Federal were still packing up around the Mindal Beach Casino in Darwin after a massive stock-take when the Northern Territory's Chief Minister, Mr Everingham, began outlining details of the new casino management structure at a 3am news conference in the casino's convention room.

Mr Everingham announced that the Territory's only public company, Henry and Walker Ltd, would have a controlling 57 per cent interest in the trust.

Japan's third largest construction company Kumagai Gumi, would have 14 per cent, leading British casino operator Aspinall Holdings and the Pratt hotel group, operator of the Sands Casino in Atlantic City, would each have 10 per cent.

"The remaining 9 per cent of the units have been set aside for further participation by Territory and Australian business interests," Mr Everingham said.

"Negotiations are continuing with Elders IXL on their possible involvement."

Mr Everingham said the chairman of the Northern Territory Development Corporation, Mr Ray McHenry, had signed an agreement last Friday with Pratts and Aspinall in London which appointed them joint operators of the two casinos.

Pratts and Aspinall had formed a company, Diamond Leisure Pty Ltd, which would operate the casinos as soon as final approval was received from the Foreign Investment Review Board.

Pending FIRB approval, Mr Everingham said this company would comprise Northern Territory shareholders.

He said the Territory Property Trust had an initial paid-up capital of $28 million.

Federal asked the Northern Territory Government for $55 million for its two properties after Mr Everingham told the group earlier this year that his Government intended bringing in new operators.

Federal has agreed reluctantly to sell the property but the compulsory legislation was brought in when negotiations broke down after the Government refused to meet the Federal price.

The Government offered $47.1 million. Under the compulsory acquisition legislation, which was passed in the August budget sessions of the Northern Territory Parliament and assented to on September 7, Government valuers will today begin determining the amount of compensation to be paid to Federal.

The Government will make *independent compensation* determinations to Federal lenders, including the Commonwealth Bank, Westpac and Standard Chartered Finance.

Mr Everingham said the signing of the London agreement and the establishment of the Territory Property Trust as owner of the casino properties paved the way for multi-million dollar hotel developments in Darwin and Alice Springs.

It is understood that Kumagai, which is a competitor with Federal for a casino licence in Adelaide, will be heavily involved in a proposed $250-million redevelopment scheme.

However, Mr Everingham gave no details and did not give reporters the chance to question him on this.

He ended the news conference about ten minutes after it began, walking away from a number of questions with an invitation to journalists to join him in a drink at a celebration party.

The news conference was attended by a vice president of Pratts, Mr Chris Raphael; directors Neville Walker, Fraser Henry, Ted Bailey, Richard Ryan from the local company; and Kumagai's managing director, Mr Tony Mitani.

Mr Ryan said he would be interim chairman of the board of Diamond Leisure.

Mr Everingham handed Mr Ryan the new gaming and liquor licences just before he ended the news conference. The gaming licence will be renewable each year, breaking the 15-year monopoly Federal was given six years ago.

Diamond Leisure will pay 8 per cent gaming tax on gross profits compared to the 20 per cent paid by Federal in Darwin and 15 per cent in Alice Springs.

The company will also pay 10 per cent of the final purchase price per annum.

After five years the Territory Government will share one third of the profits from the casinos.

FEDERAL: WE DIDN'T WANT TO SELL

Federal Hotels revealed today they were "reluctant" sellers of their two NT casinos.

Managing director, Mr John Haddad, said the Government told his company if it did not sell it would be putting back tourism in the Territory.

He said Federal Hotels had intended to stay in the Territory for many years.

"We are long-term developers, we did not initiate this project," he said.

Mr Haddad said there was no question of Federal Hotels pulling out of the Territory altogether.

Investment

He said the investment in the Don, Marrara and Crossways (Katherine) hotels would remain.

Mr Haddad said he wanted to put to rest any suggestion that his company was getting out of the casinos because of financial losses.

"The Mindil Beach is doing very well. We have 90 per cent occupancy.

"If the Chief Minister scrapped this plan tomorrow we would still be here."

Mr Haddad said he had no doubt the casinos as they were established had be . catalyst for the intere. of "these overseas people."

"I am only putting a personal view but I'm not sure that they would have had the same interest if the casinos themselves were not established the way they are at the present time," he said.

"I might also say that we thought we would have been here a lot longer time than we have been."

Mr Haddad said he believed the marketing emphasis might change under the proposed joint venture.

He said his group had concentrated on drawing a mix of local and overseas people to the casinos and concentrating on a spread o gambling activities.

The big NT casino gamble: How Federal Hotels were finessed and the Government went international. PETER WILSON — Page 6.

"We have established unique controls in our casinos that are not in these casinos that Mr Everingham is talking about," he said.

"When they come here they will have to perform under the conditions established by the NT Government. That is a plus for Australia. English casinos do not have anything like the controls in Australia and the casinos in Atlantic City are totally different to ours.

"They rely tremendously on poker machines. Sixty per cent of their business comes from the 'slots' as they call them.

"Aspinalls do have a good reputation although they have very small casinos in London. They concentrate on high-rollers ... they concentrate on four or five people that may be capable of turning over a million pounds on one table."

The Chief Minister, Mr Everingham, said Aspinalls had world-wide contacts with the wealthy gamblers of Asia and the Middle East.

It was reputed around the world to be the place where the "highest of the high rollers resort when they go to London and London, in money terms, is probably the serious gambling capital of the world."

He said the NT Government had letters of commitment from Aspinalls and Pratt Hotels of the U.S. on the joint venture agreement and hoped to be in a position within three to four months to table Heads of Agreement in the Legislative Assembly.

"These people say they want to get into Asia because they believe there is a great market there," he said.

He said Hong Kong, Macao, Malaysia, and Indonesia were closed to them for various reasons so they had decided on the NT.

Marketing

Mr Everingham said evaluation teams of accountants would be appointed by the Government and the Federal Hotels group to price the two casinos.

The Territory project participants would pay to Federal Hotels within 45 days of those valuati.. being delivered the average of the two valuations.

Both parties had agreed on this.

Mr Everingham said under the proposals substantial additional hotel and tourist unit accommodation would be built in Darwin and Alice Springs.

In Darwin, upwards of 900 additional hotel rooms would be established in a staged development on the old

• Cont. Page 2

Casino deal

• From Page 1

Darwin hospital site overlooking Mindil Beach.

In Alice Springs more than 300 additional rooms would be built on a site at the Alice Springs Golf Course next to the casino.

Marketing would be undertaken by the Swiss-owned international condominium marketing organisation, Propinvest (UK) Limited.

This accommodation would be largely marketed overseas.

Mindil Beach, built at a cost of more tha. $30 million will be one year old on Saturday, while the Alice Springs complex cost about $18 million

Casinos meeting planned

A director of Henry & Walker Ltd will soon meet the British and American interests which will take on the operation of the two Territory casinos later this year.

Mr Neville Walker said yesterday arrangements were in hand to meet representatives of Aspinalls in London and the Pratt Hotel group of the United States.

Mr Walker said he thought it would take more than four months to set up the company — with the NTDC — which is to buy the Darwin and Alice Springs casinos from the Federal Hotels group.

Talking about the property trust to be set up to own the casinos and the $200 million tourism development at Darwin's old hospital site and next to the Alice Springs Casino, Mr Walker said it all looked very exciting.

He said that his company would almost certainly be buying equity in the proposed property trust.

N.T NEWS
17/4/84

N.T. NEWS 18/4/84

9

Pratt plans review for NT casinos

The American Pratt Hotels group is poised to send a company official to the Northern Territory next week to review the financial structure of the casinos.

By PETER WILSON

The foreign operations head of the Pratt group, Mr Chris Raphael, told The NT News this morning that someone was on stand-by to come to the Territory to conduct the review.

Mr Raphael said that both his company and Aspinalls of London were well placed in the "Middle-East and Asian gambling market."

He said those interests, especially in Asia, would be interested in coming to Darwin and Alice Springs to gamble rather than flying to Atlantic City or London.

"Aspinalls and ourselves are in a financial situation to be able to cope with super high-rollers who are prepared to use a million dollars a night," Mr Raphael said.

The redevelopment of the hospital site in Darwin and the development next to the Alice Springs Casino were necessary adjuncts to the full utilisation of the casinos.

Operations

Mr Raphael said the two operations were at present too small — in terms of accommodation — to use the gambling facilities fully.

He discounted the part the local population could play in turning the gambling operations into an attractive, viable position.

Mr Raphael said the joint venturers would review the controls imposed by the Northern Territory Government on the casino operations.

He said that they would do that with the Government's blessing.

"But let me stress this. There is nothing wrong with the strict controls as they stand," he said.

"We expect to be able to bring substantial new and foreign business to the Northern Territory."

Complete plans for the highly secret redevelopment of the old hospital site project were found by Mindil Beach Hotel security men on top of a poker machine about four weeks ago.

The plans were drawn by Darwin architects, Hans Vos Planning Consultants.

The plans show the proposed marina facilities, the hotel and the siting of the condominiums.

The plans were apparently meaningless to security staff at Mindil Beach until Tuesday morning when they were retrieved from the safe in which they had been lodged after being found.

Sir James Goldsmith: 'Attila the Hun with financial genius: Page 6

Centralian Advocate

COMMENT

Thinking big: the way to go

18/4/8

SALE of the Alice Springs and Darwin casinos in a development deal involving the golf course estate in Alice Springs and the old Darwin hospital site marks the start of a very bold venture indeed for the Northern Territory. Let's hope that it all works, for the sake of the developers and the NT Development Corporation, which is backing the loan for the Australian interest.

New management of the two casinos and the involvement of the NT public company, Henry and Walker, is certainly of enormous significance to the Territory. More significant, perhaps, is the opportunities for promoting two of the Territory's major tourist attractions through the involvement of overseas interests.

It was a bold move by Federal Hotels to apply for the casino licences and invest in the bricks and mortar to make them a reality. While the Darwin casino is doing reasonably well, the Alice Springs casino really hasn't taken off in terms of revenue. The hordes of "wealthy Asian gamblers" that were expected just haven't materialised in Alice Springs — and not too many in Darwin either.

The failure to promote both establishments worldwide cannot be entirely blamed on Federal Hotels. The relatively few overseas tourists is both a reflection of Australia's isolation and the complicated logistics of promoting overseas without a network and back-up to make it effective.

Pratt Hotels and Aspinalls are experienced operators on an international scale, with the links to make promotion work. The Federal Government and the airlines must now work on the same sort of scale to develop both Alice Springs and Darwin as international tourist destinations. We will need more international and domestic flights to cater for the needs of visitors — and surely, at last, not just upgrading but total re-development of the Alice Springs and Darwin air terminals.

EDERAL WILL
F CASINOS
SELL

/o

CENTRALIAN ADVOCATE 18/4/84

Federal Hotels has agreed to sell out of the Darwin and Alice Springs casinos in preference for a multi-million dollar development scheme.

It has been proposed that two U.S. and British casino operators take over management of the Alice Springs and Darwin casinos.

As part of the scheme, 12.12 ha of land on the new golf course estate in Alice Springs, next to the casino, will be compulsorily acquired by a property trust to be formed soon.

This land will be used for a $40 million condominium development being financed by a Swiss-UK consortium, Propinvest UK Limited.

The 300-room development will include a central hotel facility of 180 rooms, 120 mini-townhouses, two artificial lakes, undercover swimming pools and tennis courts.

Golf course developer, Mr Gary Hunt, said he was pleased with the scheme but it would mean redesigning a major part of the golf course estate.

"We're working on that now," Mr Hunt said.

He said the land would be bought at a price determined by the Land Valuation Tribunal.

HOSPITAL

In Darwin, it is proposed that Propinvest will also develop a $160 million condominium complex including 900 hotel rooms, to be built next to the Mindil Beach casino on the proposed hospital site.

In the meantime, the two casino properties will be bought initially by a company, made up of the only Territory public company, Henry and Walker, and the Northern Territory Development Corporation.

A property trust will be formed to take over the casino properties from the company.

The trust will then appoint new operators to the casino, proposed at this stage to be a joint operation between the US company, Pratt Hotels, and a UK company, Aspinalls of London.

Pratt Hotels, a large chain of hotels operating under the Holiday Inn flag, operators of the Sands Casino in Atlantis City.

Aspinalls is a leading British casino operator.

The major new developments were announced at a joint press conference on Monday by Chief Minister, Mr Paul Everingham, and Federal Hotels.

However, the proposed property trust will also take up an interest in the large condominium developments proposed to be built in Alice Springs and Darwin.

The trust will be 51 per cent Australian controlled — that is Henry and Walker.

The remaining 49 per cent will be owned by Aspinalls of London and Pratt Hotels.

Mr Everingham said the trust deed would contain a provision where the Territory Government could, within the first seven years of operation, require share units to be offered to the public on the basis that Territory residents would have first option.

He said the involvement of leading overseas casino operators would attract substantial numbers of overseas visitors to the Territory.

It would open up new opportunities for marketing Territory attractions outside Australia and particularly in Asia, he said.

"The additional employment to be generated by the project will run into thousands," Mr Everingham said.

"The marketing of accommodation units overseas will increase world-wide awareness of

Cont P9

CASINO SALE...

From P1

an interest in the Territory and its development opportunites."

Chairman of Federal Hotels, Mr Greg Farrell, said he was delighted that an agreement was able to be reached so that the existing successful casino developments could be made part of the overall plans for development of the two areas.

"It is not my company's policy to sell casino assets, but I was persuaded by the logic of incorporating the two properties in the overall development scheme," Mr Farrell said.

To ensure an effective changeover, Federal Hotels have agreed to be retained as consultants to the new owners and operators for at least 12 months.

12

'Key' to the gamble

The success or failure of plans for the $200m Dasrwin gambling centre plus more than a thousand extra hotel rooms will depend entirely on the city being included on the "international network."

Chief Minister, Paul Everingham displayed a model to the media on Tuesday and gave details of development plans on the old Darwin Hospital site taking in Myilly Point.

They included two huge hotel towers featuring 900 rooms and additional casino facilities, plus condominium style units to be offered as investments to foreign investors in the project.

The government have to negotiate with the private owners of land and fine houses on Myilly Point, many of whom will not want to move.

Mr Everingham explained after displaying the model of the main development that the buildings were in "Mexican style."

They would not be built to that style here but in typical "frontier town" but of modern style.

Getting the deal together involves Federal Hotels selling both the Darwin and Alice Springs casinos and other facilities to a joint company involving the NT Development Corporation and the big local company of Henry and Walker.

NTDC will hold 51 per cent of the interest, and the price for the Federals properties is expected to be around $50m.

Henry and Walker could not be contacted yesterday to confirm whether they will be borrowing or spending from their own resources to find its share.

Operators of the casinos and hotels will be one of Britain's top casino businesses, Aspinalls of London, and Pratt Hotels of America.

Concern for casino control

Federal Hotels managing director, Mr John Haddad this week said he had been worried about outside interests controlling gambling.

He told an ABC reporter there had always been this concern.

"We feel we've established unique controls and, you know, in the Victorian inquiry the judge found that our casinos were scrupulously run and when he went overseas he found others were not.

"Now it's not for me to criticise overseas operators, all I can say is that our casinos have never had any insinuation of malpractice leveled against them and we want to make sure, we need to make sure, that this does not occur in other states.

Asked if the NT government threatened to withdraw Federal's casino licence and change the conditions if he didn't agree to hand it over, Mr Haddad replied ... "No they didn't."

"I don't think they'd be in a position to do that, but they made it perfectly clear that if we didn't agree we would be charged with seriously inhibiting what they consider to be the master tourist plan for the Northern Territory, and we as a company are not prepared to be placed in that sort of invidious situation."

Earlier Chief Minister Paul Everingham was asked why his government had put pressure on Federal Hotels?

"Well there's a provision in the agreement whereby the NT Can acquire anywhere up to 100 per cent of the Federal's property at anytime within seven years of the signature of the agreement.

He further added: "I'm not saying that Federals are overjoyed but they in fact signed the agreement and this provision has always been available to the NT and we'd be happy if Federals continued with it."

Mr Everingham said Federal Hotels "will probably come out at least with what it cost them."

DARWIN
ADVERTISER 19/4/84

25

$200m CASINO DEAL FACES COST PROBLEMS

Mr Everingham

By Patrick Cusick

The NT Government has run into difficulties in negotiations with overseas casino operators to establish a $200m casino complex in Darwin.

A leaked negotiating document prepared by the US-based Pratt Hotels has highlighted major differences between the parties as to how the complex will be funded and operated.

Chief Minister Paul Everingham announced last April that a deal had been agreed to between Pratt Hotels, Aspinalls of London, the Territory Government and the Swiss marketing group, Propinvest Ltd.

Mr Everingham said in an ABC interview that the government would be involved to "the minimal degree" and would provide only "roads and sewerage and similar works."

In return the government was "asking 33⅓ per cent" equity in the project.

But the Pratt document presented to the Legislative Assembly on Tuesday by Opposition Leader Bob Collins showed a sharp contrast in how Pratt Hotels envisage the NT Government's involvement.

CHIEF DENIES LOAN OFFER

Pratt Hotels, according to the document, are seeking:

- $25m government loan at six per cent interest.
- 15 years tax exempt operation.
- 30 years gambling monopoly.
- One third direct purchase by the Northern Territory Development Corporation.

The leaked document further states that the Territory Government will be pressed to provide almost 50 per cent of the working capital for the first property trust and purchase a third of a second trust.

Mr Everingham replied that "Pratt Hotels can prepare all the negotiating documents it likes. Pratt Hotels' negotiating documents have no bearing on the position of the Northern Territory Government.

The Chief Minister denied that Pratt Hotels had been offered any loan.

"I do not know yet what particular terms our negotiating team in London has arrived at on any particular point.

"I know that certain principles were arrived at in the discussions that I had overseas," he added.

A top level Territory negotiating team -- headed by NTDC chairman Ray McHenry -- is currently in London holding discussion with the casino operators.

ADVERTISE DARWIN

THURSDAY, JUNE 7 1984

FROM P1

Casino dealings

Mr Everingham said there were three stages in the negotiations: the principle, the heads of agreement and the final agreement.

During question time the Treasurer Marshall Perron said the Assembly will be advised of "certain information relating to the contingent liabilities of the government in the period up to date."

"It would be inappropriate to try and and assess the extent of government contingent liability when these matters have not been finalised," he added.

Mr Everingham said the negotiations are expected "to take several further months to complete."

In answer to a question referring to the Darwin Performing Arts Centre project Mr Everingham said the financiers with whom Asia North had been dealing "have queried the situation because of the announcement of the additional major hotel projects in Darwin.

"Bankers and financiers tend to become extremely nervous.

"Unfortunately, they do not have the confidence in the Northern Territory Government . . . in our ability to develop the tourist industry in the Territory."

His statement contrasts with remarks he made in last month's ABC interview in which he stated that there "are people falling all over themselves, banks, at the moment to lend money to us on this project."

Meanwhile company executives involved in the planned Sheraton Hotel complex in Mitchell Street said Mr Everingham had assured them that after completion of the project there would still be 100 beds short in the tourist season.

A spokesman for the group said that work will begin in October.

Much of the finance for the hotel project i;s being provided by NTDC loans.

DEAN'S VIEW...
NT RAILWAY
WEST LANE CAR PARK
PERFORMING ARTS CENTRE
MINDIL BEACH CASINO
PLEASE DO NOT TOUCH THE EXHIBITS
MUSEUM OF ARTS AND SCIENCES
WHITE ELEPHANT COLLECTION
Courtesy of
NT GOVERNMENT
DEAN.

12 days to leave town

ADVERTISER 19/9/86

Who is taking over?

The Casino Affair
by Malcolm Ormiston

With only 12 days to go before Federal Hotels vacate their premises the NT Government appears to have only found between $10 and $20 million towards the purchase of the Territory's two casinos.

A reliable source has told The Advertiser the government's major funding hope, Elders IXL, is only prepared to get involved to the tune of more than $10 million and less than $20 million.

Asking

The price of the casinos, which the government is compulsorily acquiring, will presumably be somewhere between Federal's asking price of $55 million and the government's offer of $47.1 million.

The new, foreign operators of the casinos take over from 3am on October 1 and will lease the buildings from a yet-to-be formed trust of nebulous composition, which will own the casinos.

Elders IXL chairman, Mr John Elliot, was in a board meeting yesterday and unavailable for comment. Northern Territory Development Corporation chairman, Mr Ray McHenry, said he wouldn't discuss the trust, but it was shaping up.

Mr McHenry said the new operators, Pratts and Aspinalls, were still meeting on the final details and an agreement was expected soon.

Personnel from the two operators will be arriving shortly to manage the casinos after Federals' departure.

Elephant

The question as to who will form the trust, and whether or not the government will have to become involved in the purchase of the two casinos, still remains unanswered. There is very little time left to stop the casino affair becoming a white elephant hanging from the government's neck.

Casino stakes full of intrigue

N.T.N 27/9/84

WILSON PLACE

NOW that we are in the final run of the casino stakes intrigue bites the heel of intrigue — the Borgias look positively pale by comparison and my word, wouldn't they have turned it to advantage.

Rumor and counter-rumor are flung across the gambling table and if the participants play correctly the stakes are worth collecting.

Federal Hotels have presented a doleful countenance as unwilling sellers.

Methinks the tears the tears are not as salty as they look.

An interesting document has fallen the way of this column — prepared, Wilson Place understands, by a chartered accountant of some note.

To quote: " At the outset we must say that the latest public information available on the IPEC group (now TAL Holdings Ltd of which Federals is a subsidiary) is the accounts for the six months ended September 30, 1983.

"These were lodged with the stock exchange on December 30, 1983, one day before IPEC share trading would have been suspended by the exchange.

"These disclose a consolidated operating loss for the six months of $10.2 million."

The report goes on to say that normally the next set of accounts lodged for public scrutiny would have been for the full year to March 31 1984 which would have been lodged by June 30 1984.

"However, for some reason which could only be guessed at, IPEC, Federal and TAL changed their accounting period from a year ended March 31 to June 30.

"In consequence the full-year accounts (which will be for a 15-month period to June 30 1984) do not have to be lodged until September 30, 1984."

And would you believe, by some strange coincidence, that is the date the Federal casino properties are to be handed over at a price yet to be determined.

There is also some remarkably funny business about the new holding group TAL buying for $6.5 million the IPEC debts arising from the re-insurance guarantees — estimated value $32.5 million.

No wonder that a director of the company, a Mr McClure has said: "It is all too complicated sometimes even for the directors!"

NORTHERN TERRITORY **The News** 57

OPINION

Only time will tell

N.T.N 27/9/84

THE Casino take-over by the Government on behalf of the property trust which is in the process of being set up is very widely misunderstood.

The Financial Review yesterday led the pack by quoting a $300 million plan for the acquisition of the Territory casinos.

It is unclear where the $300 million figure comes from but it is suspiciously like the figure mentioned in an unsolicited report to the Prime Minister, Mr Bob Hawke, by a Melbourne freelance journalist who writes mainly for the Toorak Times.

The report is a farrago of nonsense characterised by the heading of $300 million casino robbery.

The Government is not saying so but it is almost certain that the official take-over in the early hours of Monday will be surrounded with a degree of confusion.

Federal Hotels have offered several key executives positions elsewhere and those executives have reacted to those offers in a perfectly understandable way.

They have accepted the offers to move in the light of the fact that they were uncertain of their future under the new arrangement.

Federal Hotels as a company has not been exactly forthcoming with the Northern Territory public about its financial background — a background which may well have justified the Government's move to acquire the casino properties in order to put them into the hands of operators who will fulfill the goals originally set by the agreement to introduce casinos to the Territory.

The Opposition Leader, Mr Bob Collins, has gone on record as saying that the new operators, Aspinalls of London and Pratt Hotels of the U.S.A. clearly know what they are doing.

Mr Collins has been visiting the United States and London to gain first-hand knowledge of the way these casino operators conduct their business.

He appears to have been impressed.

DRAMATIC

The Chief Minister, Mr Paul Everingham, has made a dramatic move by calling a press conference at 3 am on Monday.

That is when Federals will lose control of the casinos in Darwin and Alice Springs.

The names of the new senior executives have yet to be announced; there are still T-s to be crossed and I-s to be dotted.

It is a bold move by the Government, one which has been widely criticised and will have to be seen to be justified in a period that will not allow much leeway.

Whether Federal Hotels has been the friend of the Territory, as the group has claimed to be, only time will tell.

58

A/S ADVOCATE 28/9/84

CASINOS' STILL DEAL TO BE SIGNED

With only two days to go before Federal Hotels must get out of its two Territory casinos, the final deal between the proposed new operators, Aspinalls, of Britain, and Pratt Hotels, of the U.S., still hasn't been signed.

By ROSS IRBY

According to Chief Minister, Mr Paul Everingham, the deal will be signed in London "sometime before 3 am Monday".

Federal Hotels were directed earlier this month to be out by Sunday.

Mr Everingham announced in April that Federal Hotels had agreed to sell its casinos in Alice Springs and Darwin, but it was expected the deal with Aspinalls and Pratt Hotels would be signed well before Federals moved out.

Mr Everingham said on Wednesday he would make an announcement on Monday "of the arrangements in existence".

It is still not clear who will be operating the casinos from Monday, but it will be under a trust, probably controlled by the large Australian conglomerate, Elders IXL.

However, hotel employees who are staying with the new operators have signed contracts with Diamond Leisure Ltd, a company operated by Pratt Hotels and Aspinalls.

On Wednesday, Mr Everingham did not deny a report in the Financial Review that Elders IXL may become the major shareholder in a control trust, with a 50 per cent share.

Pratt Hotels and Aspinalls could have up to 20 per cent total, with the rest going to the Territory's only public company, Henry and Walker Ltd, with units made available to Territorians.

However, Mr Everingham said the whole scheme still had to be "vetted and approved by the Foreign Review Board".

He said a lot was still to be negotiated.

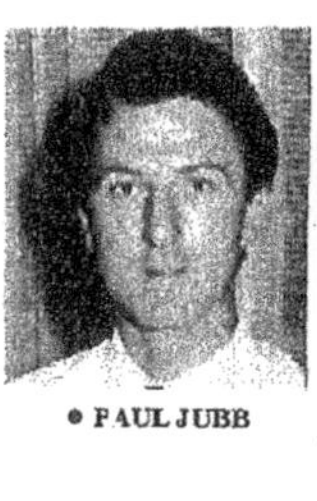

• PAUL JUBB

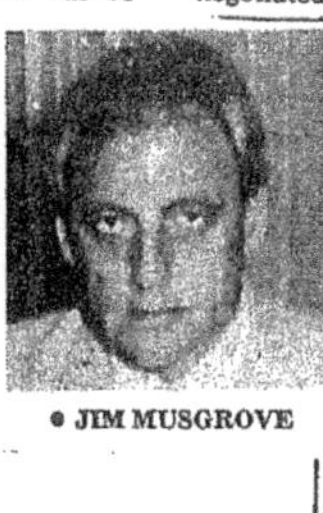

• JIM MUSGROVE

Mr Everingham said it was up to Elders IXL to confirm their involvement, but admitted the Government had been talking to them for some time.

He confirmed Elders were one of a number of parties involved.

Mr Everingham announced earlier this year that the casinos would first be sold to the NT Development Commission and Henry and Walker Ltd.

This was to be a stop-gap measure until Pratt Hotels and Aspinalls took over.

Aspinalls and Pratt Hotels would be appointed by a trust.

Federal Hotels said this week they couldn't say much because under the Federal Hotels Compensations Act, set up by the Territory Government, they must "cooperate".

Federals managing director, Mr John Haddad, said from Sydney: "No-one is sure what's happening after we leave.

"It's become an extraordinary situation.

"The Government wants to introduce new operators, but where are they?

He said he didn't believe it was a satisfactory state of affairs.

"We had two major projects in the Northern Territory which were running successfully which we didn't want to sell, and it's now incumbent on the Government to see they continue running successfully."

Mr Haddad said Federal Hotels would not be staying on as consultants to the new operators.

He said it was almost insulting that the skill of what was required in operating the casinos was being taken so lightly by the Territory Government.

He said his company turned 100 next year.

Mr Haddad is in Sydney for the National Tourism Awards, in which he and Federal Hotels, including Darwin's Mindil Beach Casino, have been nominated for three awards.

Mr Haddad said the Mindil Beach casino was nominated in the "most outstanding" accommodation section of the awards.

The awards are to recognise the diversity, quality and excellence of the Australian tourisam product.

The NT Government is on record as saying "it is our opinion Federal Hotels lack the professional administration and management expertise one would expect in an organisation of its size".

Alice Springs Federal Casino manager, Mr Jim Musgrove, said they had no idea what was happening.

He said the casino and hotel will operate as normal until 11 pm Sunday."

Mr Musgrove said he would be returning to Wrest Point Casino in Tasmania and hotel manager, Mr Paul Jubb, would be working with Federal Hotels in Melbourne.

The key staff will remain with Federal Hotels, while other staff will stay with the new operators.

NT casino trust scramble

By CHRISTINE BECKINGSALE

DOUBTS surround the property trust being set up by Northern Territory Chief Minister Mr Paul Everingham to take control of Federal Hotels Ltd's two NT casinos — only three days before legislation formally removes Federal as owner and operator.

It would appear that Mr Everingham is fast learning the risks and pitfalls of free enterprise as his quest to turn the Northern Territory into the Las Vegas of the southern hemisphere, hits a few last minute snags.

Based on information from impeccable sources in the Northern Territory Government, *The Australian Financial Review* on Wednesday reported that at 3am next Monday, the Northern Territory Government would remove Federal Hotels as the owner and operator of the two casinos, and would deliver the properties into a trust with Elders IXL Ltd as the major unitholder.

Federal Hotels will be removed — Mr Everingham's draconian Federal Hotels Casinos (Compensation) Act will see to that — but there apparently is some doubt as to who or what will own the Darwin and Alice Springs casinos after 3am on Monday.

Yesterday the managing director of Elders, Mr John Elliott, denied that Elders had agreed to step in, while a spokesman for Mr Everingham maintained that "your story was fine, it was right".

During the afternoon Mr Everingham told the *Financial Review* that the story had Elders "all steamed up" — but he did not say that the situation had altered. Later in the day, he could not be contacted as he was in-flight on his way to Melbourne.

Mr Elliott yesterday said: "There's a whole package of development up there as well as casinos and there's no doubt we have had some extensive discussions with them.

"But under no circumstances are Elders going to run casinos and at this point we've made no decisions.

"We have been looking at parts of the package and we could well be interested in part of that, through our construction and finance arm, but at this moment there's been no proposal put forward to me, nor have we made any decisions at this stage," said Mr Elliott.

When Mr Elliott's comments were put to a spokesman for Mr Everingham last night, he said: "The situation with Elders is that they haven't made their announcement — we can't be precise about Elders until they make their announcement.

"What he (Mr Elliott) is trying to say is that they've been negotiating with a trust for property — of which the casinos happen to be part."

"It's all a question of legal nicety," Mr Everingham's spokesman said.

"The problem is that negotiations are going on across a very wide stage — some in London, some in New York, some in New Jersey, some in Melbourne and some in Sydney. It's all got to come together at the last minute, and it may not do so.

'So there may have to be some sort of holding situation for a week or so."

Interestingly, Federal Hotels also had plans to put the properties into a property trust and, indeed, they were close to finalising a deal in March this year when Mr Everingham decided to buy them out.

Speaking of moves to find a partner, Mr Everingham said in Parliament during the recent Budget session: "It appears that our casinos have been unsuccessfully touted around the world like a rag doll for the last one and a half years."

It would seem that he is now doing a bit of last minute scrambling to seek out equity participants.

It is all part of a grandiose plan — worth as much as $300 million — to redevelop the two existing casinos, build two new international hotels and a major complex of investor-owned villa units.

Federal, which was given a 15-year licence to operate the casinos and which has been removed under the most extraordinary circumstances after only five years, will be out at 3am on Monday, along with most of its key people.

The Financial Review asked Mr Everingham yesterday when Aspinalls and Pratts — the two overseas casino operators which will be running the casinos under the new arrangements and which are supposed to be taking up 20 per cent of the trust units — would be taking over. He explained that they had yet to obtain Foreign Investment Review Board approval.

"Well, Pratts and Aspinalls will probably take a couple of weeks to be approved by the FIRB," he said.

Nevertheless, he said there would be people on the ground on Monday to keep things rolling.

Mr ELLIOTT

FIN/REVIEW
28/9/84

61

'Malicious falsehood' claim by hotel group

FEDERAL WRIT FOR CHIEF

TNT 29/9/8

NT NEWS 29/9/84

Operators of the Mindil Beach casino, Federal Hotels, have issued a writ against the Chief Minister, Mr Paul Everingham.

The writ was issued late yesterday.

It alleges malicious falsehood by Mr Everingham.

Federal Hotels managing director, Mr John Haddad, said the writ had been issued to allow the company a chance to defend itself against claims it was experiencing financial problems.

"Mr Everingham has been saying a lot about our financial situation," Mr Haddad said.

"We haven't been saying too much, but we just couldn't let these sorts of comments go on any longer.

"Federals are in a sound position.

Suggestion

"By issuing the writ we are simply saying any suggestion that the Alice Springs and Mindil Beach casinos are in financial trouble are not true."

With only two days left before legislation formally removes Federal as owner and operator of the NT's two casinos, Mr Haddad said his staff were busy working around the clock to ensure a smooth handover.

The takeover will be 3 am Monday. However there are doubts about the property trust being set up by the NT Government to take control of the casinos.

It is believed the NT Government will deliver the properties into a trust with Elders IXL Ltd as the major unit holder.

Elders managing director, Mr John Elliott, has denied Elders will step in.

Mr Elliott confirmed extensive discussions over "development" in the NT have taken place.

But he said under no circumstances were Elders going to run casinos.

He said Elders have been looking at parts of the package, but no proposals had been received by him.

"No decision has been made at this stage," he said.

Pratts and Aspinalls the two overseas casino operators, which under the new arrangements, will be running the casinos have yet to get Foreign Investment Review Board approval.

The Chief Minister, Mr Everingham, says he expects this to take a couple of weeks to be approved.

Mr Everingham

Pratts and Aspinalls are expected to take up 20 per cent of the trust units.

Sighted

While Federal has 10 senior staff handling takeover transactions, Mr Haddad said he had sighted only one representative for the new operators. "That's the ironic thing about it. We're the ones losing the casinos and we've had to provide most of the staff to make sure everything goes through on time," Mr Haddad said.

"I only wish the NT Government told us two or three years ago about their plans.

"We would never have invested our money in a new casino if we had known it was going to be taken away from us."

Everingham evasive on the changeover

By CHRISTINE BECKINGSALE

WHO now owns the Darwin and Alice Springs casinos is one of many questions the Northern Territory Chief Minister, Mr Paul Everingham, failed to clarify at yesterday's 3am press conference.

At the press conference Mr Everingham said the casinos "would be" owned by the Territory Property Trust. But who owns them now?

Mr Everingham could not be contacted yesterday on this matter.

Despite his 3am conference — which apparently fell a little flat — Mr Everingham had a busy day, riding a powered exercise bike at a local shopping centre in the morning to celebrate 50 years of electricity in Darwin, and flying off to Groote Eylandt for a cabinet meeting in the afternoon.

But when a spokesman for Mr Everingham was last night asked whether the trust was formally in place, he replied: "I don't know — I'm not sure I can answer that."

Federal Hotels Ltd, the former owner and operator of both casinos, was ejected at 3am according to the Federal Hotels Casinos (Compensation) Act, without having received one cent in compensation.

Mr Everingham did announce that the casinos would be operated by Diamond Leisure Pty Ltd, a company owned by two of the world's best known casino operators, Pratts and Aspinalls.

However, Diamond Leisure has yet to obtain Foreign Investment Review Board approval and some local participation may be needed to get the FIRB nod.

Mr Everingham also said the trust would have an initial capital of $28 million.

This is likely to be much less than the two properties are worth. The tribunal set up under the Act has yet to determine the value, but in view of previous valuations this is expected to be at least $50 million.

It appears the problem is that Mr Everingham's plans to assemble the new equity participants have not quite come together at this stage.

Under the Act, Federal is to be paid 90 per cent of a valuation until the tribunal decides how much Federal is owed. (Even if that valuation is only $45 million, someone is going to have to come up with $40.5 million.)

Will the Northern Territory Government have to foot the bill?

The NT's only listed company Henry and Walker Ltd, would have a controlling 57 per cent stake, Mr Everingham told the press conference.

Directors of Henry and Walker yesterday issued a statement to the Adelaide Stock Exchange saying they had "agreed in principle" to take up 57 per cent of the trust's units, an investment of $16 million.

They said that facilities had been arranged for the securing of loan funds for the deal and that they intended to have the deal ratified by shareholders at a general meeting.

This is a big investment for Henry and Walker which has market capitalisation of about $10.5 million.

According to the company's 1983 balance sheet, shareholders funds were only $6.7 million. And based on that balance sheet the additional borrowings would lift gearing (total liabilities to total assets) from about 74 per cent to 136 per cent.

As the trust comes to reflect the true value of the properties (which is what a property trust is all about), the proportion of Henry and Walker's stake probably would have to be watered down.

The *Financial Review* yesterday tried to contact Mr Neville Walker, a director of Henry and Walker, on his company's proposed significant investment, but to no avail.

Apart from Henry and Walker, Mr Everingham said that other trust participants would be Northern Territory and Australian equity holders, the overseas operators, and the Tokyo-based construction group Kumagai Gumi.

Mr EVERINGHAM

"Negotiations would continue with Elders IXL Lt[d] ... but extra participatio[n] was not crucial to the succes[s] of the casino development as current indications wer[e] that the full association o[f] trust units would be take[n] up," he said.

This seems curious as th[e] NT Government previousl[y] stated its plans to fold the two casinos into the trust, along with other properties to be developed as part of its ambitious $300 million plan to put the Northern Territory on the map as a major tourist and casino centre.

As late as last week the NT Government maintained that Elders was going to take up a major stake in the trust — "close to 50 per cent", the *Financial Review* was told.

Elders' managing director Mr John Elliott, yesterday said: "Our role in it has got out of context in the need for someone to own the casinos because the licence had to change at 3.00am this morning."

Mr Elliott said that Elders was "still waiting" for the feasibility work to be completed by the Northern Territory Government and reiterated that no proposal had yet come to him.

"The feasibility would have to be economic from our point of view — and I imagine his (Mr Everingham's)," said Mr Elliott.

It would seem that Elders, as a banking licence candidate, does not particularly want its name bandied about in relation to casinos.

Yesterday Mr Elliott again stressed that the casinos were only a part of the package of development in the NT — that they were part of a big expansion "around the casinos".

Elders might be interested in the construction side and the financing side but was undecided as to what percentage, if any, it would take.

64

KEY CASINO ROLE GOES TO JAPAN

1/10/84

New firm takes over

N.T NEWS
1/10/84

Tokyo-based construction comny will play a major part in the rritory Property Trust which took er the Federal Hotels' Territory sino properties this morning.

By PETER WILSON

'he c.mpany is magai Gumi - the rd biggest construcn company in Japan terms of profits.

t a brief 3 am ceronny in the Mindil ach Hotel conference om, the Chief Minisr, Mr Paul 'eringham, presented ming and liquor linces to the chairman the new operating mpany, Mr Richard yan.

The operating comany is Diamond isure Pty Ltd.

Diamond Leisure will mprise Pratts of the nited States and spinalls of London.

Approval

Foreign Investment eview Board final aproval for this move is ill awaited, but Mr veringham said the reuest was being viewed ympathetically.

Those participating in the property trust are: Henry and Walker (57 per cent); Kumagai Gumi (14 per cent);

Aspinalls (10 per cent) and Pratts (10 per cent.)

The remaining 9 per cent of the units have been set aside for further participation by Australian interests.

Signed

The Mindil Beach casino will be temporarily managed by Mr Ryan until the arrival of management from London and the USA - also subject to FIRB approval.

The agreement appointing Diamond Leisure as operators of both casinos was signed in London on Friday by Northern Territory Development Corporation chairman, Mr Ray McHenry, and Pratts and Aspinalls executives.

Mr Everingham said the initial capital of Diamond Leisure would be $28 million.

Kumagai - which was represented in Darwin this morning by its managing director in Australia, Mr Tony Mitani - is involved in Australian projects worth $1 230million.

NORTHERN TERRITORY
The News
OPINION

A welcome investment

THE surprise at the take-over of the Territory Federal Hotels casinos was the announcement of the participation in the Territory Trust of the giant Japanese construction company, Kumagai Gumi.

The company's entree to the Territory could have far-reaching consequences for development in the future.

Kumagai is not exactly a household word in Australia but it is already involved in massive projects in New South Wales, Victoria, South Australia and Queensland.

In Adelaide it is the $150 million redevelopment of the Adelaide Station — a project which will include a casino.

The company will take a 50 per cent equity in the project.

After Henry and Walker, Kumagai has taken the biggest share of the equity in the Territory Property Trust which is to own the casinos.

It would be surprising if the company did not become heavily involved in the redevelopment of Myilly Point and the Alice Springs condominium project near the golf course.

The company has been operating in Australia for only three-and-a-half years — and has managed to chalk up business worth well over $1000 million.

The developments Kumagai is involved in range from coal mines to casinos, shopping centres to a "ski tube" railway.

An advantage of the company which would no doubt have marked appeal for the Northern Territory Government, is that it is able to raise huge sums of money to get projects completed.

Mr Tony Mitani, the company's managing director in Australia, is in Darwin at present not only to mark the change in ownership of the casinos but to set up an office.

In its Australian projects the company has striven to use Australian construction companies — no doubt it will do the same if it becomes involved in Territory projects.

INVALUABLE

Of great importance to the future of tourism in the Territory, Kumagai could prove to be an invaluable ally in attracting the mass Japanese market to visit here as part of a package.

Kumagai has a commitment to Australia and the Territory Government will be seeking to include the Territory in that commitment.

Past fears in the Territory about foreign investment have hopefully been dissipated. Such fears have no place in an economy which needs above all to develop.

Territorians should be seeking to welcome such investment.

New casino crew confident

65

WILSON PLACE

THERE was a polyglot collection of people at the pre-dawn hand-over of the casinos to the new property trust.

People with widely varying cultural backgrounds were at the early, early press conference to witness the handing over of new gaming and liquor licences to the new operators, Diamond Leisure Pty Ltd.

Apart from long-standing Territorians, there was a scattering of other accents ranging from various shades of American twang to the difficult-to-place accent of Chris Raphael, international marketing director for the Sands hotel and casino in Atlantic City.

Turns out Chris was born in Calcutta but has spent some years in the United States.

He has the utmost faith in the combined skills of his own group, Pratt Hotels and Aspinalls to market the Territory casinos effectively.

He has with him a security expert recently recruited from Caesar's Palace in Las Vegas.

The expert spoke about the enormity of the cheating carried out from time to time

He recounted one evening in Las Vegas when slick operators were involved in lifting something over $2 million in total from a couple of casinos.

The exercise now is to see nothing dramatic like that takes place here.

Chris Raphael was particularly pleased about the Japanese participation in the property trust — he feels this opens up important marketing opportunities for the operators.

As public relations exercises, lunches will be held in Darwin and Alice Springs today for the staff of the casinos.

Paul Everingham will host the lunch at Peppis and Alice Springs MLAs will host the lunch in Alice Springs.

N.T. NEWS 1/10/84

NT Government officially expels pioneer casino owner-operators

By BRIAN JOHNSTONE

AUST 2/10/84

FEDERAL Pacific Hotels was officially expelled by the Northern Territory Government as the owner-operator of the two casino-hotels it has built in Darwin and Alice Springs yesterday – with no idea how much it will be paid for the property.

The Country Liberal Government invoked compulsory acquisition legislation and handed over the licence to the new casino owners, the Territory Property Trust, which combines Australian, Japanese, American and British business interests.

Executives and key staff from Federal were still packing up around the Mindal Beach casino in Darwin after a stock-take when the Chief Minister, Mr Everingham, began outlining details of the new casino management structure at a 3am press conference in the casino's convention room.

Mr Everingham said the Territory's only public company, Henry and Walker Ltd, would have a controlling 57 per cent interest in the trust.

Japan's third largest construction company, Kumagai Gumi, would have 14 per cent and leading British casino operator Aspinall Holdings and the Pratt Hotel Group, operator of the Sands Casino in Atlantic City, would each have 10 per cent.

Casino party turns sour – Page 14

"The remaining 9 per cent of the units have been set aside for further participation by territory and Australian business interests," Mr Everingham said.

The chance of participation by Elders-IXL has virtually evaporated. The managing director of Elders, Mr John Elliott, said his company was primarily interested in the construction opportunities offered by the project. But since one of Japan's largest construction firms had taken a 14 per cent stake in the controlling trust, interest by Elders was fading.

Mr Everingham said the chairman of the Northern Terrritory Development Corporation, Mr Ray McHenry, signed an agreement on Friday with Pratts and Aspinall in London which appointed them joint operators of the two casinos.

Pratts and Aspinall have formed a company, Diamond Leisure Pty Ltd, which will operate the casinos as soon as final approval is received from the Foreign Investment Review Board (FIRB).

Federal Pacific Hotels had asked the Northern Territory for $55 million for the two properties after Mr Everingham told the group earlier this year his Government intended to bring in new operators.

Federal agreed reluctantly to sell, but the compulsory acquisition legislation was brought in when negotiations broke down after the Government refused to meet the price. The Government offered $47.1 million.

Under the compulsory acquisition legislation, passed in the August Budget session of the Northern Territory Parliament and assented to on September 7, Government valuers have begun determining the amount of compensation to be paid to Federal.

Mr Everingham handed Mr Richard Ryan, interim chairman of Diamond Leisure, the new gaming and liqor licences before the press conference ended. The licences will be renewable each year.

AAP

SUNDAY Territorian 86

EDITORIAL N.T.N

Ill-advised decision

THE festering sore of the whole casino deal was opened up once more on Friday by the Federal Treasurer, Mr Paul Keating.

Mr Keating announced that the approval of the Foreign Investment Review Board for the participation of Pratt Hotels of the U.S.A. and Aspinalls of London would be deferred for 90 days while more information was sought.

Former Chief Minister, Mr Paul Everingham, has denounced Mr Keating's eleventh hour entrance to the casino arena in the Northern Territory as "a cheap political trick."

Whether that is correct or not has to be left open to public judgment.

Federal Hotels managing director, Mr John Haddad, who was in Hong Kong last night en route to Beijing (Peking), said his company had not lodged a formal objection to Pratts and Aspinalls, but it had stated a point of view about the suitability of Federals to operate casinos.

Technically that could be regarded as an objection and Mr Keating has not been slow to slap a suspension on the FIRB proceedings.

Technically, too, Federal Hotels could not now withdraw their submission to the FIRB because that would be a tacit admission that perhaps they were not suitable as casino operators in the Northern Territory.

Obviously that would be a position which is untenable for the company just as it is setting its sights on a possible casino operation in Western Australia and possibly Queensland too.

Mr Haddad is going to China to further negotiations for his company to become involved in major hotel operations there and obviously would be doing all in his power to protect the reputation of his company.

It is unfortunate that Federal Hotels ever lodged the report with the FIRB and it is unfortunate that Mr Keating should have seen fit to take this delaying action.

No one is surprised that in one of the few seats in Australia where the outcome of the election is in doubt the Labor Party would be seeking an issue with which to beat its opponent, Mr Paul Everingham, over the head.

The action might just backfire.

The deal has been concluded with the new joint casino operators, the legislation (unfortunate as that might have been) has been enacted, the operators are here.

It is too late to go back, it is a fait accompli.

Pratt Hotels and Aspinalls have said there is no reason for them to be worried about being rejected by the FIRB.

The companies have been thoroughly investigated and Mr Keating's action is contrary to the interests of the Northern Territory and, indeed, to Australia.

The threat of the FIRB witholding approval of foreign investment of a minimal nature such as that involved in the casino deal will do nothing to enhance Australia's reputation as a mature country for investment purposes.

Mr Keating must reconsider his ill-advised decision.

Trust needs more money for casinos

ADV – 3/10/84

The Casino Affair
by Malcolm Ormiston

The new owner of the Territory's two casinos, the Territory Property Trust, has only $28 million - it will have to find at least another $20 million to buy the properties.

Federal Pacific Hotels was officially expelled as owner/operator of the casinos at 3am on Monday.

Federals' managing director, Mr John Haddad, said on Monday morning he did not know how much his company would be paid for the casinos, nor when the money would be forthcoming.

The Chief Minister, Mr Paul Everingham held a press conference/party in the casino at 3am on Monday to announce details of the new operators and owners of the casinos

Mr Everingham was reluctant to answer questions from the assembled media who wanted to know more than the sketchy press release which was issued to them prior to the conference.

The bare bones of the press release were that: the new operator will be Diamond Leisure Pty Ltd (comprising the Pratt Hotel Group and Aspinall Holdings), the trust which now owns the casinos is made up of Henry and Walker, Pratts and Aspinalls, the Japanese construction company Kumagi Gumi and NT and Australian equity holders.

Despite a bleary-eyed Mr Everingham saying, "I think you guys are not very lively this morning - what say we go and have a drink" the media did manage to drag some further information out of the Chief Minister.

Henry and Walker will have a 57 per cent stake in the trust, Kumagi - 14 per cent, Pratts and Aspinalls - 10 per cent each and nine per cent will be available for local and interstate equity.

Diamond Leisure will lease the casinos from the trust for 10 per cent of the final purchase price per year.

To make up the difference between the trust's capital and the purchase price of the casinos, Mr Everingham said the money would probably be borrowed.

The purchase price is subject to another valuation, as it stands now the government has said $47.1 million is a fair price while Federals are hanging out for $55 million. After the valuation Federals will be paid 90 per cent of the price and can then appeal to a tribunal for what Federals consider to be a fair balance.

On the subject of Federals credit list, which the Government and Federals were fighting over, Mr Everingham said, "It's been fixed."

At a Federals' "wake" in the Don Hotel after the press conference Mr Haddad said he had agreed to sell the list to the new operators.

The pigeon list, as it seems to be known in gambling circles, contains details of credit allowed to Federals' customers. Mr Haddad said there were 2000 names on the list with one Australian having a credit limit of a mere $1 000 000.

When asked if there were any media magnates on the list Mr Haddad said nothing.

On the government's compulsory acquisition of the casinos he said, "The government can't just ride roughshod over a national company and not expect some reaction."

Mr Haddad said members of the business community he had spoken to in the southern states were "staggered - nobody believes it's happening."

NT Govt has $10m at stake on high-rollers

S.M.H 4/10/84

The Northern Territory Government will lose more than $10 million in gaming taxes over the next five years unless there is a significant increase in gambling turnover at the two NT casinos.

The Government faces the multi-million dollar paper loss due to a drastic reduction in levies to be paid by the new operators of the Darwin and Alice Springs casinos.

According to a senior NT Treasury official, the Government agreed to the new overseas operators paying 8 per cent gaming tax in the belief that high-rollers could not be attracted if they were any higher.

But according to Mr John Haddad – managing director of evicted casinos owner-operator Federal Pacific Hotels Ltd – the Government has made a major mistake.

The Treasury official, who refused to be named, said the new operators, Pratts and Aspinalls, would pay about $1.1 million a year in gaming taxes on present gambling turnover for the first five years of their agreement with the Government.

Federal paid 20 per cent tax on its gaming operations at Mindil Beach Casino in Darwin and 15 per cent at the Alice Springs Casino.

It paid $2.4 million last year in gaming taxes on its Darwin operation, $800,000 from Alice Springs and had projected this would increase to more than $3 million this year.

Mr Haddad said the Treasury official had no idea how a casino operated.

"Any suggestion the gaming odds are locked into the tax rate is totally wrong," he said.

"The odds are worked out between the operators and the Government on an actuarial basis and have nothing to do with gaming tax.

"If they were related, why didn't the Government cut our tax rate so we could offer better odds?"

AAP

S.M.H. 4/10/84

IT seems the assessors over at Mindil Beach have found that the roulette equipment is old and unreliable.

What is more they say the equipment is "tamperable."

They are not, of course, saying the equipment has been tampered with. No, they are only saying that somebody unscrupulous could work a point a two by getting to the equipment.

It would be interesting to know what sort of price the new operators are going to be asked to pay for the equipment.

WILSON PLACE
5/10/84

71

Finance contract signed

A financing agreement has been signed by the new casino owners – Territory Property Trust – and the Australian Bank group was signed in Darwin yesterday.

Northern Territory Development Corporation chairman, Mr Ray McHenry, made the announcement on behalf of Fernbank Pty Ltd which is the name of the trustee company.

Mr McHenry said that under the financing agreement up to $30 million would be available to the trust.

"This amount together with monies to be subscribed by holders of the trust units, including Walker and Henry Ltd, the overseas operators and other trust participants, puts the trust in funds to meet its obligations," Mr McHenry said.

Those obligations would include the purchase price of the casinos which is to be paid for the casino properties.

In reply to an editorial in the Financial Review, the Chief Minister, Mr Paul Everingham, has commented to the editor of the paper that TAL Holdings which is now the parent of Federal Hotels, had advised the Sydney stock exchange on August 1 that it had paid $6.5 million to acquire judgement debts against IPEC Holdings (now Eslea Holdings) of approximately $32.5 million. N.T.N 6/10/84

N.T.N. 6/10/84

30 million reasons why Paul was right

92

BUSHRANGER

TERRITORIAN 4/11/84

□**Bushranger has just returned from a foray to the big smoke.**

Your columnist must admit to feeling a little humble among all the shocking headlines in the big city press proclaiming Mr Robert Trimbole's activities as well as the allegations by Mr Costigan of vast criminal conspiracies and Mr Kerry Packer's strenuous denials of any involvement.

So it was with a sense of some relief that Bushranger settled back into more familiar pastures, to find a remarkable thing had happened.

A company called TAL Holdings Ltd has written down its investment in the Ipeç Transport group by $13.7 million to just $1 million in the face of a thundering great $30 million-plus loss for the subsidiary in the 15 months ended June 30.

Readers might just recall that TAL Holdings is somewhat associated with Greg Farrell and John Haddad of Federal Hotels and NT Casino fame.

Now things start to get too complicated to explain fully in this space.'

In effect Ipec lost its shirt in the international re-insurance business. There then followed lots of corporate restructuring and forced sales of assets. TNT bought Ipec Transport Europe for $40 million, for example.

PAUL EVERINGHAM

Among the tactics were a reverse take-over which delayed the balance date and therefore public disclosure of the extent of the disaster.

TAL has also left the unsecured crediters of Eslea Holdings Ltd (formerly Ipec) out in the cold by deciding to welch on any financial support by way of formal undertakings.

This no doubt will be of some relief to TAL shareholders who already have seen net tangible asset backing reduced by one-third from $2.32 to $1.55 a share.

Bushranger believes Mr Farrell approached Paul Everingham with another great idea to raise some cash — flog off the NT casino properties owned by Federal Hotels in a property trust.

Paul couldn't have taken too kindly to that idea because he promptly decided if things were that bad he could flog them off himself. The licences, after all, do belong to the Territory.

Everybody knows things got pretty nasty and ended up with heaps of writs flying around. But the upshot of it is that Paul Everingham was right after all, 30 million times to be precise.

And he looks like being right again. Eslea Holdings is the main shareholder in finance company Direct Acceptance Corporation Ltd which had loans outstanding to Eslea of $31 million at March 31.

There are still large but unquantified re-insurance claims against Elsea over and above the $30 million already down the drain.

The Lizard of Oz

□A new nickname doing the rounds for Kerry Packer, alias the Goanna. These days he is being called the Lizard of Oz.

Bushranger can attest to the fact revealed in the latest Costigan report that Packer is a pretty big gambler. He's been known to drop the odd hundred grand or so at Mindil Beach.

By-election notes

□Jingili by—election notes. This weekend the candidates — around 18 of them — are being grilled by the CLP pre-selection committee.

Veterinarian Jan Hills and North Darwin branch president Rick Setter are favorites. Jan apparently has a few noses out of joint having distributed some personal puff around the electorate already. Naughty.

Digging deep at casino

□Operators of the new Diamond Beach Casino were left digging deep into their coffers this week.

Three lucky gamblers walked away with $47 000 in loot between them. The first of the trio, a Japanese business man collected $20 000 playing Keno on Tuesday night.

The second man collected $7000 the next day while yesterday afternoon the NSW tourist picked $20 000 again playing Keno.

Despite the windfall for the gamblers the Casino operators still managed to raise a smile, saying "It's all good for business".

83

Henry and Walker capital 'sewn up'

S/T 7/10/84

By MALCOLM ORMISTON

Henry and Walker, the largest shareholder in the new trust which will own the Territory's two casinos, has its share of the capital "sewn up".

Mr Neville Walker said on Friday his company had arranged loans for the $16 million needed to acquire 57 per cent of the Territory Property Trust.

Mr Walker said the money was sewn up but it wouldn't be needed for a couple of weeks.

The borrowing places Henry and Walker in a delicate position with regard to its gearing ration (total liabilities to total assets). The company now has a gearing ratio of about 136 per cent - liabilities are 136 per cent of assets.

Companies with this sort of gearing are often likely take over targets because of their inability to defend themselves but Mr Walker said as he and Mr Fraser Henry owned the majority of the company's shares this was not a matter for concern.

Meanwhile, the Territory Property Trust and the Australian Bank has signed a financing agreement which would make up to $30 million available to the trust. The trusts shareholders have already committed $28 million and the extra finance will be used to make up the purchase price of the casinos - at least 47.1 million.

The trust consists of: Henry and Walker - 57 per cent, Kumagi Gumi - 14 per cent, Pratts and Aspinalls (the new operators) - 10 per cent each and the remaining nine per cent will be available for Territory and interstate shareholders.

The newest entry in the equation is the Japanese construction company Kumagi Gumi. Kumagi is Japan's fifth largest construction company in terms of revenue but third in the profit stakes.

In 1983 Kumagi's revenue wa $3.16 billion and profit was $74.5 million.

Two of Australia's leading construction companies pale into insignificance in comparison: Leighton Holdings made $11.5 million profit on sales of $620 million and Jennings Industries turned over $325 million last year for a profit of $14 million.

Although Kumagi has only been operating in Australia since 1980 it is involved in projects and proposals worth $1.2 billion in this country.

The projects range from coal mines to casinos. Kumagi has joined with Meekathara Minerals in a proposal for a $300 million coal mine in South Australia. It is also joint venturer with the South Australian Superannuation Fund Trust in the $160 million redevelopment of the Adelaide railway station as a casino/hotel complex.

Kumagi's Australian exposure has mainly been as a source of funds although its construction expertise is likely to play an increasing role.

The company has tended to get involved in projects where there is no local competition. One recent media report suggested this might be because the projects Kumagi was interested in were relatively high risk.

Kumagi is likely to end up as project manager (with Henry and Walker) of the proposed Myilly Point development.

Report threatens NT-Haddad pact

AGE 15/10/84

A newspaper report is threatening the fragile truce called this weekend between the Northern Territory Government and Federal Pacific Hotels over the compulsory acquisition of the company's two Northern Territory casinos.

The Northern Territory's Chief Minister, Paul Everingham, and Federal's managing director, John Haddad, issued a joint statement late yesterday which stated they had reconciled their differenced on the issue.

In the statement Mr Everingham said he had seen Federal Hotel's annual report released to stock exchanges on Friday and was happy to accept a company assurance that their group assets exceeded their liabilities by more than $30 million.

"It seems likely that the difficulties Federal Hotels had been experiencing last year are now behind them," he added.

Mr Haddad said he was delighted to accept Mr Everingham's assurances and in a "spirit of goodwill" Federal would take no further issue with past events. He said writs issued in New South Wales and the Northern Territory against Mr Everingham for malicious falsehood would now be dropped.

His company was now looking to a speedy completion of an independent valuation to determine the amount of compensation his company would be paid for the Darwin and Alice Springs casinos.

The statement appeared to end public acrimony on the most extraordinary takeover in the Territory's brief corporate history.

From Mr Everingham's viewpoint it would stem a spate of adverse southern newspaper reports in his run to the Federal election.

From Federal Hotel's viewpoint it would stop Mr Everingham continuing to question the group's financial and managerial wherewithal while it sought casinos licences in Western Australia and South Australia.

However, Mr Haddad said today the writs would be reissued unless Mr Everingham and his advisors corrected statements which appeared yesterday in a front-page story and editorial in the 'Sunday Territorian'.

'If they don't fix it, we will be back where we were," an angry Mr Haddad said in Melbourne.

The report said it was believed that Mr Haddad had "made the first approach to end the bitter war of words which has accompanied the takeover.'

It went on to say Mr Everingham had responded by declaring the Government was happy to accept Federal Hotels' assurances that their financial position was secure.

A lengthy editorial repeated the statement that Federal Hotels was understood to have made the first approach to offer the olive branch and "the Government was not slow to accept, recognising that a war of attrition could do neither side any good.'

Mr Haddad said Mr Everingham's solicitor, Lex Silvester, had made an approach to his company to drop the writs.

"We were asked whether we would stop the war if Mr Everingham issued a statement to say he was satisfied the company was in a strong financial position,' he added.

New Northern Territory casino manager Mr John Aspinall

Casino man is counting on Islam

From DAVID TROUNCE

DARWIN. — John Aspinall, a British millionaire whose company has taken a 10 per cent equity in the Northern Territory's two casinos, is gambling on the Islamic revival in South-East Asia to deliver big spenders to Australia.

Mr Aspinall, 57, founder and director of the glamorous Aspinall Club of London, said in Darwin yesterday that he found conditions in South-East Asia "curiously helpful".

"The fundamentalist Moslem revival in South-East Asia has closed all Indonesian casinos," he said. "All four have been slapped shut. The one casino in Malaysia is probably going to close under the influence of the Islamic fundamentalist revolution and so on."

Darwin and Alice Springs would become attractions for Asian punters because the casino in Manila was "laughable", he said. Macao's casino was under threat of closure from China and Singapore would never have a casino under the "stringent puritan regime" of the Prime Minister, Mr Lee Kuan Yew.

"Brunei has no casino and nor will it have as a Moslem State."

Mr Aspinall was speaking at a Press conference in Darwin where he and Mr Bill Weldner, a representative of Pratts, the other company in the new management, announced their plans.

The Territory's Chief Minister, Mr Everingham, announced last week that Mr Aspinall and Mr Pratt would manage the casinos under a new company, Diamond Leisure Pty Ltd, pending Foreign Investment Review Board approval.

The two new operators yesterday formally changed the names of the existing casinos to Diamond Beach Casino Hotel (Darwin) and Diamond Springs Country Club (Alice Springs).

AGE TUES 9/10/84

75

Casino turnover crucial

N.T.N 8/10/84

The new Territory casino operators, Diamond Leisure, will have to increase turnover at Mindil Beach by $1.5 million a year to break even, one of the partners in the venture, Mr John Aspinall, said today.

Mr John Aspinall

Mr Aspinall's company, Aspinalls of London, are now operating the casinos jointly with Pratt Hotels of the United States.

Mr Aspinall said a 20 to 25 per cent increase in turnover was needed to cover the rent of the two casinos — which would be 10 per cent of the total final purchase price — as well as the cost of refurbishing and marketing the casinos.

N.T.N 8/10/84

President of the Greate Bay Casino Corporation, Mr Bill Weidner (Greate Bay is Pratt Hotels holding company) said the company would be spending at least $3 million in refurbishing Mindil Beach in the next year.

Mindil Beach Hotel will be renamed the Diamond Beach Hotel/Casino. The Alice Springs operation will be renamed Diamond Springs Casino and Country Club.

Mr Aspinall said betting limits on the gambling tables would be doubled immediately.

He said the joint operators' main contribution would be to make the casinos attractive to Territorians and to the South-East Asians.

Effort

There would be no point in making a major marketing effort in South-East Asia until the refurbishing of the casino had been completed.

The new general manager of the Territory operation is an Australian resident, Mr Roger de Lima, who has been working in a Monte Carlo casino for several years.

Mr de Lima has close family ties with Darwin.

POLITICS

HOW A $10,000 INVESTMENT WON CONTROL OF NT'S CASINOS

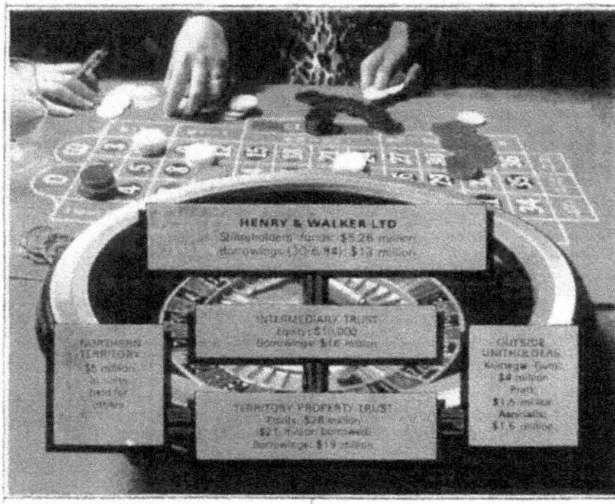

Many questions are still unanswered about the change in ownership of the $50 million operations

By IVOR RIES

The Northern Territory public company Henry & Walker Ltd has invested just $10,000 to buy 57 percent of the Territory's two casinos, valued at $50 million.

It has long been known that the Northern Territory Government, led by former Chief Minister Paul Everingham (now federal MHR for the Northern Territory), took the casinos from Federal Hotels Ltd for a sum of slightly more than $50 million in the early hours of October 1 last year.

The political backlash of the NT Government's attack on Federal Hotels Ltd continued in Federal Parliament last week when Treasurer Paul Keating called the expropriation "this confiscation, this unprecedented piece of vandalism" and pointed to "the obvious waste of taxpayers' money involved".

But it has not been revealed just how little the shareholders of Henry and Walker Ltd have put at risk. Last week H&W company secretary Patrick Armitstead confirmed for *BRW* that his company had invested a total of $10,000 to buy 57 percent of the two casino properties, through the Territory Property Trust.

Armitstead also confirmed that $10,000 was the maximum H&W shareholders had at risk in the casino venture. He said that the remainder of the company's so-called "equity" contribution to the casino purchase, orchestrated by the Everingham Government, had been borrowed from banks.

Questioned by *BRW*, Armitstead said that these loans were off the balance sheet and not secured on H&W's other assets — which include civil engineering, property development, vehicle dealerships and prawn fishing in and around the NT.

BRW pointed out to Armitstead that it was possible, in the early years at least, that the casino operations would not generate a cash flow sufficient to make all the interest payments on the loans.

Armitstead replied that Henry & Walker Ltd would not have to pick up the cost of any interest payment shortfall. However, he said he could not explain how any possible shortfall would be met. "It's not something I'd like to see in print," he said.

Armitstead, when asked by *BRW* whether the Northern Territory Government or the Northern Territory Development Corporation would pick up the cost of any interest shortfall, said he could not comment further.

The latest revelation from Henry & Walker Ltd shows that there are still many questions unanswered about Everingham's casino decision, dubbed by Treasurer Keating in Parliament as "what is probably one of the most infamous episodes in the history of Australian public administration".

BRW has attempted to find answers for many question about the viability of the new casino structure during the past two weeks. Although many details are still shrouded in mystery — such as who is guaranteeing Henry & Walker's $16 million "equity" loan — it is now clear that the Australian taxpayer is several million dollars out of pocket and the new NT casino organisation has the appearance, in financial parlance, of a stack of champagne glasses.

The base of the stack of champagne glasses is Henry & Walker itself, a company with shareholders' funds of less than $6 million and debts of $13 million according to its last balance sheet (June 30, 1984). The company lost $1.42 million last financial year but according to Armiststead it is now trading profitably.

On top of this row of glasses is the $16 million in borrowings — not guaranteed by Henry & Walker — used to take up the 57 percent equity in the Territory Property Trust, owner of the two NT casino properties. The final layer of glasses is the Territory Property Trust itself, with unitholders' equity of $28 million ($21 million of which is borrowed) and further borrowings of $10 million.

This complicated structure involves total borrowed funds of at least $40 million (disregarding H&W's on-balance-sheet debt) — much of which is guaranteed by the NT Government and at current money market rates would be costing about $6 million a year in interest payments.

The large interest costs of these borrowings throw some doubt on the ct rent commercial viability of the NT casino set-up, even though both are said to be trading at near capacity due partly to heavy promotion during the past few years (thanks to Federal Hotels).

Although the casinos themselves may be able to cover their interest bill, there seems to be considerable doubt as to whether there would be sufficient profits to cover the interest charges on Henry & Walker's $16 million "equity" loan (assuming normal bank interest rates are being charged).

At 15 percent, Henry & Walker's $16 million equity" would cost $2.4 million a year in interest. Yet the guaranteed income from the Territory Property Trust is only 10 percent, generating $1.6 million a year. This would leave a shortfall of $800,000 a year.

The Everingham Government seems to have anticipated this shortfall by making a provision that the Territory Property Trust would in its early years have a half share of the profits of the casino operators (Aspinalls of Britain and the Pratt Hotels group of the US).

Northern Territory Development Corporation chairman Ray McHenry told *BRW* that Henry & Walker had made arrangements concerning its $16 million "equity" financing with the Japanese construction giant Kumagai Gumi Co Ltd (also an equity participant in the trust) and the Midland Bank of Britain.

This raises the possibility that Kumagai Gumi will pick up any possible interest shortfall for Henry & Walker, most likely in return for sharing in property development joint ventures connected with the two casinos. The NT Government is proposing to substantially enlarge the accommodation and entertainment facilities of both casinos and Henry & Walker and Kumagai Gumi would appear to be leading contenders to win this work.

Considering the high level of debt, and the fact that the NT Government (and thus the Australian taxpayer) is having to do the groundwork for expanding the casinos, it is important to remember the reasons the NT Government gave when it turned against Federal Hotels.

Everingham said that Federal Hotels had stood in the way of $300 million expansion plans for the casinos and that the company's financial position was precarious.

At the time Federal Hotels were ejected by Everingham the company had shareholders funds of at least $30 million and its casinos were operating profitably (the company paid more than $750,000 in casino taxes to the NT Government in its last quarter in operation).

But as a result of the expropriation, beneficial control of the two casino properties rests with Henry & Walker, a company with less than one quarter the shareholders' funds of the Federal Hotels group.

According to figures provided by Federal Hotels, the new casino operators paid only $245 in casino taxes in their first quarter of operations (the period between October 1 and December 31 last year). Thus, the NT Government appears to have created a structure which is far less financially secure and is generating far less revenue for the government.

Under the old system with Federal Hotels in operation, the NT Government had an agreement to take 18 percent of the gross gaming win at the Darwin Casino and 15 percent of the gross gaming win at the Alice Springs casino. To attract the new operators the NT Government reduced the gaming tax on both casinos to 8 percent of the gross win, in return for a share of the operating profits in the later years of operations.

However the NT Government has committed itself to waiving the gaming tax in case the operations are marginal. NT Chief Minister Ian Tuxworth told the NT Legislative Assembly recently: "If after payment of rental to the tust and all other expenses, the operator has insufficient funds to meet its casino tax requiremens, the Territory will waive some or all of that tax. If there is an operating loss then NTDC will lend to Diamond Leisure (the operators) the amount of such loss . . . these loans will be secured . . ."

The forgone taxes are not the only costs to the Australian taxpayers, who provide about 87 percent of the NT Government funds. Other examples are:

☐ The NT Government lost at least $2.5 million on the deal whereby it paid Federal Hotels more than $50 million for the casinos and transferred the properties

continued next page

Neville Walker and Fraser Henry, left and Paul Everingham: A huge political backlash

from previous page

to the trust for $47.5 million.

The NT Government granted the trust a $2 million interest-free loan to be repaid over 15 years.

$5 million has been borrowed — effectively guaranteed by the NT Government — to set aside five million equity units in the Territory Property Trust for later investment by the operators (Aspinalls and Pratt Hotels) and possibly the public.

The NT Government spent some $1.38 million on various costs associated with the transfer of ownership.

The NT Government and the NTDC have spent $3.14 million to buy land and do preliminary planning work for extra accommodation and other facilities to be built alongside the existing casinos, although no investors or developers have yet given written assurances that the projects will proceed.

As a result of these moves, the taxpayer has chipped in more than $14 million to subsidise and improve the economics of an enterprise which, when previously in the hands of Federal Hotels, had no taxpayer assistance and was generating substantial tax revenue.

One of Paul Everingham's main stated reasons for ejecting Federal Hotels was that the company was "standing in the way" of a $300 million proposal to expand the casinos. Everingham said that the two new casino operators — Aspinalls and Pratt — and a Swiss company Propinvest would be involved in this scheme.

However the $300 million proposal has evaporated. In a recent statement to the NT Legislative Assembly Chief Minister Tuxworth said that the Government had spent $801,351 on consultancy fees, legal fees and other costs and $2.347 million on land purchases with a view to getting the casino expansion projects off the ground. Tuxworth also said that discussions were taking place with developers and "prominent among the parties is the Territory's only public company, Henry and Walker".

If these new developments are to get off the ground, Henry and Walker will need substantial financial assistance and guarantees. Some assistance may be forthcoming from Kumagai Gumi, which in the past two years has committed more than $1 billion to various property developments around Australia because of the decline of construction activity in Japan.

Unless Kumagai Gumi or another big investor provides the backing, the new projects would have difficulty proceeding. Given this state of affairs it is not surprising that Federal Hotels and its managing director, John Haddad, are still extremely upset about the forced exit from the NT casino business — despite having a legal agreement that should have covered a further 14 years.

Haddad recalled for *BRW* last week that Federal Hotels was attracted to the NT casino business by advertisements placed by the NT Government, calling for tenders to design, build and operate the casinos. Federal Hotels defeated 16 other tenders with a proposal for a $9 million casino at Darwin and a $4.5 million casino at Alice Springs.

Haddad said that because of the 15-year licence granted by the Everingham Government, Federal Hotels decided to substantially increase the size and facilities of both casinos. On completion, $32 million had been spent at Darwin and $14 million at Alice Springs, plus other costs.

Haddad said that after some difficult times during the construction — involving cost over-runs and interest rates of more than 20 percent — the casinos began to run very smoothly and a strong marketing campaign lifted occupancy at both to near capacity.

Haddad said Federal Hotels paid the NT Government $3 million in tax in 15 months before the sell-out, tangible evidence that the casinos were operating well. However, just as the casinos and the associated hotel operations were running at their peak, Everingham began expressing displeasure with the way Federal Hotels were operating. Haddad said that Everingham had said that Federal Hotels was verging on bankruptcy, that not enough "high rolling Asian gamblers" had been attracted to Darwin and that Federal Hotels was "standing in the way" of Everingham's $300 million expansion proposals.

"The whole thing was an absolute fiasco and if the whole thing wasn't so serious it would be funny. There is as, ‥r of Don Quixote about it," Haddad sa d. He said that Federal Hotels' bankers — including the Commonwealth Bank and the Standard Chartered Bank of Britain — were "absolutely shocked" by the expropriation.

Northern Territory opposition leader Bob Collins says he is concerned about the extent to which the NT Government and the NTDC have been acting as guarantors, not only to the two casino projects but to several other large hotel and tourism projects in the Northern Territory.

Between the casinos, two Sheraton hotels in the NT, and the Yulara project, the government seems to have guaranteed to project investors a rate of return or, failing that, capital repayments of at least $150 million, Collins says. "The Territory Government is going to underwrite all of it," he says.

Haddad says that Federal Hotels took a $50 million risk on setting up the NT casinos — "We had no government loans or government guarantees" — and endured the financially difficult establishment period, only to have operating control of the casinos handed to a US/British joint venture, and ownership of the properties handed over to a company with an indebted balance sheet and a close relationship with the Everingham government.

"The US and English companies have walked in with little money and will pick up a big return. They have not had to bear the establishment costs," he said. Haddad says that the new operators simply took over Federal Hotels' trained staff and unique casino operating systems (some of which were patented). ▪

MOTOR INDUSTRY

MITSUBISHI TAKES A HUGE PUNT UP FRONT

Magna is a worthy rival to Telstar and Commodore but fleet reaction to its front-wheel drive will decide whether it's a winner

By BILL TUCKEY

Mitsubishi's $54 million each-way bet was unveiled this week in the shape of the new Magna range of cars. It is an each-way bet because the Adelaide company is keeping a two-model, rear-drive Sigma going as well, albeit with sales half those expected.

The front-drive Magna is a huge punt for MMA. It is the first medium-large, front-drive car built in Australia, and it is aimed directly at stealing sales both from the Ford Telstar, the top-selling four-cylinder cars, and the Holden Commodore. If it fails — although that seems unlikely because, apart from the pending Toyota Corolla, it is the only all-

continued page 96

THE AGE, Wednesday 10 October 1984 1

HOW THE HOUSE LOST THE LOT

By BILL BIRNBAUER

KERRY PACKER was in Darwin's Mindil Beach casino eager to spend big. The management stopped him. They needed approval to lift the gambling and credit limits before the big money could be laid on the table.

Mr Packer, one of Australia's richest men and a big gambler, waited while calls were made interstate. By the time approval was gained, Mr Packer was seething at the delay. He was so angry that the next day he complained to the Chief Minister of the Northern Territory's Country Liberal Party Government, Mr Paul Everingham.

The story is used in NT Government circles as a justification of one of the most extraordinary business takeovers in Australia's history. At 3am on 1 October legislation passed by the NT Parliament compulsorily acquired Federal Pacific Hotels' Mindil Beach and Alice Springs casinos. The legislation acquired trademarks used by Federal on cutlery, carpets, gambling chips, linen and glasses as well as the company's registered-design two-up tables.

John Haddad, Federal's managing director, recalls the 3am takeover with bitterness. "Mr Everingham had the insensitivity to have a party at the time virtually to gloat over the acquisition while, one floor down, we were having a wake," he said. "If that's the nature of the man, then I think Bob Hawke ought to welcome him into Federal politics." Mr Everingham is expected to contest the Federal seat of Northern Territory at the coming elections.

Apart from its apparent concern over Federal's financial position, the NT Government has been critical of Federal's failure to accommodate big gamblers, like Mr Packer, and to attract those in Asia. However, Mr Haddad said that the attraction of high rollers was not a condition of the act the casino operated under nor was Darwin airport equipped to cope with such "sophisticated" people. The act set limits on gambling and credit, he said.

The events leading to the takeover are simple, according to Mr Haddad. Federal won a tender in 1978 to build and operate the two casinos under a 15-year licence. The casinos, which included hotels and cabaret and other entertainment facilities, cost about $40 million to build. Construction took place while interest rates were high — 22 per cent — and the tourist industry was down about 20 per cent.

Mr Haddad admits Federal Pacific Hotels and its parent company, then Ipec Holdings Ltd, struggled financially for a time. However, just as the operation started making profits, he said, Big Brother trampled in with acquisition legislation and plans, which included the casinos, for a $300 million tourism project in the Territory. He stressed that because of its assets, which included the two Tasmanian casinos, the Ipec group at no stage faced liquidation.

Correspondence between Federal and the NT Government reveals a higher level of concern in Mr Everingham's office about the casinos' finances. The Territory's Treasurer, Mr Marshall Perron, received a confidential assessment from the Australian Bank on the financial position of Ipec Holdings in January last year. Mr Everingham quoted part of the report to Parliament during a censure debate on 21 August this year.

"The Ipec group is in poor financial condition being highly geared and illiquid," he said. "In such a situation, the combination of high interest rates experienced by the Ipec group for the first six months of the current financial year and reduced economic activity can be severely debilitating to the company's financial viability."

In July, Federal's chairman, Mr Greg Farrell, wrote to Mr Everingham advising him of the sale of Ipec Europe to TNT for $30 million and the sale of Skypak to TNT for $20 million payable over four years. Despite the "rosy picture" this painted, Ipec still suffered a loss for the year to 31 March 1983 of about $8.5 million. Mr Farrell went on to say that while the Mindil Beach complex was doing better than budget, it was losing about $20,000 a week because of finance and leasing costs amounting to $80,000 a week.

Mr Farrell said additional bedrooms were needed at the Alice Springs casino to give it a chance of breaking even. The only way they could be built was with a Government guarantee. The response to this proposal, if there was one, is unknown.

In August last year, Mr Farrell advised the Government that the two casinos were worth $47.1 million and that the company had been talking to several groups regarding an equity partner.

On 8 March this year, Mr Everingham received a report from Martin Corporation Ltd on the feasibility of financing "particular developments" in NT by a property trust. On the same day Mr Farrell wrote to the Chief Minister informing him that a Malaysian group headed by Dato K.C. Koh — "a delightful man" — was negotiating to buy 38 per cent of the Federal group. The interpretations placed on this proposal differ widely.

Mr Haddad: "We would have come out with something superb. It would have put all his (Mr Everingham's) fears to rest. We would have had $27 million of funds, would have had a Malaysian partner, would have had an infrastructure of marketing that would have been sensational. Not only did he refuse that, but I think it set the panic button because he had in his mind that this would go against some of the excuses he was to put to us for asking us to leave."

Mr Perron told Parliament: "It appears that our casinos have been unsuccessfully touted around the world like a rag doll for the past 1½ years. One wonders if the reasons for the lack of success stem from the condition imposed by the sellers that they remain the operators."

On 14 March, Mr Everingham, Mr Perron and Federal's Mr Farrell lunched at the American Club in Sydney. Talk inevitably turned to the casinos. After the lunch Mr Farrell made notes — undisputed by the Government — on the conversation. 'The Age' has obtained a copy of the notes.

Mr Farrell told his two lunch companions that the casinos were not for sale. He pointed out that most of the group's financial problems with the casinos had been resolved and that Mr Koh's involvement would assure their viability.

At this stage, Mr Everingham is reported to have said that the Government could buy out Federal through section 16(3) of the act. Mr Farrell replied:"You must be kidding." Mr Everingham and Mr Perron said they had the power to acquire 100 per cent of the casinos. Talk then turned to Mr Koh.

"I again spoke of Koh and P E (Mr Everingham) said it could only work for his Malaysian mates. G P F (Mr Farrell): 'Not so, Koh is Chinese and has interests throughout the East. I will be fronting up with Mr Koh in about four weeks' time or less and you tell him you don't want him.' P E: 'It's not Koh we don't want, it's Federal as operators and you will force us to invoke s.16(3) if you do that.'

"I was on the point of losing my Irish so I said nothing ... There was very little conversation over coffee."

Several days later, Mr Farrell sent Mr Everingham a letter containing his recollections of the conversation. He concluded: "The board of Federal has decided, only in view of what is implicit in your proposals, they would agree to sell the fixed assets of the two NT casinos for $55 million plus the usual adjustment for consumables and stock."

Mr Perron replied the same day by expressing surprise at the amount sought for the casinos "bearing in mind the price of $47.1 million contemplated by you late last year". He proposed that an independent firm act on behalf of both parties to prepare a valuation.

A formal heads of agreement was signed on 16 April to determine a price for the casinos. Two valuators were to assess the properties and the average of their valuations, so long as it was no less than $47.1 million and no more than $55 million, was to be the agreed sale price.

On the same day, Mr Everingham announced that the Territory's only publicly listed company, Henry and Walker Ltd, which had assets of $6.7 million, would establish with the NT Development Corporation a property trust to buy the casinos. They would be operated by Pratt Hotels, which runs the Sands casino in Atlantic City, and a casino company, Aspinalls of London. He added that 600 extra hotel rooms would be built in Darwin and another 300 in Alice Springs.

Mr Haddad welcomed the proposal cautiously but said that if Mr Everingham scrapped his plan "tomorrow, we would still be here". He pointed out that occupancy at the Darwin casino was averaging 90 per cent.

The Government's valuers came up with a figure of $44.2 million. Federal's valuation was $44.5 million but another $28.8 million was added for the cost of land and improvements. The average of the figures was $59.4 million, which in Federal's eyes, set the amount at the $55 million in the agreement. The Government's final offer was $47.1 million.

Mr Everingham announced on 7 September that Aspinalls and Pratt had formed Diamond Leisure Pty Ltd to operate the casinos as soon as approval was received by the Foreign Investment Review Board. The casinos would be owned by the Territory Property Trust in which Henry and Walker would have a 57 per cent stake. This would cost the company $16 million.

Other participants in the trust would be the Japanese construction group, Kugamai, which would invest $3.9 million, Aspinalls, with a 10 per cent holding ($2.8 million), and Pratt, which would also hold 10 per cent. Nine per cent is yet to be placed but has been reserved for Australian investors. The trust is being capitalised at $28 million and will use debt funding to acquire the balance of the as yet undetermined purchase price.

The Government's Federal Hotels Casinos (Compensation) legislation was passed after a valuation could not be agreed to. Under the act, a Government valuer would determine a price, 90 per cent of which would be offered to Federal Hotels. The reason for not paying the total valuation is unclear.

The casino operators would be required to pay an 8 per cent tax to the NT Government, while the Federal group paid 20 per cent.

Mr Haddad said his company would be willing to sell the casinos for $47.1 million if it retained the management. "But they are asking us to leave our goodwill, they are asking us to forgo what we had in the 15-year licence and they want us to leave for a figure they are going to determine," he said. Mr Haddad said he found it hard to believe that the NT Government's legislation could be introduced in a democracy.

He said he had received calls from overseas business acquaintances who had asked whether Bob Hawke was at last sh[...] his [...]e colors. "I say on the con[...] [...]beral government," he said.

Paul Everingham: concern over casinos' finances.

John Haddad: recalls the takeover with bitterness.

DEFERMENT 'CHEAP POLITICAL STUNT'

N.T.N 20/10/84

Everingham slams casino decision

Former Chief Minister, Mr Paul Everingham, last night described attempts by the Federal Government to defer the takeover of the Territory's two casinos by the Territory Property Trust as a "cheap political stunt."

Federal Treasurer, Mr Paul Keating, said late yesterday the Government wanted "more information" about foreign participation in the trust before approval would be given by the Foreign Investment Review Board (FIRB).

"It's nothing more than a stunt motivated by the election," Mr Everingham said.

"Creating jobs or anything else obviously doesn't matter. Whatever scant respect I had for the Hawke Government — I've got not one scintilla now."

He said the FIRB had recently approved a $45 million project in South Australia.

"Yet here they're holding back.

"There was no indication (before the election was announced) of any problems.

"It was indicated to me by my officials that FIRB approval would be forthcoming.

"There is certainly been no problem between the owners and the operators."

The international marketing director of Pratt Hotels, Mr Chris Raphael, said his company had nothing to worry about over the delay in the FIRB deferment:

"We feel optimistic that at the end of the day their agreement to our participation, and that of our partners, Aspinalls, will be forthcoming," he said.

"There is absolutely no reason why we should be turned down and we are not worried about the delay at all," Mr Raphael said.

Chief Minister, Mr Ian Tuxworth, was unavailable for comment last night, but has called an urgent meeting of all parties for 9 am today.

Mr Everingham, who pushed the compulsory acquisition legislation through the NT Parliament before his resignation this week to contest the federal election, will also attend.

Opposition Leader, Mr Bob Collins, said last night Federal Hotels' formal objection to the FIRB was no surprise.

He said the move by the Federal Treasurer made a mockery of Mr Everingham's statement on April 16 that preliminary details of the proposed development had already been notified to the FIRB and all necessary consent and approvals would be granted at the appropriate time.

The Sydney Morning Herald, Thursday, October 11, 1984

79

Casino owners breach the House limit

KERRY PACKER was in Darwin's Mindil Beach casino eager to spend big. The management stopped him. They needed approval to lift the gambling and credit limits before the big money could be laid on the table.

Mr Packer, one of Australia's richest men and a big gambler, waited while calls were made interstate. By the time approval was gained, Mr Packer was seething at the delay. He was so angry that the next day he complained to the Chief Minister of the Northern Territory's Country-Liberal Party Government, Mr Paul Everingham.

The story is used in NT Government circles as a justification of one of the most extraordinary business takeovers in Australia's history. At 3 am on October 1 legislation passed by the NT Parliament compulsorily acquired Federal Pacific Hotels' Mindil Beach and Alice Springs casinos. The legislation acquired trademarks used by Federal on cutlery, carpets, gambling chips, linen and glasses as well as the company's registered-design two-up tables.

John Haddad, Federal's managing director, recalls the 3 am takeover with bitterness. "Mr Everingham had the insensitivity to have a party at the time, virtually to gloat over the acquisition while, one floor down, we were having a wake," he said.

Apart from its apparent concern over Federal's financial position, the NT Government has been critical of the company's failure to accommodate big gamblers like Mr Packer, and to attract those in Asia. However, Mr Haddad said that the attraction of high-rollers was not a condition of the Act the casino operated under nor was Darwin Airport equipped to cope with such "sophisticated" people. The Act set limits on gambling and credit, he said.

The events leading to the takeover are simple, according to Mr Haddad.

Federal won a tender in 1978 to build and operate the two casinos under a 15-year licence. The casinos, which included hotels and cabaret and other entertainment facilities, cost about $40 million to build. Construction took place while interest rates were high — 22 per cent — and the tourist industry was down about 20 per cent.

Mr Haddad admits Federal Pacific Hotels and its parent company, then Ipec Holdings Ltd, struggled financially for a time. However, just as the operation started making profits, he said, Big Brother trampled in with acquisition legislation and plans, which included the casinos, for a $300 million tourism project in the Territory. He stressed that because of its assets, which included the two Tasmanian casinos, the Ipec group at no stage faced liquidation.

Correspondence between Federal and the NT Government reveals a higher level of concern in Mr Everingham's office about the casinos' finances. The Territory's Treasurer, Mr Marshall Perron, received a confidential assessment from the Australian Bank on the financial position of Ipec Holdings in January last year. Mr Everingham quoted part of the report to Parliament during a censure debate on August 21 this year.

"The Ipec group is in poor financial condition, being highly geared and illiquid," he said.

In July, Federal's chairman, Mr Greg Farrell, wrote to Mr Everingham advising him of the sale of Ipec Europe to TNT for $30 million and the sale of Skypak to TNT for $20 million, payable over four years. Despite the "rosy picture" this painted, Ipec still suffered a loss for the year to March 31, 1983, of about $8.5 million. Mr Farrell went on to say that while the Mindil Beach complex was doing better than budget, it was losing about $20,000 a week because of finance and leasing costs amounting to $80,000 a week.

Mr Farrell said additional bedrooms were needed at the Alice Springs casino to give it a chance of breaking even. The only way they could be built was with a Government guarantee. The response to this proposal, if there was one, is unknown.

In August last year, Mr Farrell advised the Government that the two casinos were worth $47.1 million and that the company had been talking to several groups regarding an equity partner.

On March 8 this year, Mr Everingham received a report from Martin Corporation Ltd on the feasibility of financing "particular developments" in NT by a property trust. On the same day Mr Farrell wrote to the Chief Minister informing him that a Malaysian group headed by Dato K. C. Koh — "a delightful man" — was negotiating to buy 38 per cent of the Federal group. The interpretations placed on this proposal differ wildly.

Mr Haddad: "We would have come out with something superb. It would have put all his (Mr Everingham's) fears to rest. We would have had $27 million of funds, would have had a Malaysian partner, would have had an infrastructure of marketing that would have been sensational. Not only did he refuse that, but I think it set the panic button because he had in his mind that this would go against some of the excuses he was to put to us for asking us to leave."

Mr Perron told Parliament: "It appears that our casinos have been unsuccessfully touted around the world like a rag doll for the past 1½ years. One wonders if the reasons for the lack of success stem from the condition imposed by the sellers that they remain the operators."

On March 14, Mr Everingham, Mr Perron and Federal's Mr Farrell lunched at the American Club in Sydney. Talk inevitably turned to the casinos. After the lunch Mr Farrell made notes — undisputed by the Government — on the conversation.

Mr Farrell told his two lunch companions that the casinos were not for sale. He pointed out that most of the group's financial problems with the casinos had been resolved and that Mr Koh's involvement would assure their viability.

At this stage, Mr Everingham is reported to have said that the Government could buy out Federal through section 16(3) of the Act. Mr Farrell replied: "You must be kidding." Mr Everingham and Mr Perron said they had the power to acquire 100 per cent of the casinos. Talk then turned to Mr Koh.

"I again spoke of Koh and P. E. (Mr Everingham) said it could only work for his Malaysian mates. G. P. F. (Mr Farrell): 'Not so, Koh is Chinese and

BILL BIRNBAUER eports on one of the most extraordinary business takeovers ...tralia's history — the acquisition of the Mindil Be... and ...Springs c...nos by the NT Government

79A

has interests throughout the East. I will be fronting up with Mr Koh in about four weeks' time or less and you tell him you don't want him.' P. E.: 'It's not Koh we don't want, it's Federal as operators and you will force us to invoke S.16(3) if you do that.'"

Several days later, Mr Farrell sent Mr Everingham a letter containing his recollections of the conversation. He concluded: "The board of Federal has decided, only in view of what is implicit in your proposals, they would agree to sell the fixed assets of the two NT casinos for $55 million plus the usual adjustment for consumables and stock."

A formal heads of agreement was signed on 16 April to determine the price for the casinos. Two valuators were to assess the properties and the average of their valuations, so long as it was no less than $47.1 million and no more than $55 million, was to be the agreed sale price.

On the same day, Mr Everingham announced that the Territory's only publicly listed company, Henry and Walker Ltd, which had assets of $6.7 million, would establish with the NT Development Corporation a property trust to buy the casinos. He added that 600 extra hotel rooms would be built in Darwin and another 300 in Alice Springs.

Mr Haddad welcomed the proposal cautiously.

The Government's valuers came up with a figure of $44.2 million. Federal's valuation was $44.5 million but another $28.8 million was added for the cost of land and improvements. The average of the figures was $59.4 million, which in Federal's eyes, set the amount at the $55 million in the agreement. The Government's final offer was $47.1 million.

Mr Everingham announced on September 7 that Aspinalls of London and Pratt Hotels had formed Diamond Leisure Pty Ltd to operate the casinos as soon as approval was received by the Foreign Investment Review Board. The casinos would be owned by the Territory Property Trust in which Henry and Walker would have a 57 per cent stake.

Other particulars in the trust would be the Japanese construction group, Kugamai, which would invest $3.9 million; Aspinalls, with a 10 per cent holding ($2.8 million), and Pratt, which would also hold 10 per cent. Nine per cent is yet to be placed but has been reserved for Australian investors. The trust is being capitalised at $28 million and will use debt funding to acquire the balance of the as yet undetermined purchase price.

The Government's Federal Hotels Casino (Compensation) legislation was passed after a valuation could not be agreed to. Under the Act, a Government valuer would determine a price, 90 per cent of which would be offered to Federal Hotels. The reason for not paying the total valuation is unclear.

The casino operations would be required to pay an 8 per cent tax to the NT Government, while the Federal group paid 20 per cent.

Mr Haddad said his company would be willing to sell the casino for $47.1 million if it retained the management. "But they are asking us to leave our goodwill, they are asking us to forgo what we had in the 15-year licence and they want us to leave for a figure they are going to determine.".

Mr Haddad said he found it hard to believe that the NT Government's legislation could be introduced in a democracy.

He said he had received calls from overseas business acquaintances who had asked whether Bob Hawke was at last showing his true colours. "I say on the contrary, it's a Liberal Government," he said.

The Age

The protagonists . . . Chief Minister of the Territory, Mr Everingham, and Federal's managing director, Mr Haddad.

Casino row is over, but freeze will remain

A/S 14/11/84

Federal Treasurer, Mr Paul Keating, will not be making a decision on the casinos takeover until he receives a report from the Foreign Investment Review Board.

This is despite the Territory Government and Federal Hotels reaching agreement on a takeover price of $49.5 million for the Alice Springs and Darwin casinos.

Mr Keating blocked the takeover for 90 days about a month ago.

And a spokesman for Mr Keating said the deferral would remain until the Foreign Investment Review Board reported back to Mr Keating about the takeover deal.

The board is a statutary body, set up to advise the Federal Government on foreign investment.

The spokesman said the board's report should be given to Mr Keating within two to three weeks.

Federal Hotels, in accepting the new offer, has agreed not to have any part in future operations of the casinos or to have equity in the trust being set up to run them.

Federal Hotels had lodged an objection with the board over Aspinalls and Pratts' involvment in the trust but withdrew it after reaching agreement with the Territory Government.

DETAILS

However, the spokesman for Mr Keating said it wasn't known if the board had received details of Federal Hotels withdrawing its complaint.

The spokesman said if the board had received the details then it was possible the report would be given to Mr Keating in the next few days.

Meanwhile, Territory Opposition Leader, Mr Bob Collins, has demanded the Territory Government tell the public where the money is coming from to pay Federal Hotels.

"There are still many unanswered questions about the entire casino deal including just what financial backing the Territory taxpayer will be making towards the $49.5 million purchase price," Mr Collins said.

"It's also a fair question to ask as to exactly who now owns the casino and whether the present property trust is the same composition as the one set up originally.

"It's obvious that the Territory Government wants to keep as much information about the casino fiasco as quiet as possible for as long as possible."

Casino cash puzzle stays

N.T.N 14/11/84

The $50 million casinos mystery continued today as all doors to the corridors of power stayed closed.

Despite several attempts The NT News was unable to make any headway in discovering who came up with the cash which yesterday paid Federal Hotels for the Darwin and Alice Springs casinos.

Federal Hotels managing director, Mr John Haddad, said from Melbourne the money had been paid into a company bank account in Sydney late yesterday by telegraphic transfer from Darwin.

He said his company had received a telex beforehand from Northern Territory Under Treasurer, Mr Richard Madden, informing the company the payment would be made.

Details

Mr Haddad was unable to say who had paid the money to his company.

Details of the scheme were initially released seven months ago by former Chief Minister, Mr Paul Everingham, and it has been almost two months since the Government forcibly evicted Federal Hotels and handed the casinos to a consortium of Australian, American, British and Japanese gaming and construction companies.

88

Keating asked to relent on casinos

N.T.N TERR 21/10/84

Federal Treasurer, Mr Paul Keating, has been asked to urgently reconsider his decision to block the NT Government's take over of the Darwin and Alice Springs casinos.

Territory Property Trust, chairman Mr Richard Ryan, made the request in a telex to Mr Keating yesterday.

The Territory's newly elected Chief Minister, Mr Ian Tuxworth, also sent a message to Mr Keating asking for the decision to be reconsidered.

Mr Ryan said the trust was the owner of the two casino properties in the Northern Territory which were compulsorily acquired by the NT Government from the pioneer owner-operator Federal Pacific Hotels Limited on October 1.

The trust is a consortium comprising the Territory's only publicly listed company, Henry Walker Limited, The British casino operator Aspinall Holdings and the Pratt Hotels Group of the United States, which operates the Sands Casino in Atlantic City, and the giant Japanese construction group Kumagai Gumi.

Aspinall's and Pratt's have formed a company, Diamond Leisure Pty Ltd, to operate the casinos.

Mr Keating announced yesterday he had an interim order under the foreign takeovers act prohibiting for 90 days proposals by the foreign interests to lease and operate the two casinos.

This followed a formal objection to the Foreign Investment Review Board by Federal Pacific Hotels.

'Technical' says Haddad

Speaking exclusively to the Sunday Territorian from Hong Kong last night, Federal Hotel's Managing Director Mr John Haddad said "our solicitors put in a report to the FIRB on our behalf."

"We argued our suitabilty as operators of the Territory casinos against the suitablity of the new operators," he said.

"Technicallly I suppose Mr Keating is correct in saying we lodged an objection. As far as we're concerned, we were just *making a point of view*."

Success

Mr Ryan, who is also chairman of Diamond Leisure, pending FIRB approval, said he noted with dismay reports of Mr Keating's decision.

Mr Ryan, who is also a director of Henry and Walker, said the success of the substantial Australian investment in the trust, hinged on early reorientation of the casino enterprise. (Henry and Walker plan to take a 57 per cent controlling interest in the property trust).

In the absense of any Australian operators with demonstrated ability to access the international markets, (the) introduction of wide ranging expertise is vital to our success, the telex said.

I am therefore at a loss to understand your position and to fathom what can be gained by delaying a final decision.

A great deal of work has been put in to structure an arrangement under which the interests of this trust, those operators, and the public are all served.

I am fearful that this whole balance may now be disturbed by the uneasiness which has now been caused.

In a statement issued in Darwin Mr Tuxworth said there was no valid reason for any holdup.

The Federal Treasurer, Mr Keating, has in front of him all the information he needs to go ahead with approval.

He said the proposed new operators and the Territory Government had supplied all the information requested by the FIRB and his Government had detailed the reasons for not allowing Federal Hotels to continue as the casino operators.

He said he understood Mr Keating was supportive of foreign investment in casinos in Western Australia, South Australia (Kumagai) and Queensland.

What possible objections could there be to similar investment in the Territory? he asked.

Meeting

Mr Tuxworth said while the deferral of FIRB approval would not affect existing operations it could delay the immediate plans for upgrading the casinos.

Mr Tuxworth and Mr Ryan both attended a meeting in Darwin yesterday which was called when Mr Keating's decision became known.

FIN REV 24/6 85

Henry, Walker in rationalisation

By MIKE TAYLOR

HENRY and Walker Ltd, the company at the centre of the Northern Territory Government's controversial expropriation of the Darwin and Alice Springs hotel-casinos from Federal Hotels, has moved to rationalise its operations.

The company, which was been confronted by a $1.42 million loss for the past financial year and the necessary commitment towards its purchase of a 57 per cent share in the Darwin and Alice Springs Casinos, intends selling off about $6 million of its assets in the Northern Territory.

Today, in Sydney, the company will auction an estimated $6 million worth of property as part of the rationalisation. The catalogue includes a fleet of prawn trawlers, the big Nathan River cattle station, a prime Darwin waterfront property and the Darwin Crocodile Farm.

Several Australian and overseas groups are expected to be vying for the properties, with South African and US syndicates having already expressed an interest.

The move to rationalise is expected to give the group a sizable cash-flow after its involvement in the expropriation of the Darwin and Alice Springs casinos from Federal Hotels.

Henry and Walker will subscribe for units in the Territory Unit Trust set up to by the Northern Territory Government to own the two casino-hotel complexes.

The properties to be auctioned in Sydney today are indicative of Henry and Walkers' spread of interests resulting from its role as the Northern Territory's largest public company.

As well as its interests in pastoral properties, prawn trawling and tourism, the company is also involved in civil engineering, automotive retailing, property development and air charter.

The auctioneers, Richardson and Wrench Surfers Paradise, expect the fleet of four ocean-going prawn trawlers operating out of Darwin to fetch close to $2 million, while a prime Darwin waterfront holding facility will be offered separately.

The facility, which covers six hectares and includes a small ship repair and building facility and a slipway, is expected to sell for about $1 million.

The Nathan River Station, situated 100km north-west of Boorroloola, and covering 4,000 square kilometres and running 3,000 head, is expected to sell for just under $1 million.

The Darwin Crocodile Farm and tourist complex, one of Darwin's best-known tourist attractions, is also for sale and is expected to bring about $1.3 million.

Richardson and Wrench's Mr John McKay-Roberts is managing the sale.

He said that particular interest had been expressed by a South African group, a large US group and South Australian fishing interests.

ASPINALL TAKES OVFR THE REINS OF THE TERRITORY'S TWO CASINOS

N.T.N 2/12/84

A flamboyant 'King' moves into Darwin

"If you are Australian and a gambler, bet ... ie," crowed English gambling personality ohn Aspinall when he heard he would take ontrol of our Northern Territory casinos.

"Australians, God bless them, are a nation of amblers — I love 'em," the undisputed king of nglish gambling said.

I spoke to Mr Aspinall in the office above his plush ayfair gambling club, where he brandished the ficial telex "hot off the presses" from the Federal overnment.

"You are now the owner of two casinos," said the tter, which ended months of speculation and zarre wrangling over the future of the casinos at lice Springs and Darwin's Mindil Beach.

The ultimate owner- ip of the gaming uses had been thrown to limbo when the orthern Territory ad- inistration under Mr aul Everingham iceremoniously threw it the previous tenant, ederal Hotels, claim- g it was unhappy with e company's financial sition.

After a bitter public inging match between e chief of Federal, Mr hn Haddad, and for- er Chief Minister, Mr veringham, the threat a legal brawl was erted and Federal ap- ased with a cheque for 7 million in compen- tion.

The Chaplinesque an- s of the affair ilminated in Mr veringham holding a m press conference at Darwin casino to nounce the end of the deral Hotels regime.

It was the Northern rritory adminis- ation which ap- oached Mr Aspinall d the United States mbling group, Great y Casino Corporation, take over the management of the two casinos jointly.

Mr Aspinall and his U.S. counterparts each paid $3 million for the licence under their new joint company, Diamond Leisure.

It is fitting the extraordinary events surrounding the change of ownership should involve such an extraordinary figure as Mr Aspinall. He has two great loves, gambling and animals.

A flamboyant character, the 57-year-old millionaire zoo owner and socialite has been in the news since the early '60s when he opened his first casino in London.

From
JANINE
PERRETT
in London

The exclusive gaming club in Berkley Square was the haunt of dukes, MPs, tycoons and wealthy playboys. He left it 10 years later to concentrate on his private zoo and wildlife park.

The lure of the gaming tables called him back and he set up the Curzon St Club in partnership with financier James Goldsmith. Last year they floated 20 per cent of the shares in the club on the unlisted securities market, valuing the operations at more than $90 million.

'He has two great loves, gambling and animals.'

While his gambling interests create the most attention in Australia, in London the Aspinall name has more recently been linked with the unfortunate incidents surrounding his zoo in Kent.

The Aspinall zoo has a sorry track record for difficult animals which have led to the deaths of three of his staff. Two were mauled by tigers and one crushed to death by an elephant. Only last month one of his tigers escaped and had to be shot in a suburban backyard.

But, despite the obvious dangers, the inimitable Mr Aspinall is known to venture into his tigers' cage for a friendly frolic on occasions, undeterred by the damage the dangerous claws do to his expensive clothes.

It was animals he first wanted to talk about when the casino appointment was confirmed.

"I had a letter from the Northern Territory Government asking me if I was interested in taking some animals, but the quarantine laws are so strict here I won't be able to," he said.

His love of animals is prevalent throughout the Mayfair club. Numerous wildlife paintings adorn the tastefully decorated walls of the six gaming rooms.

The air of opulence which pervades the club is something he hopes to bring to the Australian casinos. He is quite emphatic there will be changes and they will reflect his reputation for dealing in high stakes.

"We are specialists in big gamblers and we hope to attract the big players from the Far East," he explained.

This will involve building a special private gaming room with more than 20 luxury suites for the sole use of the big gamblers from as far away as Tokyo and Seoul. Mr Aspinall believes he can lure Muslim gamblers from South-East Asia where Islamic fundamentalists are forcing the closure of casinos in several countries.

Obviously proud of his reputation, he points out that already the Darwin casino is being inundated with Asians who have heard he has taken over and say: "Ah, Mr Aspinall, you know how to treat us."

As yet, the facilities for these gamblers are not there, so all he can do is "cover them with apologies" and tell them to come back in a year when it is finished.

When John Aspinall talks about the "big gambler", he is talking from the experience of his own club which allows only that select group of "established gamblers who are prepared to risk at least $3000 a night".

The Aspinall team has already started to move into the Australian casinos and has successfully applied to raise the minimum limit from $50 to $200.

He is quick to assure Australians the small punter will not be pushed out. It was for this reason the Northern Territory Government wanted the U.S. partner, which operates the Sands chain, in the deal.

'We, are specialists in big gamblers and we hope to attract the big player from the Far East.'

"They specialise in the 'bedrock' or 'grind' action as it is known in the States. They are experts on the games for small players such as slot machines," he said.

Mr Aspinall believes Federal Hotels was not running the casinos "with any imagination".

For a man whose club reported pre-tax profits of around $22 million last year, and is expected to do even better when it reports in the next few weeks, he is incredulous that Federal "could not even make a profit" from the Australian operations.

For this reason he totally supports the Northern Territory administration and Australian gaming authorities which he describes as "sensible".

(9) Janine Perrett, NT News, 2 December 1984

Appendix F

Portion of KPMG report covering strategic positioning for the future Northern Territory University

3 The imperative for change

At the highest level, the consultations with stakeholders and the other research and analysis found an imperative for change, and confirmed that the issues of resourcing and stakeholder perceptions lie at the heart of the strategic positioning project. Both issues need to be addressed in tandem. A solution to resourcing issues without dealing with client and stakeholder perceptions will be less than half an answer, while a failure to confront resourcing issues would inevitably compound the concerns that dominate stakeholder perceptions.

The *Overview of the NTU's financial and operational position* report revealed that the university faced a serious financial situation at the end of 1999. Although the financial results for the year 2000 appeared to show some improvement in the financial situation, the university's ongoing financial viability would appear to be problematic without longer-term reform.

The consultations across all stakeholder groups identified a substantial reservoir of goodwill towards the university. Those consulted were passionately committed to its presence, to its independent existence and to working with the university to position it at the forefront of innovative approaches to education, training and research that build upon its unique position.

The Northern Territory community, to the extent consulted, also expressed a common view that the university will not succeed if it continues to attempt to try to be responsive to all needs and demands for education and training in the Territory. That objective is felt to be unsustainable, and this realisation in turn provides an opportunity to recalibrate and sharpen the vision and direction of the NTU.

The views of those consulted also covered many specific issues, from vision and resources, through quality, client focus and communication, to administration, infrastructure management and leadership. Where relevant, views on these issues are explored in greater depth in later parts of this report.

3.1 The preferred future direction

The research and analysis points to a possible preferred future direction for the Northern Territory University.

That direction is grounded in the Steering Committee's view of the key principles that should underpin the future strategic direction of the NTU.

The direction acknowledges the issues related to the NTU's current fields of study and course offerings, and evolves them to propose seven areas of competitive advantage for the NTU.

Northern Territory University
Strategic Positioning for the Future
August 2001

It examines how the NTU can maximise its competitive advantage and build its capacity by:

- Capitalising on its market potential (including in relation to product development);
- Developing the enablers of competitive advantage (being partnerships, alliances and resourcing); and
- Enhancing its operational effectiveness in the areas of structure and governance, planning and budgeting, administrative infrastructure, organisational culture and relationship management.

Diagram 1 below shows this framework, which is used for the remainder of the report.

Diagram 1: Strategic positioning project framework

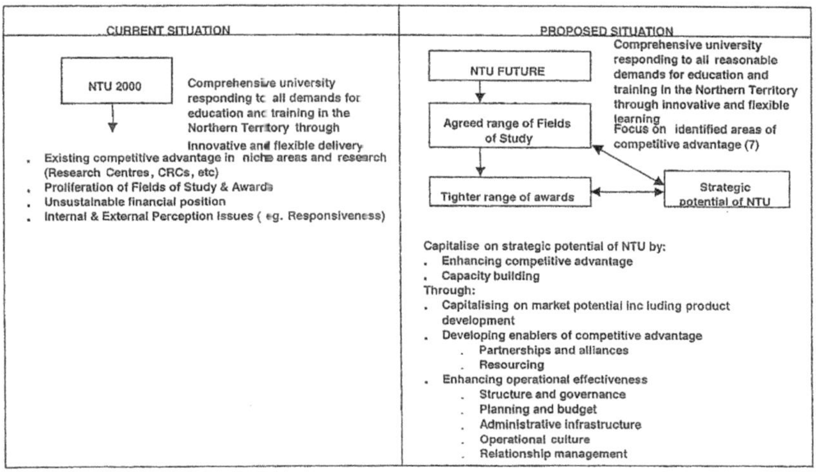

4 Key principles to underpin NTU's future directions

The Steering Committee deliberated at length about the overarching principles that should underpin the NTU's future strategic direction. The committee was conscious in these deliberations of:

- The significance of the foundation of the NTU as a symbol of the Territory's 'coming of age', and its role in providing the full range of course and program offerings to reflect the opportunities Territorians believe their Territory offers them;
- The emerging view within the Territory that the NTU cannot continue to remain faithful to an objective to meet all the needs for education and training in the Northern Territory; and
- The great diversity of views about what areas might be rationalised.

The Committee concluded that the NTU should be responsive to all *reasonable* demands for education and training in the Northern Territory, including innovative approaches to teaching and learning. What is 'reasonable' is examined later in the report, but among the criteria considered were the NTU's research strengths and the opportunities the NTU has to enhance Australia's regional engagement.

The Committee also emphasised the strengths and opportunities represented by the dual-sector nature of the NTU's operations (with neither sector subordinate to the other); and, within the dual-sector approach, how the needs of the individual learner drive the university's commitment to a seamless approach to their education and training experiences.

Finally, the Steering Committee was aware that charting a strategic direction for an organisation in the business of learning and skill acquisition requires an understanding of future trends in that business, and the forces that drive them. It was widely recognised that the arrival of the knowledge age poses a major and fundamental change to all society's institutions, and especially its learning institutions. In terms of promoting lifelong learning, new learning technologies and new knowledge processing skills (such as problem solving, communications, emotional competence, team work, technological literacy and the ability to think systemically and innovate), the Committee was determined the NTU should be at the forefront of the knowledge age.

Recommendations

1 The Northern Territory University Council (the Council) notes that a number of key background papers were prepared as part of the Strategic Positioning

Project and that the findings of the papers, and the consultations through the focus groups, workshops, written submissions and interviews, have informed this set of recommendations.

2 The Council notes the very tight financial position of the NTU, as highlighted in the review paper 'NTU financial position and operational overview', and the conclusion that the future financial position of the NTU is not sustainable without the implementation of long-term reform measures.

3 The Council note the view of the Steering Committee that statements of overarching principle should underpin the future strategic direction of the NTU, and agree that these statements be reflected in future strategic directions documentation for the NTU. These statements follow.

- In serving the people of the Northern Territory, the NTU will maintain a dual focus on their intellectual and vocational needs.
- The NTU will respond to all reasonable demands for education and training in the Northern Territory, including innovative approaches to teaching and learning.
- The NTU will be guided in all its activities by the role of education, training and research in the knowledge age through the use, for example, of innovative technology, and the opportunities and challenges this presents for the staff and students of the NTU.

Appendix G

Interview with Chancellor Richard Ryan ex CDU archives, 2007

TRANSCRIPT WEB PROFILE

Richard Ryan:

Deputy Chancellor and former Chancellor CDU

01 Richard Ryan on: The 1980s, Darwin Community College & Darwin Institute of Technology

I was involved with a couple of charities in the NT. As a result of that I was asked by the Everingham Government to go on the board of what was then the Darwin Community College. But within a month or two of my going onto it, it evolved into the Darwin Institute of Technology.

It was a major revelation because, I think we're talking the early 80s, if my memory serves me correctly. I can remember graphically going to this meeting which would have been my second or third council meeting, if we take DCC into account, and being asked to resign, along with all the other Council members. And Nan Giese, god bless her soul, stared them all down - the people who wanted us to resign. The reason they wanted us to resign was the new principle didn't meet some of the education criteria that the academics thought.

And I can understand it , it was an impingement on the freedoms of the institution . That there should be a proper process rather than Government saying that Kevin Davis had the job. And he subsequently, Kevin Davis did a wonderful job.

02 Richard Ryan on: 1989 & the formation of NTU

The history making event was NTU. Because it was the first university. It gave you a real buzz to be involved. Where else in Australia could you do that? At that particular stage I don't think there'd been any other institutions created and it was just wonderful. It was a great experience and it actually made you feel that you were contributing.

I remember the first council meeting was quite huge. I remember thinking this is too many people because you can never make a decision when you've got an audience that's listening to every word. But Austin did a good job. Nan did a good job and it all settled down.

03 Richard Ryan on: Vice-Chancellor Mal Nairn

Of course the huge advantage in all that was the choice of Vice-Chancellor in Mall Nairn was a perfect choice

Mal, because he was a VET fitted into the community extremely well. He had wonderful skills in terms of handling people. I remember graphically him coming to the University council meetings and using his presence to get things through without forcing them. I think his tenure, which was five years, was really revelationary to where the institution went.

04 Richard Ryan on: the transition from NTU to CDU

In the later years of NTU, after Austin Asche had resigned to become Administrator, Nan Giese became Chancellor and I became Deputy Chancellor. We really had some quite severe financial difficulties. We brought in a series of controls to make sure that we could pay wages. And I can remember graphically going with Ron McKay, who was the then Vice-Chancellor, to see Dennis Bourke, to get money to be able to pay wages in two months time. It was a whole series of compounding factors. It was nobody's particular fault. It was part of the growing up process that we as an institution had to go through. It was the federal Government restricting funds. It was the NT Government wanting to develop other avenues. so it was getting fairly difficult.

And all of this was occurring around the time Ron McKay had fallen ill and put his resignation in. So Charles Webb became the acting Vice-Chancellor . And I can remember graphically going down to Sydney to see the then Federal Mistier for Education, Nelson, with Peter Plummer who then headed up the Education Department and being given a series of ultimatums by the Federal Minister that if the Northern Territory didn't change some of the things that it did that he would consider holding back funding.

They wanted the institution to be more self-supporting, get more students, and the way to do that was to put together with what was then NTU, Centralian College and Menzies School of health research. And it was all very difficult at the time. As all this was occurring we started looking for a temporary Vice-Chancellor.

And Ken McKinnon was brought into this institution on the basis that he would be here for twelve months. he would effect change and then he would wander off into the wilderness. And he did exactly that.

05 Richard Ryan on: CDUs economic benefit to the NT

The economic benefit to the Northern Territory. And if you would allow me a bit of poetic licence with this, It's the third to major employer, it has a huge impact on the GDP, And if it didn't exist we would really regret it economically. It is quite relevant to all this

06 Richard Ryan on: the changes in tertiary education in the NT

If you take the changes in education from the Darwin Community College days to today, we have Darwin Community College, Darwin Institute of Technology, the University College of the NT, Centralian, Menzies School of health Research, NTU and now CDU, that's six and I've possibly missed one. the changes are enormous .

It's hard to comprehend that in the mid-eighties there was a small country town institution that turned into an institution that has 20,000 students, that has campuses right throughout the Northern Territory, it has campuses in Sydney and Melbourne. It has Menzies School of Health research that is the leader of its type in the country. And all that has been done with a population of 220,000 people. If I sound parochial it's because I am - it's true actually!

07 Richard Ryan: reflections on CDU

The University today is a long way ahead of where I ever thought it would be. We had lots of very difficult years and suddenly it's all come together

Everybody honestly has tried to do the right thing for the institution. Now often people haven't agreed on the method, or even the process.

There are some people that to the detriment of their health have stayed and fought for CDU against those dreadful people down south that existed at one stage.

The main thing that we've got going for us is our staff is dedicated. The people really want to do things and I think the future is really something - I do actually.

Appendix H

Assorted papers relating to GST and NT budget review, 2024

Capital city Indigenous: population on the move, 2016-2021

Capital city	Indigenous population 2016	Indigenous population 2021	Total population 2021	Indigenous population 2021	Change Indigenous population 2016-21
GREATER SYDNEY	87,755	90,954 ▲	5,231,104	2%	4% ▲
GREATER MELBOURNE	31,907	33,020 ▲	4,917,717	1%	3% ▲
GREATER BRISBANE	60,522	76,940 ▲	2,526,268	3%	27% ▲
GREATER PERTH	36,439	42,055 ▲	2,116,648	2%	15% ▲
GREATER ADELAIDE	19,340	23,782 ▲	1,387,276	2%	23% ▲
ACT	6456	8903 ▲	453,868	2%	38% ▲
GREATER HOBART	8544	11,226 ▲	247,083	5%	31% ▲
GREATER DARWIN	11,961	14,527 ▲	139,927	10%	21% ▲
RURAL, REGIONAL & REMOTE	439,115	511,303 ▲	8,402,786	6%	16% ▲
AUSTRALIA	702,039	812,710 ▲	25,422,677	3%	16% ▲

The latest five-yearly national census records significant steps towards the goal of reconciliation

BERNARD SALT

Politics Federal GST

— Opinion

Why the GST fiasco won't be fixed

Fights about the distribution of GST revenue aren't just about the money – they also reflect the political death of major tax reform. It's a policy fiasco.

Jennifer Hewett
Columnist

Mar 27, 2024 – 4.55pm

Ferocious arguments between the states over their shares of the GST aren't just typical squabbles over money. They are another signpost to the dead end of major tax reform [https://www.afr.com/policy/economy/slash-income-tax-hike-gst-and-levy-tech-giants-comyn-s-growth-fix-20240326-p5ffbt] in Australia.

The outrage from any other state government – and certainly most economists – about the inequity of Western Australia's special deal on the GST won't change that paralysis.

The Albanese government appreciates that any change to the Coalition's guarantee [https://www.afr.com/policy/economy/we-re-paying-more-tax-for-liberals-gst-fiddling-20240213-p5f4j7] to WA of a minimum 70 per cent of GST per head of population – rising to 75 per cent in July – would be electoral poison in a key state.

WA's mining royalties, worth more than $11 billion last financial year, have transformed it into a remarkably wealthy state.

But problems with the GST formula go much deeper than predictable screams about who should get what. The 1930s concept of "horizontal fiscal equalisation" supposedly allowing states to provide equal levels of service seems badly out of touch with the needs of a modern, competitive economy.

Ironically, greater Commonwealth assistance to weaker states was in part due to the need to assuage Western Australia after it voted to secede. WA benefited from this formula for decades. The difference now is that WA's mining royalties, worth more than $11 billion last financial year, have transformed it into a remarkably wealthy state.

The resources boom may also be propping up the federal budget and national economy but the cost of Canberra's commitment to "top up" other states on GST to ensure they are no worse off amounts to far more than anticipated. Around $5 billion a year and counting.

Yet this is just the most spectacular of contradictions in this arcane policy. Why should a wildly profligate Victoria, for example, that also refuses to allow gas exploration or development be rewarded because it doesn't have a coal or iron ore industry it can tax? Why should any state government be rewarded if it makes lousy policy choices that make it increasingly less appealing for business investment and therefore more reliant on stronger economies that also manage their finances better?

The Productivity Commission will report on the GST design and allocation in 2026. But this is another example of how it's increasingly beyond the reach of Australia's politicians to get agreement in a federal system. Polite suggestions from business that general policy inertia can be neatly resolved by "independent" experts are negated by the Grants Commission's own record.

Treasurer Jim Chalmers is naturally keen to shelter behind the independence of the commission's latest recommendations on how to divide up near $90 billion of GST next financial year.

That can't stop the political blame game spreading. [https://www.afr.com/policy/economy/mathematically-challenged-states-spat-over-gst-gets-personal-20240315-p5fcoy] Cue fury from NSW and Queensland whose GST dollars have been slightly reduced due to higher royalty payments from coal while Victoria will get $3.8 billion more.

Victorian Treasurer Tim Pallas describes NSW Labor Premier Chris Minns as "mathematically challenged" and a "tool" for describing Victoria as a "welfare state receiving a whole bunch of money from the pockets of NSW families". Queensland will become a donor state for the first time in more than a decade, receiving just over 95¢ in the dollar. Expect a desperate Premier Steven Miles to shout loudly about that in the October election campaign.

Despite the mutual insults, bigger states do have a mutual interest in the pool of GST money being divided largely on a population basis. Back in 2012, NSW, Victoria, Queensland and WA signed a declaration to this effect – with no real traction since. For obvious reasons, smaller states like South Australia and Tasmania as well as the Northern Territory fear losing out from their current level of subsidy providing about 10 per cent extra of the total GST pool redistributed from larger states to them.

According to Victorian Premier Jacinta Allan's complaint, there's nothing fair about Victoria subsidising any other states. NSW Treasurer Daniel Mookhey wants to use anger about an "absurd" system to challenge Canberra's attempts to negotiate reform partnerships with the states in other contentious areas like the National Disability Insurance Scheme.

Due to its attempt at political insurance for WA, the Albanese government extended the "no worse off" pledge to other states to 2030 precisely to try to avoid this sort of stand-off. But this political fix is clearly unstable, as well as eye-wateringly expensive

The intensity of feelings – on both sides – has been building for years. After the iron ore boom began to push up state royalties 15 years ago, then WA premier Colin Barnett warned a succession of federal governments about the impact on WA's share of the GST.

Compounding local community anger, delay in the timing of payments meant WA's share fell to 30¢ in the dollar in 2015 after iron ore prices had fallen dramatically, its economy had suddenly slowed, and the budget was in deficit.

Without Canberra's guarantee, the state would by now be receiving around 12¢ in the dollar. But the view from outside WA's borders is of a fantastically rich state getting billions of dollars it doesn't need from other Australian taxpayers. That's even though the state's boom bust history in resources demonstrates how volatile such funding is.

Former WA premier Barnett is one of those arguing Australia can't afford to keep ignoring a broken, unpredictable system. The most logical and simple reform, he says, would be to allocate around 90 per cent of the GST money to states based on population – with 10 per cent kept aside to subsidise the smaller states. The floor of 70¢ should be retained, he says, but there's no need for the imminent rise to 75¢.

"We are prepared to support the other states but not to an unlimited degree," he says. "This system is archaic. We can do something to give stability to all the states."

The enraged spluttering from across the Nullarbor will only get louder.

Have your say

We are always interested to hear your views on current topics. Guidelines for how to write an opinion article are **here** [https://www.afr.com/companies/media-and-marketing/how-to-write-an-opinion-article-for-the-afr-20231025-p5eey4]. Guidelines for how to write a letter to the editor are **here** [https://www.afr.com/contact-us/letters-to-the-editor]. Please send your letter to edletters@afr.com.au

RELATED

Why Comyn went 'off script' and called for a major tax shake-up

https://www.afr.com/policy/tax-and-super/why-matt-comyn-went-off-script-and-called-for-a-major-tax-shake-up-20240326-p5ffew

RELATED

The five worst decisions this century by politicians

https://www.afr.com/politics/federal/the-five-worst-decisions-this-century-by-politicians-20240319-p5fdni

RELATED

NSW needs to lead the charge on reforming GST share-out

https://www.afr.com/policy/economy/nsw-needs-to-lead-the-charge-on-reforming-gst-share-out-20240318-p5fd57

Jennifer Hewett is the National Affairs columnist. She writes a daily column on politics, business and the economy. *Connect with Jennifer on Twitter. Email Jennifer at jennifer.hewett@afr.com*

Northern Territory Budget Review 2024

GST Revenue is projected to increase $3.99 billion in 2023–24 to $4.83 billion in 2027–28, at an average growth of 4.9% per annum.

The Territory's GST revenue is expected to increase by an average of $188 million per annum, reflecting higher forecast growth in the GST collections pool; an increase to the Territory GST relativity from 4.98725 in 2023–24 to 5.06681 in 2024–25; partially offset by higher interstate population growth, reducing the Territory's GST share of national population.

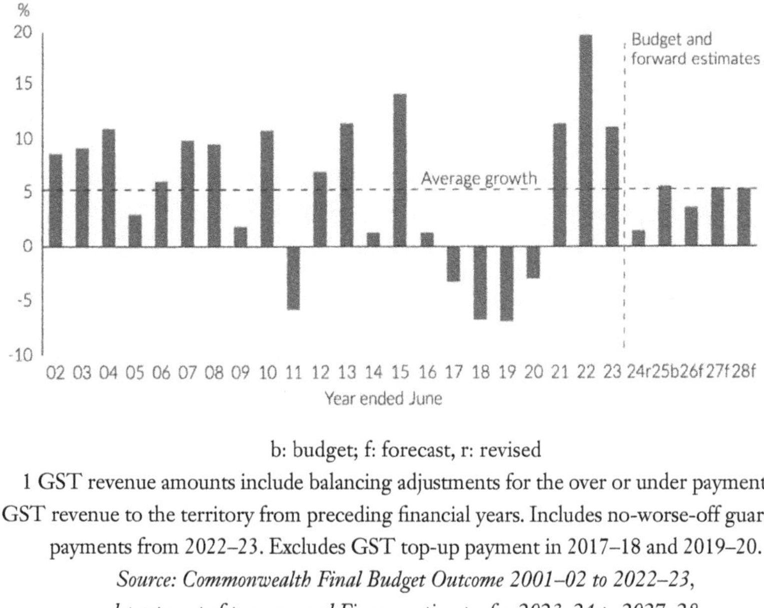

b: budget; f: forecast, r: revised

1 GST revenue amounts include balancing adjustments for the over or under payment of GST revenue to the territory from preceding financial years. Includes no-worse-off guarantee payments from 2022–23. Excludes GST top-up payment in 2017–18 and 2019–20.

Source: Commonwealth Final Budget Outcome 2001–02 to 2022–23, department of treasury and Finance estimates for 2023–24 to 2027–28.

Chart 5.1: Territory GST revenue annual growth.

Chart 5.1 shows actual annual GST revenue growth for the Territory from 2001–02 to 2022–23, and estimates across the budget cycle to 2027–28. It highlights the volitivity of Territory

GST revenue, mainly due to fluctuations in the national GST collections pool and Territory and relativity , with actual annual growth rates ranging from -6.9% to 19.7% across 2001–02 to 2027–23. Since the introduction of GST, the Territory's GST revenue has averaged annual growth of about 5.2%.

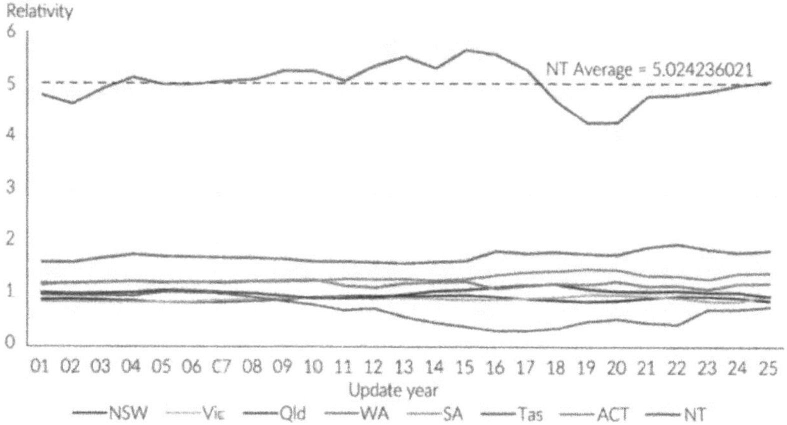

Source: Commonwealth Final Budget Outcome, 2000–01 to 2022–23, CGC Annual Update 2023–24 and 2025.

Chart 5.3: GST relativity, 2000–01 to 2024–25

In March 2024, the Commonwealth Grants Commission (CGC) released its 2024 Update, which recommended increasing the Territory's GST relativity to 5.06681 in 2024–25, from 4.98725 in 2023–24, Chart 5.3 sets out the Territory's GST relativity over time and illustrates its greater volitivity compared with other states.

The 2024–25 GST relativity recognises that the Territory is assessed as having the lowest fiscal capacity of the states reflecting:

- Above average assessed expenditure needs due to a relatively high share of disadvantaged populations groups, including people living in remote and very remote areas, diseconomies of scale in administration and above-average infrastructure requirements, primarily for roads (higher GST relativity)

- Below average assessed capacity to raise own-source revenue across most revenue lines, particularly property taxes (higher GST relativity)
- Above-average assessed investment requirements and construction costs (higher GST relativity).
- Above average share of relevant Commonwealth payments (lower GST relativity).

The main contributors to the increase in the Territory's GST relativity in the 2024 Update as assessed by the CGC were:

- Large increases in coal prices and royalties, which decreased other states GST requirements
- Increased Territory wage costs relative to other states
- Updated socioeconomics data following the 2021 Census showing greater Territory disadvantage and a more
- dispersed population, which particularly increased the Territory's assessed health and housing needs.

Changes to the way GST is distributed among states came into effect in 2021–22 following passage of the Commonwealth Treasury Laws Amendment (Making Sure Every State and Territory Gets Their Fair Share of GST) Act 2018.

The GST distribution reforms are being transitioned in stages from 2021–22 to 2026–27, and comprise four elements:

- staged implementation from 2021–2022 to 2026–27 of a new equalization standard, being the stronger of New South Wales or Victoria
- a minimum GST relativity floor of 0.7 from 2022–23 increasing to 0.75 from 2024–25
- Commonwealth funded top-ups to the GST pool of $600

million from 2021–22 increasing by $250 million from 2024–25, and indexed in line with the GST pool growth

- A temporary no-worse-off guarantee to the end of 2029–30.

The impact of these reforms have increased Western Australia's GST share, which is the only jurisdiction with a relativity below the minimum floor due to its significantly greater ability to raise own-source revenue from mining. As the amount distributed to Western Australia by this reform is more than the amount of GST pool top-up payments, all other jurisdictions are worse off, and require the Commonwealth to make a no-worse-off guarantee payments. Due to the no-worse-off guarantee, the reforms currently do not have a net impact on Territory GST revenue.

Table 1.3: Commonwealth revenue

	2023-24	2024-25	2025-26	2026-27	2027-28
	Revised	Budget	Forward estimate		
	$M	$M	$M	$M	$M
Untied Commonwealth revenue	3 989	4 208	4 356	4 589	4 830
Tied Commonwealth revenue	1 802	2 076	1 853	1 697	1 620
Total Commonwealth revenue	5 791	6 284	6 209	6 286	6 450

Chart 2.1: Non financial public sector fiscal balance - medium-term outlook[1]

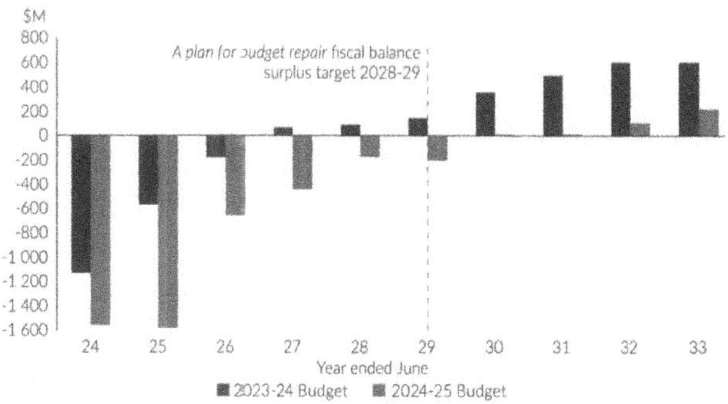

Table 2.12: Non financial public sector – variation in net debt and net debt to revenue ratio since 2023-24 Budget

	2023-24	2024-25	2025-26	2026-27	202
	Revised	Budget	Forward estimate		
	$M	$M	$M	$M	$I
Net debt					
2023-24 Budget	9 231	9 849	9 984	9 861	r
2023-24 Mid-Year Report	9 178	9 938	10 190	10 138	r
2024-25 Budget	9 396	11 046	11 776	12 210	12 3
Variation from 2023-24 Budget	165	1 197	1 792	2 349	r
Net debt to revenue (%)					
2023-24 Budget	113	118	122	118	r
2023-24 Mid-Year Report	111	119	123	121	r
2024-25 Budget	115	126	132	135	1
Variation from 2023-24 Budget	2	8	10	17	r

n/a: not available at the time of publishing the 2023-24 Budget and 2023-24 Mid-Year Report

Table 4.8: Non financial public sector – net debt to revenue ratios

	2024-25	2025-26	2026-27	2027-28	Target on track
	Budget	Forward estimate			
	%	%	%	%	
2024-25 Budget	126	132	135	133	no

As shown in Table 4.8 above, the non-financial public sector's net debt to revenue ratio is projected to be 126% in 2024–25, increasing to 133% by 2027–28. Its anticipated the net debt to revenue ratio will remain above 100% over the medium term, and therefore this fiscal strategy objective and target is not likely to be met.

The Fiscal Integrity and Transparency Act 2021 (FITA) incorporates a cap on accessible debt at the non-financial public sector of $15 billion (the debt ceiling). The legislated debt ceiling increases accountability for financial performance and supports improving the Territory's credit rating and net debt to revenue ratio.

Table 4.9 presents the assessable debt for the 2024–25 Budget in accordance with the FITA debt ceiling and shows that total borrowings, excluding leases, are projected to increase over the budget cycle but remain below the $15 billion cap in all years.

Table 4.9: Non financial public sector - debt ceiling assessment

	2024-25	2025-26	2026-27	2027-28
	Budget	Forward estimate		
	$M	$M	$M	$M
Total borrowings	14 401	15 196	15 759	16 006
Less: leases	1 777	1 673	1 546	1 433
Total assessable debt	12 624	13 523	14 213	14 573
Target on track	yes	yes	yes	yes

Operating balance surplus indicates government can finance the cost of services from revenue generated in that financial year. Conversely, operating deficits indicate revenues are insufficient to fund current operations. While in the short term cyclical operating deficits may be appropriate during periods of economic downturn, persistent or structural operating deficits subsequently pass debt relating to current services to future generations. Operating deficits also provide no capacity for investment in infrastructure beyond depreciation levels without further borrowings.

Table 3.1: Territory key economic indicators (%)

	2022-23a	2023-24e	2024-25f	2025-26f	2026-27f
Gross state product[1]	- 5.3	4.9	2.3	7.1	4.1
State final demand[1]	1.9	1.7	1.9	- 0.2	2.1
Population[2]	0.9	0.8	0.9	1.1	1.1
Employment[1]	2.6	1.5	1.1	0.9	1.3
Unemployment rate[3]	4.3	4.4	4.6	4.8	4.7
Consumer price index[1]	6.4	3.6	2.9	2.5	2.4
Wage price index[1]	2.8	4.1	3.2	3.1	3.1

a: actual; e: estimate; f: forecast
1 Year-on-year percentage change.
2 Change in June quarter compared with June quarter the previous year.
3 Year average.
Source: Department of Treasury and Finance, ABS

The Territory economy contracted by 5.3% in 2022–23 due to the decline in net exports. This was driven by a reduction in LNG exports, as major maintenance work at the LNG plant ceased production for a number of weeks. Lower exports were also reported from the Darwin LNG plant in 2022–23.

In 2023–24, GSP is expected to be 4.9% reflecting the positive contribution from net exports, primary due to upgrades to LNG production capacity at the Ichthys LNG project, and low imports due to weak household consumption, and lower machinery and equipment imports. Exports have been impacted by Cyclone Megan, with Groote Eylandt Mining Company (GEMCO) ceasing manganese ore exports while the site is remediated and brought back on-line.

Chart 3.1 Territory gross state product and state final demand

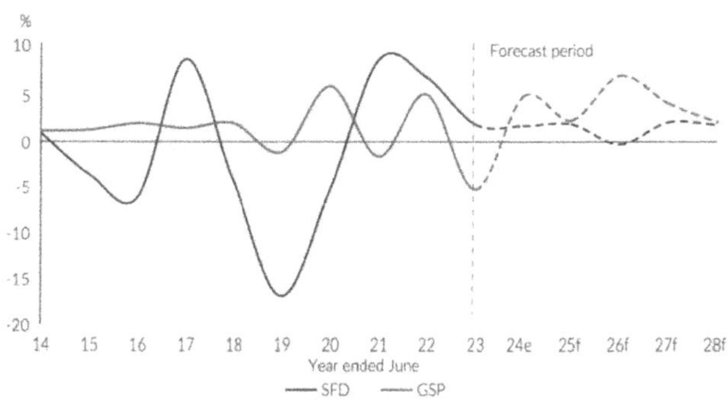

e: estimate; f: forecast; GSP: gross state product; SFD: state final demand.

Source: ABS, Australian National Accounts: State Accounts, Cat. No. 5220.0; Department of Treasury and Finance.

Chart 3.4: Population growth

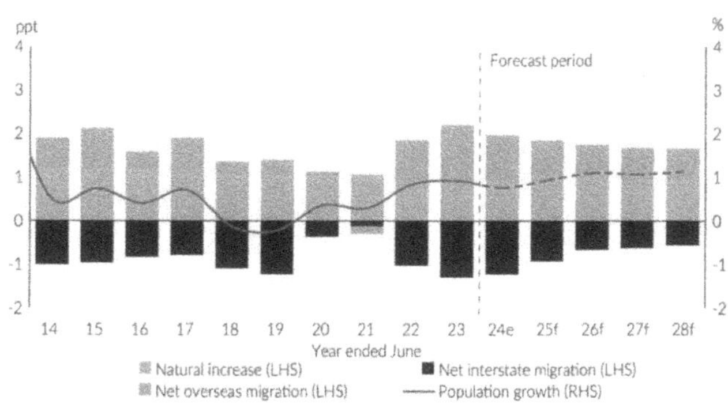

e: estimate; f: forecast; LHS: left-hand side; ppt: percentage point; RHS: right-hand side

Source: ABS, *Australian Demographic Statistics*, Cat. No. 3101.0; Department of Treasury and Finance

The Territory's population forecast remains broadly unchanged from 2023–24 budget. Growth over 2023–24 and 2024–25 has been revised down slightly to 0.8% and 0.9%, respectively, reflecting the weaker than expected natural increase outcomes.

Risks to the Territory's population forecasts remain elevated with significant volitivity in migration flows over recent years.

Operating balance surpluses indicate government can finance the cost of services from revenue generated in that financial year. Conversely operating deficits indicate revenues are insufficient to fund current operations. While in the short term cyclical operating deficits maybe appropriate during periods of economic downturn, persistent or structural operating deficits subsequently pass debt relating to current services to future generations. Operating deficits also provide no capacity for investment in infrastructure beyond depreciation levels, without further borrowings.

Table 4.6: Taxation effort by jurisdiction, 2022-23

	NSW	Vic	Qld	WA	SA	Tas	ACT
	%	%	%	%	%	%	%
Total taxation effort	97.1	108.0	95.1	98.6	96.0	84.2	135.3

Source: CGC 2024 Update

The Territory's taxation effort decreased from 86.2% in 2021–22 to 82% in 2022–23 largely due to lower stamp duty on conveyances and fewer large one-off commercial transactions in 2022–23 compared with 2021–22.

Appendix I

Proposed merger between SA and NT

Former NT minister backs SA merger

News

Adelaide

A former Northern Territory minister will talk to former deputy premier Vickie Chapman about building a grassroots campaign to unite South Australia with the Top End it relinquished more than a century ago, after she urged the move in her farewell speech from parliament.

ADVERTISER.COM.AU SATURDAY MAY 21 2022 NEWS 17

Why SA + NT is not a croc

Support for ex-deputy premier's plan to create one big central state

EMILY OLLE

REUNITING South Australia and the Northern Territory into one big state would be a tourism "bonanza" that would "offer very good prospects", according to leading experts.

They have backed former deputy premier Vickie Chapman's call to remove the 115-year-old border and create a single central state.

Associate Professor Michael O'Neil, from the University of

Adelaide's Centre for Economic Studies, said there was plenty to like about the proposed reunification.

"Both the states have a lot of space and natural climate that's very well set up for the 21st century in terms of solar and wind power. You could have extremely large solar farms in the middle of SA and the NT," Prof O'Neil, pictured, said.

"It would also offer very good prospects in terms of tourism and assets – mining assets such as minerals, rare earth and nickel – that are going to be incredibly in demand in the future."

Tourism Industry Council of SA chief executive Shaun de Bruyn said Ms Chapman's idea – which she outlined in her farewell speech to state parliament – would be "a bonanza" for SA and NT tourism industries.

Ms Chapman likened her proposed new state to "reunification in Germany after the Berlin Wall came down".

She said SA "gave away" the NT in 1907.

"Personally, I would like to see the artificial line dividing the central desert people forever removed," she said.

Prof O'Neil said the idea would boost mining and natural resources opportunities.

Darwin's trade ports could also provide the perfect hub for SA to tap into the burgeoning Asian economy. "It would have a boost at the start – it's like saying, 'Here is a new state, here is a new beginning,'" he said.

But he warned SA would suffer the fiscal burden of the NT, which received up to 80 per cent of its funding from the commonwealth. "SA would be taking on a millstone around its neck financially," he said.

Mr de Bruyn said SA and NT tourism industries would benefit from combining into one state. "Arguably we would be the No.1 state in terms of tourism product offering," he said.

He said it could become a "super hub" for international travellers and workers, who would be able to switch between seasonal spikes.

In an online poll conducted by The Advertiser, 65 per cent of 760 voters agreed the decision would make sense for tourism, assets and facilities.

Appendix J

Ronald and Ena Ryan and Reginald Gross photos and press releases

Both of Richard Ryan's uncles worked diligently in the Northern Territory and each in his own way made a significant contribution to the Territory … hence Richard's enduring relationship with both men and it.

James Ronald Ryan
(Library & Archives NT)

Ena Ryan (née Harvey)
(Library & Archives NT)

Ron Ryan with an Indigenous Woman
(Library & Archives NT)

Reg part of air history

Public servant
Born: August 18, 1916
Died: April 27, 2003

REGINALD William Stuart Gross was a remarkable man who loved his country in a very Australian way.

He was an important contributor to the golden age of civil aviation in Australia during which time we had a safety record second to none in the world.

In his capacity as a Commonwealth public servant with the Department of Civil Aviation he was involved in three significant events in Australia's 20th century history.

Firstly, he was the regional director of civil aviation for the Northern Territory.

He was present at Darwin airport in April 1954 when the aircraft bearing Mrs Petrov, the wife of Vladimir Petrov, the Russian diplomat and spy who had defected to Australia, landed.

Mrs Petrov had been forced on board a Russian-bound plane at Sydney airport by two armed KGB agents.

The plane was obliged to refuel at Darwin where police, who had been alerted to the situation, succeeded in disarming her guards and releasing Mrs Petrov to join her husband.

The chief of police handed Reg a KGB gun with some comment like "It's all yours, mate". Legend

Reg Gross

Secondly, in December 1967, when Reg was the regional director for civil aviation of the Victorian and Tasmanian region, he helped co-ordinate the search for missing Prime Minister Harold Holt.

While watching television on a Sunday afternoon, his younger daughter, Kay, came running into the room with the message there was a Mr D24 on the telephone.

The phone call brought Reg the news of the disappearance of Mr Holt while swimming in heavy surf off Portsea.

For some time thereafter Reg became involved in the co-ordination of the unsuccessful air-sea rescue operations for the Prime Minister.

Third, on Christmas Eve, 1974, news broke of the devastation of

found himself involved in co-ordinating the evacuation of homeless families from their home town to the southern states and liaising with the then Minister for Civil Aviation, Mr Charles Jones.

At this time he made a number of trips to Darwin and was overwhelmed by the amount of damage. Strangely, his former home in Mitchell St, Darwin, was untouched by the cyclone.

Reg's mother was Janet, born in Rutherglen, northern Victoria, who prior to her marriage had assisted her mother and sisters run a guest house named Dudley House in Hepburn Springs. It is still going strong today.

Reg's father was Frederick Gross, who was born in Wurtemberg, Germany, and migrated to Australia in 1902 and became a citizen in 1906.

After completing his education at Adelaide High School, Reg worked as a clerk at the Adelaide firm of Horwood Bagshaw where his father had worked as an engineer.

Reg enlisted in the RAAF on the outbreak of World War II. He was posted to 10 Squadron based in Plymouth, England, where he trained as a navigator and attained the rank of Acting Squadron Leader.

The job of his squadron was patrolling the English Channel and Bay of Biscay for U-boats. In

plane was able to evade the enemy and return to base — though not without loss of some crew and injuries to others, including Reg. For this action, he was awarded a Distinguished Flying Cross.

After his discharge from the air force in 1947, he returned to Australia and joined the Department of Civil Aviation. He and a colleague were charged with the establishment of the school for air traffic controllers.

Reg rose through the ranks to the position of first assistant secretary in charge of ground facilities, that is, airports and navigational aids.

He was in this position when Tullamarine Airport was opened.

He ended his career as the Australian member on the council of the International Civil Aviation Organisation based in Canada for six years.

He served also as senior vice-president of ICAO, which at times required him to chair council meetings.

Reg retired to Mount Eliza in Victoria where he enjoyed golf, tennis and squash as well as spending time with his beloved family. He was a keen Melbourne fan and was actively involved in establishing Neighbourhood Watch in the Mount Eliza area.

Reg was married twice, first to

Don Charlwood

Until his last years, Reg Gross was a man of seemingly inexhaustible energy and joie de vivre, whether on the squash court or in pursuit of his life's work with the former Department of Civil Aviation — this during the golden age of Australian air transport.

Reg, who died in Mornington, Victoria, on April 27, was one of that generation whose life changed direction after aircrew service during World War II.

Born in Adelaide and educated at Adelaide High School during the Depression years he became a clerk in an Adelaide firm where his father, Frederick Gross, was an engineer. His mother, Janet, helped run a family guesthouse at Hepburn Springs before her marriage, a guesthouse that still exists: Dudley House.

In 1939, nine days after the outbreak of war, Reg enlisted in the RAAF. Trained as a navigator, he was posted to the renowned 10 Squadron, stationed at the time at Mount Batten, on Plymouth Sound.

The squadron's Sunderland flying boats and their 11-man crews were engaged in anti-U boat patrols from the English Channel down to the Bay of Biscay; they in turn were hunted by packs of long-range German fighters.

For Reg there was some irony in the situation: his father had migrated from Germany to South Australia in 1902 and had been naturalised four years later. It would have been hard to find a more typical Australian than his son.

When the slow-flying but well-armed Sunderlands came under attack, the navigator took up the position of fire-controller, standing in the astrodome. From there, with the advantage of wide visibility, he directed the pilot's evasive action.

This was Reg Gross's lot on various occasions, but mostly on August 3, 1943, when their Sunderland was attacked in the Bay of Biscay by seven JU88s, three to each side, the

to take off in marginal weather conditions and crashed into defence booms; two of the crew lost their lives.

Reg was not repatriated until 1947. On the homebound ship he met Dorothy Young, a young Scottish dentist, also bound for Australia. He and Dorothy were married in December of that year. Already Reg had joined the fledgling air traffic control branch of the Department of Civil Aviation.

In those pioneering days he was given the task of setting up a training school in accordance with provisional international standards. It was his good fortune that his pupils were all former aircrew men, eager to establish themselves in civil life.

At home Reg was overjoyed by the birth of his first child. His wound as fire-controller on their Sunderland had put fatherhood in some doubt for him. It gave rise to his favourite expletive: "By my tattered left agate."

In 1952, Reg was appointed Civil Aviation's regional director of the Northern Territory, a region seen to be in need of strong leadership as it was showing a tendency to go its own way. Reg's unannounced visits to all NT stations were cyclonic in nature and were followed by a deluge of telegrams and teleprinter messages demanding that shortcomings be set right before his next visit. These became known as Grosso-grams. Despite reverberations throughout the Northern Territory, Reg never lost his popularity and the improvements were made.

He was in Darwin in 1954 when Vladimir Petrov defected from the Russian embassy. In Sydney, Mrs Petrov was forced aboard an international aircraft by the KGB with the intention of repatriating her. In those days international aircraft had inevitably to land at Darwin to refuel. There, Northern Territory police disarmed one of the guards and Mrs Petrov was enabled to return to her husband.

As regional director, the police handed Reg Gross the

operations, central office, a position he took up in 1954.

Sadly, Dorothy Gross died in August 1963 of Hodgkin's disease and Reg was left with three children still at school. During these years alone his youngest daughter took a call one Sunday from a "Mr D24". Thus Reg learnt of the disappearance of Harold Holt off Cheviot Beach; he was seconded to co-ordinate the search.

In 1970 he was promoted first assistant director-general, ground facilities. Happily, that same year, he married Jan Robinson, a Melbourne solicitor. He and Jan were to have two sons. On Christmas Eve 1974 they were planning a quiet family dinner for the next day when news came to Reg of Cyclone Tracy and his need to return to Darwin to assist in the evacuation of the homeless and the setting up of temporary services. He was appalled by the devastation but, strangely, found his home of the '50s still intact.

In 1975, Reg Gross was appointed Australian representative on the council of the International Civil Aviation Organisation in Montreal. There he and Jan and the younger family set up home for the two three-year terms, a home where Australian and international visitors found warm welcome.

Reg was appointed first vice-president of the council. To many countries in the world of international aviation, Reg Gross became the face of Australia, a man forthright and honest in his dealings, always gregarious and good-humoured.

He retired on his return home. He and Jan enjoyed 16 years of retirement, but then the scourges of Parkinson's disease and, finally, dementia became his lot — travesties of the life of so vibrant a man.

As well as Jan he has left Annie, Ian and Kay of his first family, Steven and Alan of his second, their partners and five grandchildren.

Both families combined in a death notice, which closed with the words: "A truly great Australian". He was indeed —

ME GROSS, Reginald William Stuart

d D.F.C. Reg. No. 285147 Rank F/O. Service R.A.A.F.

mmended by Governor-General on O – R

ulgated in *London Gazette* on 27.8.43. G. H. File R.A.A.F. 1A

ulgated in *Commonwealth of Australia Gazette* on 9.9.43.

ion (G. H. File RAAF 269A) Courage over BAY OF BISCAY when aircraft attacked.

nia received from London N/A PN LONDON. N/A G. H. File –

nia presented by His Majesty, The King,

Buckingham Palace, London, On 12/12/44. G. H. File ENGLAND/31.

ess of recipient on presentation date A/N/A

arks

r Awards 2876.

Appendix K

NT Chinese Museum

Short History

Did you know that at one time the Chinese population outnumbered the European population in the Top End? Many were recruited by the Government of the day and by 1878 the Chinese were the largest non-Aboriginal group of the time.

According to the Government Resident's report of 1909, there were 6122 Chinese in the NT by 1888. The "coolies" were contracted to work the goldfields and later the building of the railway line from Palmerston to Pine Creek.

These early Chinese settlers were mainly from the Kwantung Province in south China and primarily spoke the Sze Yup and Hakka dialects. The local newspaper of the time noted of the Chinese arrival in the NT: "The coolies were landed here in a poor state of health, and if they had been so many cattle, instead of human beings, their low condition would have caused their employers to feed them and to strengthen them before putting them to work."

By 1881, anti-Chinese feeling in South Australia was sufficiently strong to fix a boundary between the Northern Territory and South Australia (1000 miles north of Adelaide). The Chinese could pass south of this line only if they paid a ten pound entry tax. But it was the need for cheap labour which allowed the Chinese to continue their work in the Northern Territory and soon enough they were working their own claims, establishing market gardens and engaging in general industry and commerce.

In the 1890s the economic depression and a national campaign aimed at a White Australia mean many Chinese left the Territory but some stayed on and became Australian citizens in the brief period when it was possible and settled permanently in the Territory. These families increased and extended their commercial base in Darwin.

This description from 1897: "Chinese, who are ready and willing to work night or day and seven days a week, have ousted Europeans from many branches of trade. Hairdressing, tailoring and bootmaking are all done by them. . .The chefs are invariably Chinamen; this applies to most of the Northern Territory." But the Chinese settlement in the NT was not approved of by the rest of Australia, as Banjo Paterson wrote in The Bulletin in 1898: ". . .the Territory itself is now clamouring for the introduction of the cheap and nasty Chow, notwithstanding that it is breeding its own Chinky fast enough, in all conscience. The Territory people want more Chows and would gladly cut loose from South Australia to get them." Chinatown in Cavenagh Street had become a hive of Chinese activity and commerce. It featured many stores including a "bootmaker, tailor, baker, hairdresser, several washerwomen and many gardeners." There were also many restaurants and a seed and plant shop – the first of its kind in the Territory (even the Government Resident of the time made purchases there).

By the 1920s the Chinese had become economically poweiful in the region but it wasn't until sometime after World War Two that they were able to overcome discriminatory measures such as not being allowed to work in the public service. Nevertheless, the Chinese continued to forge ahead and as we look back to recent twentieth century history the impact of those who remained has been well noted. In politics, in business, in sport and recreation, in the development of the general lifestyle of the Northern Territory –

these areas and more have been "touched" by the Chinese. And not just those born and bred here, but those more recent arrivals who have chosen the Territory as their home.

Today in our proudly cosmopolitan community, there is a sharing of culture and blending of knowledge and roots. We pay tribute to our forefathers who helped make it so. This short history has been compiled from excerpts from the following books: *Cathay of the North* by Frances Chan, *The Chinese in the Northern Territory* by Timothy G Jones, *Beyond Chinatown* by Diana Giese, *Sweet & Sour* compiled by the Museum and Art Gallery of the NT.

Background to the Chinese in the Northern Territory

The first group of Chinese labourers arrived in Darwin in 1874 as indentured labourers or 'coolies'. Many were highly skilled tradesmen and they were employed on roads, in the mines, on the Overland Telegraph and on railway construction. In the late 19th century, there were up to seven times more Chinese in the Territory than any other ethnic group and since then, the Chinese have continued to play a very important part in the development of the NT. Their early contributions to all branches of industry and business were essential and without their enterprise, skills and the food they grew, life in the Territory would have been significantly less attractive. They faced extreme hardships and discrimination but their determination and perseverance helped them to overcome these difficulties and have earned them a very important place in Territory society and history.

Purpose of the Museum

The Museum aims to encourage greater awareness and understanding of the history of the Chinese in the Territory. The Museum is open to the public and other institutions, for general interest, research and education. The Museum is a stimulus for families and individuals to research and document their histories and serves to remind present and future generations of their heritage. The opening of the NT Chinese Museum is just the beginning. There is much more research to be undertaken; more themes to be explored and developed; many more stories to be told and photos and objects to be found and displayed. The Museum highlights the importance and explores the history of the Chinese contribution to the development of the Northern Territory and is committed to documenting and preserving the history of the Chinese in the Territory, particularly Darwin and the surrounding regions.

The Museum Project

For the Chinese, honouring our ancestors is a duty, a passion, a belief and a commitment. It was with great determination, then, that in the 1990s, the Chung Wah Society undertook a project which today stands proudly at the Society's headquarters – the Northern Territory Chinese Museum.

Born from the Chinatown '42 display which was put together as part of the Bombing of Darwin, 50th Commemorative Year, the Chinese Museum is packed with material documenting the lives and times of Darwin Chinese through the years. Small but well-appointed, the Museum is a tribute to our ancestors and contains many colou1ful insights. Elements of it featured in the 1996 Museum and Art Gallery of the Northern Territory display, Sweet and Sour. Personal histories, family trees, prominent Chinese citizen, pay tribute to the contributions made in the past to Darwin society.

A model of the old Chinatown allows the visitor to visualise that bustling street in the early days. And the history of the painstakingly hand crafted silk banner presented to William G Stretton in 1913 demonstrates the Chinese connection with the officials of the time. Photographs of times past are dotted throughout the Museum, depicting the business, social, religious and cultural elements of Darwin Chinese.

This fascinating journey of Darwin through the eyes of its Chinese inhabitants is proudly available for all to see and experience. We invite you to come and spend some time in the Chinese Museum – a tribute to our ancestors and the many who helped build Darwin's multicultural society.

Appendix L

Australian Defence Force Academy Discussion Paper

Discussion Paper – Highly Confidential

The Australian Defence Force Academy (ADFA) is a tri-service military academy that provides military and academic education for junior officers of the Australian Defence Force in the Royal Australian Navy (RAN), Australian Army and Royal Australian Air Force (RAAF).

Tertiary education is provided by the University of New South Wales' Canberra campus, known as UNSW Canberra at ADFA, which is the awarding body for ADFA qualifications. Apart from educating future leaders of the Australian Defence Force, UNSW Canberra also provides postgraduate programs and short courses both to Department of Defence personnel and the general public.

The stated purpose of the ADFA is 'to service Australia by providing the Australian Defence Force (ADF) with tertiary graduates who have the attributes, intellect and skills required of an officer'.

AWARDS

ADFA's academic offers awards at the Diploma, Associate Diploma, Bachelor's Degree, Master's Degree, and Doctorate levels.

Under its agreement with the Department of Defence, the University of New South Wales (UNSW) provides Midshipmen (RAN) and Officer Cadets (ARA and RAAF) with a tertiary education at its University College campus (UNSW@ADFA), which is located on the Academy grounds.

Midshipmen, Officer cadets and civilians undertake three- and four-year undergraduate degrees at ADFA.

MILITARY TRAINING

Year One Familiarisation Training (YOFT)

On arrival at ADFA, new Officer Cadets undertake a five-week phase of training known as Year One Familiarisation Training (YOFT), Midshipmen join the Officer cadets approximately two weeks into this training, as they have already received some basic military training as part of their first year in the Navy. Year One Familiarisation Training encompasses weapon training, physical training, first aid, drill and academic enrolments. The training culminates with the return of second and third year cadets to ADFA, and the conduct of the Chief of the defence Force (CDF) Parade in late February/early March.

Joint Military Education Training (JMET)

During academic sessions, ADFA provides basic military training to Midshipmen and Officer Cadets through the Joint Military Education Training (JMET) program.

The JMET program encompasses physical training (PT), leadership and management studies, equity and diversity (E&D), military history, defence studies, drill and ceremonial, the military communications program (MCP), first aid, military law, field craft and weapons tralning.

Single Service Training (SST)

At the end of each academic session, Midshipmen and Officer Cadets move to their respective single service colleges for Single

Service Training (SST). Such training prepares them to be officers in the ADF. Army Officer Cadets continue this training for another twelve months after leaving ADFA at the Royal Military College, Duntroon (RMC-D), to later be commissioned as Lieutenants. Most Officer Cadets and Midshipmen undertake six SST periods over a three-year period. However, Midshipmen have already completed 12 months of training in the Navy so they may not be required to train these periods.

Part of the Military training includes familiarisation in possible operations such as the tropics. It is highly probable that any future conflict that Australia has will be in the tropics.

The course could also include 'mock battles' against possible 'enemies' which would assist in general training for conflict situations.

OPPORTUNITY

The opportunity exists for the Northern Territory to provide an 'exchange programme' with ADFA.

The degree course conducted by UNSW would have components that could easily be supplemented by Charles Darwin University (CDU) on say a 6-month exchange programme.

Military training in the Tropics would provide excellent experience for Trainee Officers in all of three services due to the significant presence of Australian Service personnel together with the large (circa 1500) resident American force in the Territory.

Norforce, which is unique would also be part of the training syllabus.

PROPOSAL

A 'special' school to be created for this purpose, which can handle all the operations of the ADFA exchange students in the Northern Territory.

The school would be unique in that it would provide specialist service training in the tropics (not Canberra), exposure to Norforce, together with the possibility of sharing training with growing U.S. Armed Services and other countries. Students would be able to continue their tertiary studies in conjunction with 'in the field' training.

It is suggested that, whilst the school would be controlled by ADFA, its agenda could also include service and assistance from the U.S. Military Academy and US Naval Academy at Annapolis and also Sandhurst.

Appendix M

Richard Ryan at lunch with Richard Evans, 2016

Richard Evans' Interview with Richard Ryan: Advertiser, *Weekend Extra* March 19, 2016, *Lunch with ... Outgoing Festival chair Richard Ryan*

RE: You grew up in Adelaide but spent many years in the Northern Territory.

RR: I went there in my late 20s; it was exciting and gives you a great lifestyle.

RE: The inspiration came from within your family?

RR: Yes, Uncle Ron. He used to go into the Northern Territory bush. He'd go out to settlements where families and children had been abandoned and help relocate them. I went to the NT predominantly because of him.

He was in the 2/ 10th infantry battalion during the war in New Guinea and was out on patrol by himself when he found a badly wounded Digger. Ron heard a Japanese patrol approaching he and his wounded colleague. He lay down with the moaning wounded soldier with him.

The Japanese thought Ron was dead because he was covered in blood but hearing noise from the other soldier, they bayoneted him.

Ron decided to change his whole lifestyle as a result of this experience.

He was a genuinely good man.
My father died when I was very young and Ron became an inspiration to me.
Ron died in his early 60s. If you go to Katherine (NT), Ryan Park is named after him and if you want the 'real' Uncle Ron, at Katherine Club there's a bar named after him.

58 WEEKEND EXTRA SATURDAY MARCH 19 2016 ADVERTISER.COM.AU

Lunch with ... Outgoing Festival chair Richard Ryan

Arts, education and footy

As his stint as Adelaide Festival chairperson draws to a close this month, Richard Ryan – also the inaugural chancellor at NT's Charles Darwin University and a Port Adelaide Power board member – found time for lunch with **RICHARD EVANS**

FUNDING SQUEEZE: Outgoing Adelaide Festival chairperson Richard Ryan at lunch: "There are great people here in the arts but everyone is chasing the same money pot." Picture: DYLAN COKER

THE BILL

THE BOWERY KITCHEN AND GROCER

Total	$44.40

RICHARD EVANS: "Ryan" suggests an Irish heritage?

RICHARD RYAN: My father's family were very keen that the Irish ancestry would be invested in us. I ...

Christmas Day cyclone (1974). I'd gone out for drinks and my wife was home looking after the children. I came home about nine o'clock and had a mild disagreement with her because she was putting water into the bath which you're supposed to do in the event of a cyclone. I was wrong as usual.

During the first half (of the storm) nothing happened to us at all. In the second half the cyclone really hit...

It's why the NT is so exciting. (And) where else in Australia could you start a university?

How do you start one?

For the Territory to grow you need skills and there was a dearth of skills. To do medicine you had to come to Adelaide. There was no dental school, no engineering school. None of the education opportunities we have here in Adelaide, and consider our right, existed there.

Paul Everingham, when he was NT chief minister, was very keen to start a university.

The Federal Government was not prepared to fund it but the NT went ahead anyway. If you don't have education, the Territory won't grow properly and the development of the north will never really occur.

People forget that the

was actually taught Gaelic as a child. My mother's side were very strong Methodists.

I was in Galway recently for the Rugby World Cup and I couldn't help but feel how proud I am to be Australian.

You're in your final days as chair of the Festival. What have you been up to?

You are busy talking to people you're trying to get to help the Festival and suddenly you get a fond affection for all politicians of all parties (laughs).

This was my sixth festival ... ticket sales were the best they have been for about 15 years, and hopefully it will be the same for the cash surplus.

I attend most Festival events. In the days of the Festival Centre (where I was chairman) sometimes you'd go to the same production four nights in a row. There was nothing hard about it really – how wonderful if that's the most tedious thing in one's life.

Festival money is scarce. How do you find sponsorship?

The problem sometimes is that there are not enough outsiders involved in arts boards. When it comes to philanthropy and fundraising, it's an incredibly limited market. Boards must have a broader representation of the business and philanthropic community, so that there's a greater networking opportunity. There are great people here in the arts but everybody is chasing the same money pot.

That's not a criticism, but with sponsorship down across our state, philanthropy is doing better. The mix of boards has to become more focused on people who can network and fundraise. It's up to government as most boards are government-controlled boards.

Is a different model needed?

In the USA to chair an Arts board you actually have to be seen to donate money. I guess our whole arts scene needs to have some form of transformation. Perhaps Governments need to reappraise their criteria. When I first came on the Adelaide Festival Centre board ... there would have been four or five private enterprise individuals, all with connections. If you want to make it work properly with sponsorship and philanthropy, I think you have no choice but to be totally focused.

Everyone wants something different for their money. The Chairman's Circle (which funded *The James Plays*) was the biggest untied sponsor of the Festival this year, around $200,000 and it's based totally on philanthropy. The sponsorship decline is a combination of circumstances. Many of the businesses in Adelaide have gone – Bank of Adelaide, John Martins, they've all gone.

Is there a government role?

Partly, but I also think the industry has to get its act into gear. The arts can't expect to be fed by government all the time. It's right around the world. Arts cost so much more these days, travel, accommodation etc. What people want with a festival is for it to be successful artistically but sometimes this can be intrinsically uneconomic. It's the ability to get the balance right.

Was there a temptation to spend big at your last Festival?

You can't leave a deficit, you just can't. We take every single program and work out whether we think it will be a profit or not and then decide whether it will go in or not. One thing I can promise is that there will be a healthy cash surplus this year.

You grew up in Adelaide but spent many years in the Northern Territory.

I went there in my late 20s; it was exciting and gives you a great lifestyle.

The inspiration came from within your family?

Yes, Uncle Ron. He used to go into the Northern Territory bush. He'd go out to settlements where families had been abandoned and help relocate them. I went to the NT predominantly because of him.

He was in the 2/10th infantry battalion during the war in New Guinea and was out on patrol by himself when he found a badly-wounded Digger.

Ron heard a Japanese patrol approaching him and his wounded colleague. He lay down with the moaning wounded soldier with him.

The Japanese thought Ron was dead because he was covered in blood, but hearing noise from the other soldier they bayoneted him.

Ron decided to change his whole lifestyle as a result of this experience. He was a genuinely good man. My father died when I was very young and Ron became an inspiration to me. Ron died in his early 60s.

You were in Darwin for the Northern Territory is one sixth the size of Australia, with a population of about 250,000. I was deputy chancellor of NT University and chair of Menzies (School of Health Research), so I helped put it all together and subsequently became the inaugural chancellor of Charles Darwin University.

And then there's footy.

I'm on the Port Power board, the longest-serving by one whole month. I have been lucky enough to have the opportunity to do it.

Port has always had a strong indigenous component, and the Power community really does try hard to do all that. Part of my appeal to them was my connection with the Territory.

Port was looking to go into the NT at the time to develop a player base.

And, finally, your favourite festival year?

Roman Tragedies (2014) – something different. When (artistic director) David Sefton said he would have six hours of Shakespeare in Dutch at the Adelaide Festival Centre and you could walk on the stage, I remember thinking, "come on". I was 100 per cent wrong.

It was a spark of genius.

DREAM LUNCH GUESTS

US filmmaker **Quentin Tarantino**
Australian WWI military commander General Sir **John Monash**, pictured
Italian composer and conductor **Ennio M[illegible]ne**
Author **Eric Blair** (better known by his pen name, **George Orwell**)
American cartoonist **William Watterson** (the creator of the popular *Calvin and Hobbes* comic strip)

ADVE01Z01MA - V1

Appendix N

Charles Darwin University Honorary Award, 2021

The following is a speech made in August 2021, awarding Richard Ryan the titles of Emeritus Chancellor and Honorary Doctor of Letters at Charles Darwin University.

Chancellor, I have the honour of presenting to you Richard Ryan AO, who council has determined should be awarded the honorary title of Emeritus Chancellor.

Council has also determined that Richard Ryan should be awarded the awarded the title of Honorary Doctor of Letters.

Richard Ryan has been integral to the tertiary education landscape in the NT since the days of Darwin Community College in 1985, and then with the Darwin Institute of Technology, Northern Territory University and Charles Darwin University.

Mr Ryan, a chartered accountant and company director, has steered CDU since its inception in 2003. He had the challenging task of chairing the merger of NTU & Centralia College and bringing Menzies School of Health Research into the fold—work that consumed days and months.

Compounding his challenges were resistance to institutional name changes, the appointment of an interim VC and a new VC and Federal and NT Government requirements, to name but a few. Mr Ryan emerged as Chancellor of CDU, a position which saw him make significant contributions to University life.

Under his tenure, CDU took great strides in research, student enrolments and technology initiatives, progressing from some 9000 student enrolments to more than 21,000. Mr Ryan's recent retirement brings to a close a 24-year association with CDU and its predecessors.

In a distinguished career he has served on a number of government advisory boards, was awarded the Sir John Loewenthal award for his role as president of the National Heart Foundation, and was awarded a Centenary Medal in 2003.

Mr Ryan was made a member of the Order of Australia in 1989 for Services to the Community and was made an Officer of the Order of Australia in 1998 for Services to Indigenous People.

Mr Ryan's philanthropic endeavours have been instrumental in the University Foundation raising more than $15 million. Major projects made possible from Mr Ryan's extensive business connections include the establishment of the University Library and North Flinders International House. He has also made very generous personal financial donations to CDU and to Menzies.

The Ryan Family Prize is an internal annual award that recognises outstanding contributions to Menzies School of Health Research. It is awarded to individuals or groups who go above and beyond and help make Menzies a great place to work or to help Menzies achieve excellence.

Richard Ryan has served as director of a number of public and government boards including the Northern Territory Treasury, The Australian Government Solicitor's Advisory Board and The Adelaide Festival. Richard has certainly been a Chancellor for a new age and his association with tertiary education in the Territory will last far longer than his term in office.

Chancellor

In recognition of his distinguished service to the University through his leadership and membership of key governing bodies, Richard Ryan AO is awarded the title of Honorary Doctor of Letters. And in recognition of his significant contribution to the advancement of Charles Darwin University in his role as Chancellor and Deputy Chancellor, Richard Ryan AO is awarded the honorary title of Emeritus Chancellor.

Bibliography

Aboriginal Land Rights (NT) 1975

Aboriginal Land Rights (Northern Territory) Act 1976 (Commonwealth)
Allocation of Funds (Supply) Ordinance (No. 1) 1977–78 (NT)

Anwar, Sajid, and Bruce Prideaux. 'Regional Economic Growth: An Evaluation of the Northern Territory.' *Economic Papers* 24, no. 3 (2005): 194–214.

Arias, Cesar Rodrigo. 'Complete Broadcast.' YouTube. 1 April 2021. Documentary, 9:34. https://youtu.be/n2C0arEcncU.

Arias, Cesar Rodrigo. 'DVD Full Interview.' YouTube. 1 April 2021. Interview with Richard Ryan, 7:24. https://youtu.be/9yGB-FU08Cwo.

Australian Bureau of Statistics. *Aboriginal and Torres Strait Islander People: Census*. Accessed 10 December 2022. https://www.abs.gov.au/statistics/people/aboriginal-and-torres-strait-islander-peoples/aboriginal-and-torres-strait-islander-people-census/latest-release.

Australian Bureau of Statistics. *Census of Population & Housing, 30 June 1971*. Cat. no. 2150.0. Canberra, 1971. https://www.abs.gov.au/AUSSTATS/abs@.nsf/DetailsPage/2105.01971.

Australian Bureau of Statistics. *Census of Population & Housing, 30 June 1981: Cross-classified characteristics of persons and dwellings, Northern Territory*. Cat. no. 2450.0. Canberra, 1983. https://www.ausstats.abs.gov.au/ausstats/free.nsf/0/7F57E0BC6F25274BCA2575820014E6D6/$File/24500_1981_CCC_PD_NT.pdf.

Australian Bureau of Statistics. 'Census of Population and Housing – Counts of Aboriginal and Torres Strait Islander Australians.' Accessed 12 December 2022. https://www.abs.gov.au/statistics/people/aboriginal-and-torres-strait-islander-peoples/census-population-and-housing-counts-aboriginal-and-torres-strait-islander-australians/2021.

Australian Bureau of Statistics. Department of Treasury & Finance; ABS, Australian National Accounts: State Accounts, Cat. No. 5220.0.

Australian Bureau of Statistics, *Northern Territory Statistical Summary 1979* (Canberra: Commonwealth Bureau of Census and Statistics).

Australian Bureau of Statistics. *Northern Territory Statistical Summary 1981* (Canberra: Commonwealth Bureau of Census and Statistics).

Australian Government Commonwealth Grants Commission. '2020 Review.' Accessed 10 December 2022. https://www.cgc.gov.au/reports-for-government/2020-review.

Ball, Y. 'HWE Slammed for Poor Financial Planning.' *Financial Review*, 29 June 2005. https://www.afr.com/companies/hwe-slammed-for-poor-financial-planning-20050629-jv77r.

Berbins, Baiza, and Peter Loveday. *A University for the Territory: The Northern Territory University and Preceding Institutions (1949–1995)*. Darwin: Northern Territory University, 1999.

Biddle, Nicholas, and Heather Crawford. 'The Changing Aboriginal and Torres Strait Islander Population: Evidence from the 2006–2011 Australian Census Longitudinal Dataset.' (2015). Accessed 10 November 2022. https://researchers.anu.edu.au/publications/112976.

Biddle, Nicholas, and Francis Markham. 'Income, Poverty and Inequality.' *CAEPR Census Paper 2* (2018). Accessed 10 November 2022. https://caepr.cass.anu.edu.au/research/publications/income-poverty-and-inequality.

Carson, Dean, Doris Schmallegger, and Sharon Harwood. 'A city for the temporary? Political economy and urban planning in Darwin, Australia.' *Urban Policy and Research* 28, no. 3 (2010): 293–310.

Centralian Advocate. 'Thinking Big: The Way to Go.' 18 April 1984.

Charles Darwin University. *Annual Report 2003*. Darwin: Charles Darwin University.

Clarke, K.B. *Northern Territory Treasury Annual Report 1997–98*. Darwin: Northern Territory Treasury.

Clarke, Miranda. 'Guardian of the North'.

'Client Services,' Northern Territory Government Department of Treasury & Finance, accessed 10 December 2022. https://treasury.nt.gov.au/dtf/nttc/client-services.

Commonwealth Grants Commission Act 1973 (Commonwealth)

Commonwealth of Australia. Aboriginal Land Rights Commission, *First Report* (1973) and *Second Report* (1974).

Commonwealth of Australia. *Our Universities: Backing Australia's Future*. Canberra: Department of Education, Science and Training, 2003.

'Deferment "Cheap Political Stunt",' *NT News*, 20 October 1984.

Department of Territory Families, Housing and Communities, Northern Territory Government. 'Records 1979.' Accessed 10 December 2022. https://tfhc.nt.gov.au/heritage,-libraries-and-archives/library-and-archives-nt/cabinet-records/1979-records/nt-and-australia-in-1979.

Department of Territory Families, Housing and Communities, Northern Territory Government. 'Records 1983.' Accessed 10 December 2022. https://tfhc.nt.gov.au/heritage,-libraries-and-archives/library-and-archives-nt/cabinet-records/1983-records/about-1983-records, accessed Nov 2022.

Elferink, John. '1983 Cabinet Records Released.' Media release. 1 January 2014. https://hdl.handle.net/10070/548155.

Everingham, Barry. 'CLP Moves on Uranium', *NT News*, 20 July 1977.

Financial Agreement Act 1928 (Commonwealth)

Financial Management Act 1995 (NT)

Griffiths, Owen, *Darwin Drama*. Sydney: Bloham & Chambers, c. 1946.

Henry Walker Eltin Group Limited. *Annual Review, 1990* (Adelaide: The Group, 1990).

Howlett, Michael, and Keith Brownsey. 'Introduction: Towards a Post-Staples State?' *Policy & Society* 26, no. 1 (January 2007): 1–7.

Hyland, Anne. 'The Ghost of Neville Walker.' *Financial Review*, 2 April 2005. https://www.afr.com/politics/the-ghost-of-neville-walker-20050402-j7avs.

Johnstone, Brian. 'Casino Party Turns Sour.' *Australian*, 2 October 1984.

'Keating Asked to Relent on Casinos.' *NT News*, 21 October 1984.

Kennedy, Alex. 'Taming the Wild Henry Walker.' *Financial Review*, 2 October 1992. https://www.afr.com/companies/taming-the-wild-henry-walker-19921002-kaplu.

KPMG, *Northern Territory University: Strategic Positioning for the Future*, August 2002; see also pp. 7–10.

Lawrence, Michael. 'Keating Withdraws Ban on Casino Sale.' *Sydney Morning Herald*, 17 November 1984.

Ling, Ted. *Commonwealth Government Records about the Northern Territory*. Canberra: National Archives of Australia, 2011.

Lyons, Suzannah. 'Tropical Cyclone Tracy: December 25, 1974.' *ABC News*, 24 December 2014. https://www.abc.net.au/news/emergency/2014-12-24/cyclone-tracy/5981404

McGinnis, Mark. 'Lord Vestey "Abidingly Proud of His Australian Descent".' *Sydney Morning Herald*, 12 February 2021. https://www.smh.com.au/national/lord-vestey-abidingly-proud-of-his-australian-descent-20210210-p571ah.html.

McKinnon, Ken. *Confidential Report: The Present Situation of the Northern Territory University*. Darwin: Northern Territory University.

Montague, John. 'Speech to Treasury Corporation Members.' 15 October 2021.

Native Title Act 1993 (Commonwealth)

Northern Territory Administration. *Report of the Acting Administrator for the Year 1911*. Canberra: Government Printer, 1912.

Northern Land Council. 'Northern Land Council.' Accessed January 2023. https://www.nlc.org.au/.

Northern Territory (Administration) Act 1974 (No. 30 of 197) (Commonwealth).

Northern Territory Government. *Northern Territory Treasury Corporation Annual Report 2019–20*. Darwin: Department of Treasury and Finance, 2020.

Northern Territory Government Department of Treasury & Finance. 'Client Services.' Accessed December 10, 2022. https://treasury.nt.gov.au/dtf/nttc/client-services.

Northern Territory Government Department of Treasury & Finance. *Northern Territory Treasury Annual Report 2000–2001*. Darwin: Department of the Treasury, 2001. Accessed 14 March 2023. https://hdl.handle.net/10070/670000.

Northern Territory Legislative Assembly. 'Parliamentary Record: Part III Minutes (21 August–30 August 1984).' Accessed 16 March 2023. https://parliament.nt.gov.au/__data/assets/pdf_file/0003/367455/PR03-Minutes-21-August-30-August-1984.pdf.

Northern Territory (Self-Government) Act 1978 (Commonwealth)

Northern Territory (Self-Government) Regulations 1978 (Nos. 102, 168, 290) (Commonwealth)

Northern Territory Treasury Corporation Act 1994 (NT)

Northern Territory University. *Northern Territory University Annual Report 2002*. Darwin: Northern Territory University, 2002.

Northern Territory University. *Northern Territory University Annual Report 2003*. Darwin: Northern Territory University, 2003.

Ormiston, Malcolm. 'Henry & Walker Capital Sown Up.' *NT News*, 17 October 1984.

Parliamentary Budget Office. *Fiscal Sustainability – Long-term Budget Scenarios. Report No. 1, 01/2021*. Canberra: Commonwealth of Australia.

Pastoral Land Act 1992 (NT)

Perrett, Janine. 'A Flamboyant "King" Moves Into Darwin.' *NT News*, 2 December 1984.

Pforr, Christof. 'Tourism Administration in the Northern Territory in the Era of Country Liberal Party Governance 1978–2001.' *Australian Journal of Public Administration* 65, no. 1 (2006): 61–74.

Population Australia 'Population of the Northern Territory 2022' Accessed 31 August 2022. https://www.population.net.au/population-of-northern-territory/.

Public Service Ordinance 1977 (No. 11 of 1977) (NT)

Racial Discrimination Act 1975 (Commonwealth)

Ramsey, Alan. 'The Story of a London Dinner.' *National Times*, 9–15 November 1984.

'Records 1979,' Department of Territory Families, Housing and Communities, Northern Territory Government, accessed 10 December 2022, https://tfhc.nt.gov.au/heritage,-libraries-and-archives/library-and-archives-nt/cabinet-records/1979-records/nt-and-australia-in-1979.

'Records 1983,' Department of Territory Families, Housing and Communities, Northern Territory Government, accessed 10 December 2022, https://tfhc.nt.gov.au/heritage,-libraries-and-archives/library-and-archives-nt/cabinet-records/1983-records/about-1983-records.

Ries, Ivor. 'How a $10,000 Investment Won Control of NT's Casinos.' *Business Review Weekly*, 29 March 1985.

Reid, Brian. *The Menzies School of Health Research: Establishment, 1978–1997*. Casuarina: Historical Society of the Northern Territory, 2003.

Scanlon Foundation Research Institute. 'Australian Migration and

Population Dashboard.' Accessed 9 October 2020. https://scanlon-institute.org.au/publications/migrationdashboard.

Taylor, Andrew, Tom Wilson, Jeromy Temple, Margaret Kelaher, and Sandra Eades, 'The future growth and spatial shift of Australia's Aboriginal and Torres Strait Islander population, 2016–2015.' *Population, Space and Place* 27, no. 4 (2021): e2401. https://doi.org/10.1002/psp.2401

Transfer of Powers (Self Government) Ordinance 1978 (NT)

Transfer of Powers (Health) Act 1978 (NT)

Transfer of Powers (Law) Act 1978 (NT)

Whitlam Prime Ministerial Collection. Whitlam Institute Within Western Sydney University. https://www.whitlam.org/collection.

Whitmont, Tony. 'The Silent Invasion of Kumagai Gumi.' *Financial Review*, 5 September 1984.

Wilson, Helen, and Elizabeth Estbergs, eds. *Northern Territory Chronicle, 2nd edition*. Darwin: Northern Territory University Planning Authority, 1984.

Wilson, Peter. 'Federal: We Didn't Want to Sell.' *NT News*, 17 April 1984.

Index

Wakefield Press is an independent publishing and
distribution company based in Adelaide, South Australia.
We love good stories and publish beautiful books.
To see our full range of books, please visit our website at
www.wakefieldpress.com.au
where all titles are available for purchase.
To keep up with our latest releases and news,
subscribe to the *Wakefield Weekly* at
https://mailchi.mp/wakefieldpress/subscribe

Find us!

Facebook: www.facebook.com/wakefield.press
Instagram: www.instagram.com/wakefieldpress

www.ingramcontent.com/pod-product-compliance
Lightning Source LLC
Chambersburg PA
CBHW042030200926
51615CB00027B/1
9781923388550